SENECA

Selected Dialogues and Consolations

SENECA

Selected Dialogues and Consolations

Translated, with Introduction and Notes, by

PETER J. ANDERSON

Hackett Publishing Company, Inc.
Indianapolis/Cambridge

18 17 16 15   1 2 3 4 5 6 7

For further information, please address
Hackett Publishing Company, Inc.
P.O. Box 44937
Indianapolis, Indiana 46244-0937
www.hackettpublishing.com

Interior design by Elizabeth L. Wilson
Composition by Aptara Inc.

Library of Congress Cataloging-in-Publication Data

Seneca, Lucius Annaeus, approximately 4 B.C.–65 A.D., author.
  [Works. Selections. English]
  Seneca : Selected dialogues and consolations / Translated, with
Introduction and Notes, by Peter J. Anderson.
      pages cm
  Includes bibliographical references and index.
  ISBN 978-1-62466-369-7 (cloth)—ISBN 978-1-62466-368-0 (pbk.)
  1. Seneca, Lucius Annaeus, approximately 4 B.C.–65 A.D.—Translations
into English.   I. Anderson, Peter J., 1970– translator.   II. Title.
  PA6661.A7S48 2015
  188—dc23

                                                        2014034853

The paper used in this publication meets the minimum requirements of
American National Standard for Information Sciences—Permanence of
Paper for Printed Library Materials, ANSI Z39.48–1984.

♾

Cum potuero, vivam quomodo oportet.

For my family.

CONTENTS

Acknowledgments

I offer my gratitude to Brian Rak, Charles Brittain, Margaret Graver, R. Scott Smith, William O. Stephens, Emily Wilson, and anonymous readers for Hackett who labored over my translations, offering both encouragement and criticism. I could not have hoped for better critical support in producing this translation. Thank you to my wonderful colleagues at Grand Valley State University, especially William Levitan, Diane Rayor, and the late Barbara Flaschenriem, for encouragement and sage advice.

Institutional support for this project was provided at various stages by Grand Valley State University, through a summer research stipend and a precious sabbatical leave, and by The Margo Tytus Visiting Scholars Program at the University of Cincinnati, Classics Department.

Of the many people who have labored in hidden ways, sometimes even unknown to themselves, I must mention two of my teachers: William Johnson, who taught me to value my own work and still keep revising, and Rick Powell, who helped teach me to value myself and also to appreciate the ways in which energy properly applied can produce interesting results. Many students have read Seneca with me, in Latin or in English, and each of them has taught me something that benefited the whole. Most of all, and in all things, my heartfelt gratitude goes to the wonderful Gretchen Galbraith, who has probably read these translations more often than I have and certainly with keener eyes. Even all of these people were not sufficient to catch every one of my errors. For the errors that remain I ask for your patience and understanding.

INTRODUCTION

Seneca's Life

Little is known about the early years of Seneca's life, although much can be surmised about its general course from its historical and social contexts. Seneca's family was wealthy and prominent, part of the provincial equestrian elite of Spain who, along with elite families from Gaul, would come to strongly influence literary and political life at Rome from the mid- and late first century CE on. He was born in Corduba, Spain, sometime between 4 BCE and 1 BCE. The expansion of Roman power and culture into Spain began during the Punic Wars in the third century BCE, although Roman dominance was strongly resisted by certain tribes for over 200 years after that. Corduba was captured and made into a Roman garrison town when the two Roman Spanish provinces (*Hispania Citerior*, nearer Spain, and *Hispania Ulterior*, farther Spain) were established in 206 BCE. By the time of Seneca's birth, Corduba was the Roman provincial capital of *Hispania Ulterior* (from Almeria along the southern coast to Portugal, and stretching northward into the Guadalquivir), and thoroughly Romanized. His father, Marcus (or Lucius) Annaeus Seneca, was a distinguished teacher of rhetoric, and Seneca seems to have joined him at Rome before the age of ten. There he was given the normal elite education in literature, languages, rhetoric, and, as a young man, philosophy. He had two brothers, the elder of whom, Julius Annaeus Gallio, entered politics and rose to a distinguished rank. The younger brother, Annaeus Mela, lived a life apart from politics; his son (Seneca's nephew) was the famous poet Lucan, later charged with treason in the plot of 65 CE that also led to Seneca's compelled suicide. Seneca's father's and his father's family's position and talents ensured him access to patrons who supported early political activities, but Seneca's career seems to have started only under Emperor Tiberius in 33 CE and progressed quite slowly. Even so, he eventually reached senatorial rank and must have been an astute politician. To be active in politics during the reigns of four emperors very different in style and character—Tiberius (14–37 CE), Gaius Caligula (37–41 CE),

Claudius (41–54 CE), and Nero (54–68 CE)—was no mean feat. Our best and most certain knowledge about Seneca's life comes from the period starting with his exile on Corsica under Emperor Claudius (41–49 CE) until his death in 65 CE.

The reasons for Seneca's exile are not fully discussed in any of his works, but he seems to have been implicated in an adulterous affair with Julia Livilla, a member of the imperial family, either as a facilitator or a participant. But none of the other sources that mention it consider Seneca actually guilty, and there are good reasons from Seneca's several comments about the charge and trial to suppose that the charge was exaggerated. Indeed, Emperor Claudius reduced the sentence from death to exile. In 49 CE Seneca was recalled by Claudius to Rome through the machinations of Agrippina, mother of Nero. Shortly afterward, he began as the young Nero's tutor and advisor (Nero was about twelve years old), a role that he maintained through Nero's adoption as heir by Claudius and into the first years of his reign. Seneca, now a senator, continued to give political advice, write speeches, and offer moral guidance to the young and talented Nero; he seems to have helped shape policy along with other *amici* (friends) of the emperor, who served as a sort of informal court; and he seems to have been key in securing positions for people of talent and for his family and friends, many of whom were also people of talent. Seneca's deep involvement in political affairs is consonant with his Stoic principles. His attempts to finally withdraw from Nero's circle of advisors were similarly motivated: Seneca seems to have perceived that his influence over the increasingly erratic emperor was entirely gone. Seneca's first attempt to withdraw in 62 CE was refused, as was a second in 64 CE, although at that point Seneca secluded himself anyway, using ill health as a reason to not attend Nero. In 65 CE a failed plot revealed extensive opposition to Nero among high-ranking members of the Senate and his own advisors, and Nero ordered many suicides. Seneca was ordered to commit suicide in late spring 65 CE—an order he obeyed, modeling his death on that of Socrates. The death scene itself, as described in Tacitus (who is sympathetic) and Cassius Dio (who is not) clearly displays Seneca's own thinking about suicide—namely, that it should be an entirely rational decision, undertaken only when every other option has been exhausted, and even then only when circumstances are such that one's life may not be lived in accordance with virtue. The scene also displays Seneca's penchant for drama and making an impression, and the extent of his affection for his family and friends (both of which we also see in his writings). Tacitus' description in his *Annals* 15.60–64 is quite moving; I will not paraphrase here, trusting the reader to find one of many translations available in print or online.

Literary Qualities of Seneca's Philosophical Writings

Seneca chose well-established literary genres as vehicles for his contributions to philosophy. As a result, various devices we tend to think of as superfluous to philosophical argument or even to the articulation of "pure" convictions—things such as rhetorical techniques, word-play, witty and epigrammatic statements, rhythm, sound, and style—form an integral part of his philosophical style. It would thus be absurd to attempt to treat Seneca's philosophical writings without considering their literary form, and Seneca's ancient readers would certainly have approached these texts as literature just as they would have approached them as philosophy; in Seneca, these are two sides of one coin.

Formal classical Latin was deeply influenced by a culture of elite Roman education steeped in poetry and rhetoric. By Seneca's time, the practice of rhetoric and speech-making as a pedagogical tool (e.g., through declamation training) was standard. As a result, highly rhetorical forms of argument, and the structures and techniques of artistry and persuasion they employed, were understood and appreciated by almost anyone who would have read Seneca's work. Prose writers in Seneca's time also felt the influence of the previous century—the century of such literary giants as Cicero, Sallust, Caesar, Virgil, Horace, and Ovid—not without some anxiety as to how the achievements of their own century stood by comparison. The style of the first century CE can be seen as both a perpetuation of the kinds of (often very different) styles seen in the previous century, as well as a seeking out of new and varied kinds of expression.

Seneca's own writing is a good example of the vivid style of the first century CE and is notable for its dazzling effects. Flashes of sharp or humorous wit, elegant turns of phrase, stunning verbal imagery, aural effects, stark juxtapositions of words, quick changes in tone, and admixtures of these and more all create an impression-driven style that deliberately seeks to stir up and excite the reader. Seneca's intent, however, is not merely to impress the reader with his literary virtuosity—though it is surely that too—but to rivet his or her attention to the matter at hand, all the better to persuade the reader of his argument.

Similar intentions can be seen behind Seneca's frequent recasting of ideas in slightly different—or wildly different—words. Such variations on a given theme are perhaps the most dominant feature of Seneca's style, a device he moreover uses to develop his ideas, explore subtle differences, and (like his insertion of interjections of various kinds) place emphasis on key arguments.

Another striking stylistic tactic of Seneca's is his deployment of the epigrammatic statement, in which an idea or argument is encapsulated in a clever and compressed turn of phrase—for example, "Cato did not live longer than liberty, nor liberty longer than Cato" (*On the Resolute Nature of the Wise Man* 2.2). Like a jingle for a commercial, an epigram is meant to stick with a reader for a long time, and Seneca is thus quite a quotable author. But as vivid, carefully honed, and often ironic propositions that also serve to punctuate and underscore his arguments, Seneca's epigrams serve other useful purposes: they help persuade, and do so in the interest of advancing a Stoic view of life. Seneca is a sermonizer and these are a sermonizer's tricks.

Just as the devices of Seneca's prose are deliberate, so are the genres in which he writes and his adherence to their formal conventions. Chief among these for this selection is the dialogue, sometimes called a diatribe or, in the case of a letter to a grieving person, a consolation. Seneca's *Dialogues* are not dialogues with multiple characters speaking, such as we might see in Plato or Cicero. Instead, Seneca himself speaks the words of his interlocutors (when they are given), but most often follows the generic conventions of the letter form. By Seneca's time, a sophisticated understanding of formal rhetorical structures, such as the parts every kind of speech or letter should have, could be assumed of the educated elite. While Seneca is thus quite aware of these structures, and uses them skillfully, and while the influence of formal rhetoric is pervasive in his dialogues, his use of them is far from slavish and very much his own.

Like his lavish use of literary devices, Seneca's exploitation of the generic conventions of the dialogue can sometimes seem motivated by sheer showmanship. His style as a whole was criticized in antiquity (and is today) for being excessive and undisciplined. It is better to think of it as deliberately affected—a style that, like its author, uses language for all it is worth to achieve a wide variety of literary effects, but can achieve real philosophical and humane ends with it too. As artificial in some respects as his dialogues clearly are, what Seneca has to say is always presented within the context of an ongoing conversation between persons bound by ties of affection, between friends or family. It is as if the reader is dropped into a set of conversations that started some time ago. But such is the artistry of Seneca's writing that it will quickly seem as if he wrote his dialogues with more than his ostensible interlocutors in mind.

This personal touch is quite an interesting element of Seneca's style, blurring the lines between his addressees and his readers. Seneca frequently poses rhetorical questions to the reader and raises supposed objections to his arguments, but rarely uses names or mentions specific circumstances (except perhaps in *Consolations*). In some instances, it is quite clear that he is addressing Gallio, Serenus, Paulinus, or his mother. At other times, we might feel obliged to wonder at the generalizing second person "you": does he still mean Gallio or is he talking to us now? And we *should* feel obliged, because at yet other times he fully and explicitly addresses persons outside the dramatic context of the letter. This blending of readerships is a sign of the literary nature of this kind of writing—it was perhaps intended for the original addressee but never (I would suggest) intended solely for that person. Seneca's lively engagement with a particular individual, and the playfully serious engagement with other readers, moreover lends his prose peculiarly personal qualities, some of which (e.g., its colloquial tone, interjections, and intimacy) I've touched on above.

A Note on the Translations

Because of the range of Seneca's style and stylistic effects, good translations of *Dialogues* are very difficult to produce. It often seems to me that some translations prefer to adopt a more or less uniform quality and tone, becoming normalized throughout. I have no illusions about the success of my efforts but have tried to replicate in these translations something of the wide range of effects and qualities of Senecan prose. Sometimes it was possible to replicate the same effect in English in the same place as in the Latin, with all its constraints as a language. Sometimes to replicate the effect would have meant utterly obscuring the meaning. (I have tried not to do that!) Sometimes I have broken up what is a very long sentence in the Latin: there are things that modern, readable English simply cannot do. Other times, where sense was not impaired, I tried to maintain some of the larger structures of a passage to present some of the astonishing complexity of Seneca's sentences. His writing is not a casual, quick product, but the product of the labor of his many hours and his considerable talent.

The thematic variation that is the core stylistic principle of Seneca's writing does not extend to certain terms of vocabulary, about which he is quite strict and clear. The issue for a translator is that the words available in English for rendering Seneca's moral and psychological vocabulary tend to have a wider or narrower range of meaning than in Latin. After some struggle, I decided it would be preferable, especially for the needs of those wishing to track Seneca's use of some terminology, to be very consistent in rendering six key words and their cognates even when a more naturally English phrase might have caught the flavor a bit better: *animus* (spirit), *mens* (mind), *virtus* (virtue), *otium* (retirement), *bonum* (good; a noun), *malum* (bad, badness, bad thing(s); a noun).

Some comments, then, on the terms themselves: in Seneca's writing, *animus* signifies the activating force of life that belongs not just to the body but to the universe, and could quite reasonably have been translated in some contexts as soul, courage, heart, or mind; *mens* signifies the combination of processes and abilities that make up the rational mind; *virtus* signifies a moral quality that motivates, enables, and requires proper action in a person; *otium* is a state of living in which an individual does not engage in political or public activity (*negotium* is a Latin word for work) but instead seeks betterment through study, sometimes in isolation but certainly disengaged from politics; *bonum* refers to that which is morally good, and *malum* to that which is morally bad. For a fuller explanation of the range of meanings for each of these words, a reader should consult a comprehensive Latin dictionary.

The text used as the basis for the translations was Lindsay's *Oxford Classical Text*. The order of the dialogues and consolations in that edition has been maintained.

Seneca and Stoicism

Stoicism traces its philosophical heritage directly back to Socrates, although the founder of the philosophical school known as the Stoa was Zeno of Citium. When Zeno came to Athens in the mid-fourth century BCE, he attended the lectures of the Cynic Crates. Following Diogenes of Sinope, the Cynics proposed a life according to the necessities of nature, which included a rejection of all things formed by mere convention or rule; in fact, cynic means "doglike," and the Cynics were notorious for their self-sufficiency, living in chosen poverty, and seeking only the bare necessities of life. Zeno subsequently studied in the Academy, headed by Polemo, and then with the Megarian Stilpon. All of these teachers and schools had their influence on Zeno, and he returned to Athens, teaching in the Painted Stoa (the site from which the Stoics earned their name) near the Agora.

There are basic tenets that it seems all Stoics adhere to, but as a school of thought Stoicism was articulated and developed through the interests of the individual philosophers who professed it: Zeno was known for setting out the basic principles and framework for Stoic thought; Aristo of Chios, one of Zeno's colleagues, seems to have developed a very strict theory of indifferents (see below) that was subsequently moderated by later heads of the Stoa; Cleanthes, the second head of the Stoa, was famous for refining ideas about the nature of matter, "tension," and the cosmic soul; and Chrysippus, Cleanthes' successor, was especially known for his rigorous application of logic and, as a result, for more clearly defining what Stoicism was.

In fact, it was during Chrysippus' lifetime that Stoicism came under attack, especially from the Academic Skeptics: Chrysippus' staunch defense was a watershed period for orthodox Stoic doctrine. The second century BCE saw the large-scale introduction to Rome of Greek philosophies, of which Stoicism seems to have held particular (but not singular) attractiveness. Posidonius and Panaetius figure most significantly in histories of Rome's encounter with Stoicism, and we can see clear evidence of their influence of Cicero who, although not a Stoic, presented and analyzed (and admired) many Stoic ideas. Attalus, Seneca's teacher, was one of the liminal figures of the transition from the Middle to the Later Stoa at the end of the first century BCE and into the first century CE. The Later Stoa is dominated by Rome, as she had spread her influence throughout the Mediterranean by this time.

Also, through Epictetus, Seneca, and (a century later) Marcus Aurelius, we have an enormous amount of textual evidence; we possess very little in writing from earlier authors. The incomplete preservation of texts from antiquity tends to lead us to lend more weight to the material we have, but we do know of several other important Stoics in Seneca's time and after, such as Hierocles, Cornutus, and Musonius Rufus, whose writings either do not survive whole or who, like Musonius Rufus, following Socrates' example, made it a point to not write down any of their teachings themselves (although their students did). Stoicism was a living tradition, adhering to central tenets about the nature of the universe and human happiness, but shifting focus slightly from teacher to teacher and developing over time. Indeed, Stoicism had profound influence on early Christian writers, as well as medieval, Renaissance, and Enlightenment philosophers, and even thinkers of our own time.

In such a brief introduction, little more can be done than to orient the reader to some major strands of Stoic thinking important for understanding Seneca's *Dialogues*. Curious readers are directed to the "Further Reading" section for more detailed and better introductions to Stoic philosophy. But there are three things, it seems to me, that underlie a great deal of Seneca's thought, and that should be kept in mind when reading these dialogues.

First, although much of what we find in the extant sources of ancient Greek and Roman philosophy arises from attempts to understand the nature of the universe and the world within which human beings find themselves, philosophy's purpose as a whole was to enable a human being to lead a "happy life." Not that there were not other purposes; some philosophers seem to focus on quite precise areas of investigation without referring at all to human happiness. But philosophy was a holistic practice of a set of principles and beliefs, not simply a sequence of logical arguments. This conception of philosophy applies especially to the Stoics and the Epicureans, the two major schools of thought that, along with Academic Skepticism, influenced the education and thought of the elite Romans of the late Republic and early empire. It certainly applies to Seneca.

Second, Stoicism itself was a highly integrated system of philosophical thinking that encompassed, literally, all of reality. The dialogues in this book are focused for the most part on the "right conduct of life," but the interdependence of the traditional topics in Stoic philosophy (logic, physics, and ethics) is key to understanding any aspect of Stoicism. The ancient writers themselves thought this interdependence and integration worthy of attention (and if the writer was hostile, worthy of attack). Various analogies found in our sources illustrate the essential integration of the Stoic system: logic is the bones and tendons of the body, ethics its flesh and muscle, and physics its soul; again, logic is the shell of an egg, ethics the white, and physics the yolk; and again, logic is the wall around a field, ethics the produce, and physics the soil or trees. These analogies need not be taken much further than to demonstrate that each element is an essential part of the whole. The Stoic system stands or falls as a unit. It is quite possible to read, analyze, enjoy, and benefit from these dialogues without being deeply immersed in Stoic philosophy, but it is worth keeping in mind that the assertions and arguments Seneca makes are sometimes undergirded by several centuries of thoughtful people developing their ideas about the universe.

Third, as is true for the Greeks and Romans in general, the Stoics and their ideas are like us in many ways but unlike us in many others: they are at once utterly strange, though familiar. Certain ideas and arguments in these dialogues will seem to make sense to a modern reader right away. Some ideas will seem bizarre and implausible from the outset. Others will seem reasonable until carried to their logical conclusion. As a result, students of Stoicism and Seneca must engage with the central assumptions of Stoicism and at the same time be critical and careful in examining the central arguments, all while setting aside their own assumptions and convictions about the issues being examined.

For example, Stoics are often thought to embody physical and mental endurance and rigid emotional control to such an extent that they will not allow themselves to feel anything. (The adjective *stoic* came into English with just that connotation.) Now it is true that Stoics consider many emotions (or disturbed passions) a danger to human happiness, and in need of very careful rational evaluation or even eradication. But it is also true that Stoics understand emotions to be a part of human nature: they argue that only the truly wise man can love truly—that is, (as we might say today) unconditionally—or indeed have any authentic and healthy emotion. As Seneca writes to his friend Polybius on the death of his brother, "No one should hope or desire that reason could make sorrow disappear entirely. Let reason instead preserve a limit for grief: to imitate neither irreverence nor insanity but to maintain the behavior appropriate to a reverent and steady mind. Weep, and also stop weeping; let sobs come from the deepest place in your heart, but likewise finally set them aside" (*Consolation to Polybius* 18.5). Similarly, Stoic arguments about the essential connectedness of all human beings led to a conception of universal duty to and compassion for others (*oikeiosis*) that is directly opposed to emotional isolation and rigidity. Both of these ideas run counter to a common modern perception that being stoic means controlling and suppressing emotion or having no emotion at all. Certainly, while a Stoic is progressing toward the goal of a happy life, he or she is monitoring, evaluating, and controlling his or her emotions and reactions. But this control is not the end goal of the Stoic. The goal of Stoic training is healthy and proper emotions and reactions that are predicated on the perfection of human nature and the primacy of a human being's rational capacity as represented by the Stoic sage. Until that perfection is reached, every emotion or affective reaction must be examined and rationally regulated according to the circumstance and to the proper degree.

The Providential Universe and Virtuous Living

God for the Stoics, Greek and Roman, is the active, living, conscious, rational universe. Thus, the Stoic god is not Plato's Demiurge, who exists outside the universe, ordering and directing, but the universe itself, directing and ordering itself with a rational intelligence. God and matter are always coexistent, and all matter in the universe has some degree of the divine *pneuma* (spirit). This divine *pneuma* was thought of as fiery—the "designing fire." Fire burns what it touches, and the divine fire itself burns continuously and cyclically: it builds to a conflagration of the present finite universe; becomes the stuff of an expanded (because hotter) universe of pure fire/light; then regenerates matter, producing the same present, finite universe again, in its elemental stages. This cycle of creation is a natural and inevitable succession of the exact same world-order, divinely ordered in the best possible way. In a very real sense for the Stoics, god, the rational governing intelligence of the universe and also the universe itself, lives out identical phases of a life cycle. This view of the universe has been called optimistic or providential, because it means that everything that is and that happens is part of a rational, divine order. While few would argue that Stoicism is a religion in the sense in which we frequently use that term today, it does have a clear idea of divinity (and for some Stoic writers something approaching what we would think of as a theology) that includes the divine rational universe as well as the gods themselves. Some Stoics argued that the gods were simply fuller than human embodiments of the divine *pneuma*, different from humans only in not being mortal. This last, at any rate, seems to have been Seneca's view.

Human beings, unlike other animals, have a share in this divine *pneuma*: reason. And it is this share that allows us to make right choices about our perceptions and impulses (i.e., to live virtuously). Reason, or rationality, is the essential, particularizing component of both humanity and of the divine. Rationality, as the essential nature of a human being, is, when perfected, virtue—and therefore sufficient for happiness. Stoics' ubiquitous requirement "to live according to nature" means "to live according to reason" and "to live according to vir-tue" (which are the same). In this way, Stoic ethical precepts, which is Seneca's concern in this collection, are completely integrated with and dependent on the Stoics' understanding of the universe and the divine quality of reason.

Chrysippus and Stoic thinkers after him held the view, one grounded in their understanding of the universe, that the world is ordered providentially in the best possible way, and that this best pos-sible order results from the agency of the divine *pneuma*. Under the Stoic conception of causation and responsibility (in which divine *pneuma* is both the reason we are rational beings, acting in ways that are determined, and the means by which we deliberate and choose our actions), a person must recognize what is "in our power" and what comes from external influences and causes. Everything that is external is simply a triggering cause, and so a person can only hold himself or herself, the primary cause, responsible for his or her actions through the capacity to use reason and deliberate about how to act. The Stoic philosopher Epictetus asked why god placed only this one capacity "in our power." In his *Discourses* (1.1.7–12) Zeus replies, "Epictetus, if it had been possible, I would have made your wretched body and trappings free and unhindered. But as it is, please note, this body is not your own, but a subtle mixture of clay. Since, however, I was not able to do this, I gave you a portion of myself, this power of impulse and repulsion, desire and aversion—in a word the power to use impressions. If you take care of it and place in it everything you have, you will never be blocked, never hindered. You will never complain, never blame, never flatter anyone" (Long and Sedley 1987). Using our perception of external things and of any impulses to act that might arise because of them, and engaging our faculty of reason to analyze and filter our perceptions correctly, we can act correctly, develop our minds, and change our character for the better by virtue of our share in the divine *pneuma*. If we recognize this, we will be motivated to choose the good (i.e., to act according to nature through our reasoning mind). Every rational human being therefore has the capacity, and the opportunity, to work throughout their lives at becoming fully virtuous and fully happy.

The divine *pneuma* that continuously shapes and directs the universe imparts to human beings a rational mind; this rational mind allows human beings, using impressions about what we experience, to make choices. These choices are determined in the sense that each choice is caused by everything that has come before it, especially everything that has determined an individual's character. But the very nature of what makes us able to choose also makes us able to change. Stoics argued that by using impressions, individuals can, in a very real way, alter their own character such that even when an impulse to act badly arises we will not necessarily act badly—that is, reason can interrupt the movement from impulse to action. Indeed, as we just saw, every rational human being has the capacity and the moral responsibility to do this, given the opportunity. Achieving a virtuous life, free of what has no relevance for virtue (which is everything but virtue or rationality itself, as we shall see), leads inevitably to enduring and inviolable happiness.

Oikeiosis

Another facet of human ethical development is *oikeiosis,* or a human being's self-identity and connection to community. Social organization, family, and care and love of offspring are all natural impulses of the human animal. According to the Stoics, human beings are by nature able to form relationships, communities, states, and to care for others; this ability is a natural outgrowth of the divine *pneuma*'s (or Nature's) "affectionate ownership" of humans, an ownership conceived as comparable to a skilled artisan's affection for his handiwork—though one that is even more enduring. Although blood ties and familial ties can strengthen relationships, the Stoics insisted that the basis for the affectionate ownership humans feel for each other was the connection guaranteed by the divine *pneuma*. Any single person owes "duties," or behaviors, to other humans because all humans derive their rational uniqueness from the same entity.

A conventional notion from the time of Seneca conceived of the propriety of human ties of obligation and affection as operating according to a model of proximity. As if located within a series of concentric circles, an individual was appropriately concerned first with himself, then with those closest to him, then those next closest, and so on, all the way to the whole human race—with ties to any given party typically seen as weakening according to its distance from one's self. Hierocles, a Stoic philosopher who was active just after Seneca, rejected this notion, arguing that in fact the model was incompatible with Stoic thinking: the Stoic's responsibility was to recognize that there was no real difference or distance between the circles representing the self and those representing the apparent outer limits of the concentric circles. Just as concern for immediate community (e.g., offspring, family) is a natural development of the animal's concern for its own health and safety, concern for the wider community and for the human race was the natural development of our rational self's concern. Similarly, the providential and affectionate attitude of the universe, Nature, for human beings (and of the gods for human beings) comes from this shared divine *pneuma*, the essence of our rational humanity. What is appropriate (*kathekon*) to each creature is to live according to its nature. For humans, whose nature is governed by the divine *pneuma*, living in perfect agreement with nature will result as a consequence in virtuous and correct actions, the moral intentions of which stretch far beyond the individual self to embrace all rational human beings.

Indifferents

Yet another important Stoic concept that bears on Seneca's thought is that of indifferents. The Stoics have an unconventional view of what is good or bad. In fact, they maintained that virtue is the only good (and therefore the opposite of virtue, badness, the only "bad"), and the only requirement for happiness. Virtue is the natural result of the action of the divine *pneuma* (i.e., in humans, the rational mind). The Stoics believed in the unity of the virtues. Though unitary, virtue has distinguishable spheres of practical application, such as prudence, justice, moderation, courage, etc. What is unconventional about the Stoic view as it developed is that everything but virtue (and its linguistic and practical subcategories) is indifferent—that is, nothing but virtue affects the capacity or the opportunity of the human being to live in agreement with nature or reason (i.e., to be happy). It is certainly true that some things might be preferred (e.g., good health, wealth, liberty, etc.) and others dis-preferred (e.g., illness, poverty, oppression, etc.), but the Stoics insisted that none of these circumstances undermine the capacity for rational action. The goodness of virtue is the only compelling good. The value of any other thing depended entirely on the degree of perfection of the rational mind using it: a weak or ill mind might harbor impulses that lead to not-right action, where a healthy mind would identify and discriminate between impulses and possible actions, making good use of the entire range of things and circumstances. So, one might prefer to be extremely wealthy (as Seneca was), but neither wealth nor poverty can guarantee virtuous actions and happiness. One might prefer to have liberty, but neither liberty nor slavery was considered a constraint on rational behavior. Many choices made by Seneca and those around him (e.g., maintaining a household of slaves) and their characteristic way of referring to their changeable circumstances (i.e., their fortune, or Fortune itself, personified) would seem to many in the modern world difficult to understand or even abhorrent. But they were consistent with this fundamental view that material, physical, or social circumstances were not an essential factor in a human being's motivation and capacity to be happy, living a life of reason and virtue. Only the rational mind and the use to which it can be put is "in our power"; everything else does not belong to us, and can be lost or gained in a moment. The wise man's happiness, tranquility, and security derive from his reasoning nature, and is unshakeable because he recognizes what is in his control (his reasoning and actions) and what is outside of his control (everything else).

Epicureanism

Like Roman Stoicism, Epicureanism finds its fullest expression in the Roman period in ethical teachings. The ideas of these two philosophical schools, along with several others, would have been familiar to any well-educated Roman. It is clear in some of the selections in this volume, and most explicitly in Seneca's *Moral Letters* (*Epistulae Morales*), that Seneca is at pains to contrast Stoic approaches with Epicurean ones. And it is reasonable to conjecture in such cases that his addressee may have been more influenced by the Epicureans than by the Stoics. But it bears pointing out that these dialogues are literary endeavors also, and surely were composed with a broader audience in mind: recourse to Epicurean examples and comparisons always support or contrast with Seneca's own, Stoic, arguments.

The differences between the schools of thought on all of the areas elaborated above are extensive and profound, even antithetical. Rather than a world of divine causation and determined perfection, Epicureans saw a world of random and mechanistic atomism. More to the point for Seneca's writing, the Epicurean ethical framework that determines human behavior was incompatible with that of Stoicism, although it had the same goal of happiness and tranquil living through adherence to human nature. Epicurus suggested that to live according to nature meant to avoid pain and to seek pleasure. But for Epicurus, most of what people thought pleasurable in fact brought pain or distress of some kind. So, far from advocating a life of debauchery, Epicurus exhorted his students to lead a frugal life of honor, prudence, and moderation, surrounded by friends, and using philosophy and science to dispel superstition, while remaining free of civic involvement. The Epicureans' different understanding of the primary goal of living led in turn to very different ideas about civic engagement, human community, and the path to a happy life, and Seneca frequently juxtaposes Epicurean maxims or principles to highlight Stoic ideas of virtue through reason and *oikeiosis*, both divine and human, as well as more mundane patterns of living.

The Dialogues and Consolations

The selections in this volume date from nearly the full span of Seneca's life: from the reign of Gaius Caligula (*Consolation to Marcia*, possibly

On Providence); his exile under Claudius (*Consolation to Polybius, Consolation to His Mother Helvia*); either the last years of Claudius' reign or under Nero (*On the Shortness of Life, On the Resolute Nature of the Wise Man, On Serenity of the Spirit, On Retirement*); and from the early years of Nero (*On the Happy Life*). Most of Seneca's other writings, with the exception of *De Ira* (*On Anger*), date from the very last years of his life.

Each of the selected dialogues addresses a central question of interest, although all participate in the common ideas and problems of Stoicism. The order of presentation chosen in this volume is that in which the dialogues survive in the manuscript tradition: they are not always in chronological order.

On Providence probably dates from Seneca's earliest period of writing, before the end of his exile, but this is by no means certain. The dialogue addresses a fundamental question of Stoic theology and cosmology, however, and for it to occupy the initial position in any collection (as it did in the manuscript tradition) is surely no accident. In it, Seneca elaborates the view that the universe, the gods, and the human experience are divinely ordered: human suffering, challenges, etc. stem from human misperception of the nature of the universe and a human's role within it. In a sense, this dialogue addresses the same issue that led later Christian thinkers to consider "the question of evil." The Stoic answer Seneca might have given is that humans wrongly claim events or circumstances are evil through ignorance of the divinely ordered nature of the universe. Like a parent, the universe tests and prepares its children with Fortune.

On the Resolute Nature of the Wise Man was very probably written during Claudius' reign, likely after Seneca's recall from exile, and takes up an old "chestnut," or problem, in Stoic thinking. Many such classic problems had been collected by Cicero in a work called *The Paradoxes of the Stoics*. In *On the Resolute Nature of the Wise Man*, Seneca argues that the wise man can never be injured or insulted, because he never "receives injury." Indeed, "the wise man does not receive injury or insult" seems to have been the title used for the dialogue in some manuscripts; the Latin word *constantia* (resoluteness) does not appear in the text. Instead, Seneca uses the word *firmitas* (steadfastness or consistency) to describe the wise man's endurance against injury. The basis for the arguments in this dialogue can be found in Stoic psychology of perception and in the notion of indifferents. The wise man can never be insulted, because an insult depends on the target's perception of what is true: simply put, if a critical statement is true, there can be no insult; if it is false, it is not insulting, but simply untrue. The wise man is secure in his dignity, which is not vulnerable to attack by the less wise. The wise man's *self* can never be injured (which for the Romans included damage to personal property), because nothing except his rational mind is he. What seems like special pleading on Seneca's part—that is, that "someone can do injury to my body, but I will not receive the injury" or clever sophistry, actually stems instead from the Stoic understanding of the self in relation to perception, matter, and the universe.

Consolation to Marcia was likely written between 39 CE and 49 CE. Like *Consolation to Polybius* and *Consolation to His Mother Helvia* (both also written during Seneca's exile), it follows a specific pattern of presentation, tailored to the circumstances of the individual: the consolation was an established genre of writing. Behind all three is the conviction that death is not a bad thing, that the nature of a mortal is to die, that grief is entirely natural but has appropriate limits, and that excessive grieving separates a person from her or his relationships and duties to the living. *Consolation to Marcia* was written to a famous historian's (Cremutius Cordus') adult daughter, who publicly grieved for her son for over three years. *Consolation to Polybius* was written to console an important official in Emperor Claudius' administration on the death of his brother. *Consolation to His Mother Helvia*, written to console his mother during his exile on Corsica, likens exile to death and treats her grief over his absence in a similar way.

On the Happy Life is from the later stage of Seneca's literary production, while Seneca was still active in politics under Nero (before 62 CE); it is addressed to his elder brother Gallio, a prominent politician and administrator. In this dialogue Seneca articulates the goal of philosophical living, a happy life, from a Stoic perspective: intentional rationality and an awareness of natural processes and of natural order will lead inevitably to virtue and unassailable happiness.

On Retirement, at least the beginning of which was lost in transmission from antiquity, weighs the purpose and use of *otium*, a Latin term that means time spent away from public duties. *Otium* was by Seneca's time considered to be, on the one hand, an alternative to public duties and, on the other hand, a period of rest from the rigors of public life and duties. *Otium* was not laziness, but a period occupied with a different kind of activity, and often one of learning. (As previously noted, in this volume I use "retirement" for *otium* instead of the more common but slightly misleading "leisure.") *On Retirement* dates from the same period as *On the Resolute Nature of the Wise Man* and *On Serenity of the Spirit*—after Seneca's return from exile.

On Serenity of the Spirit is a reflection on the pragmatics of living without disturbances of the soul. Both Seneca's addressee Serenus and Seneca himself are intensely introspective, focused on the practicalities and pitfalls of living into the vision of a life secure from anxiety. Even so, the rationale for behaviors and for the mindset Seneca is "prescribing" to his friend are explicitly derived from the Stoic precepts articulated above and in other dialogues.

In a similar way, *On the Shortness of Life* was likely written before these last dialogues, after his return from exile but before 55 CE. Like *On Serenity of the Spirit*, it is a reflection on the realities of living as a Stoic engaged in her or his community and especially in public life. This dialogue speaks eloquently, and repeatedly, about the necessity of self-care and appropriate discernment of duty to others. In this sense, the dialogue can be read as a meditation on *oikeiosis*: care and sustenance for the individual precedes (but does not eliminate or supersede) care and concern for community and state.

The Addressees

The cues in the dialogues indicating that the intended audience is the addressee are not always as strong as those indicating a much wider audience, a characteristic of Seneca's style noted above. Not that the addressees are not important to understanding the dialogues. On the contrary, they are real individuals who have meaningful relationships with Seneca, personally as well as in the pursuit of the life of philosophy.

On Providence is addressed to Gaius Lucilius Junior, to whom the large collection of *Moral Letters* and the set of learned inquiries called *Natural Questions* (*Quaestiones Naturales*) were also addressed. Lucilius seems in many ways to be a self-made man who rose to prominence under Claudius and Nero, accepting significant imperial appointments in Greece and Africa. A poet as well as a politician, Lucilius seems, judging from frequent comments in works addressed to him, to have been a student of Epicureanism; either he turned away from Epicureanism at some point or, like many of his time, drew ideas from both schools in the pursuit of a happy life.

Serenus, another important political appointee during Nero's principate, seems to have been a member of the Annaeus clan. He was a close friend of Seneca, to whom he likely owed his appointment as *prafectus vigilum* under Nero (probably in 54 CE); this was a senior post in the administration of Rome, and the height of Serenus' career. Serenus, even more so than Lucilius, seems to have been strongly influenced by Epicureanism. Seneca reports his death (probably in 62 CE) from eating poisonous fungi. *On the Resolute Nature of the Wise Man* provides a framework for the philosopher to interact with difficult and insulting people; *On Serenity of the Spirit* similarly advises Serenus on the most virtuous ways to pursue inner and lasting calm amid the chaos of political life. Both of these problems find similar solutions in Epicureanism, but of course through markedly different means.

The daughter of the famous historian Aulus Cermutius Cordus, whose works were burned after his conviction for *maiestas* under Sejanus, Marcia was an influential member of an important family. Her son Metilius died while still a promising youth, and she appears to have maintained public mourning for him for a very long time (three years at least, before the letter was written). Seneca's motivations for writing the consolation to her from exile, so many years past the point of death and grief, are hard to ascertain with any degree of certainty. It seems clear and inevitable that Seneca could have benefited from her influence, but he also writes with a degree of sensitivity and concern, and with a positive assessment of her ability to live philosophically, that is hard to dismiss. *Consolation to Marcia* is an especially elegant, spiritual, and compassionate work.

Seneca's older brother Gallio also entered political life, and rose to some prominence under Nero as governor of the Greek province of Achaia as well as *suffect consul* (taking over part way through the year). Like *On Serenity of the Spirit* and *On the Shortness of Life*, *On the Happy Life* is clearly aimed at enabling the politically active Gallio to nevertheless achieve virtuous living and a life balanced between the necessities of office and the security of the happy life of the philosopher.

Pompeius Paulinus was likely near the end of his very successful political career when Seneca wrote *On the Shortness of Life*; he was Seneca's father-in-law. As *praefectus annonae* from 48 CE to 55 CE, Paulinus had the unenviable position of regulating, procuring, and protecting the grain supplies with which the emperors fed the volatile urban populace of Rome.

Helvia followed Seneca's father to Rome near the beginning of the first century CE, according to Seneca while he was still an infant. A basic biography of Helvia and other important women in her family forms part of the consolation written to her, but the letter is not meant to console grief for the death of a loved one, but for Seneca's own absence during his exile. To modern sensibilities this might seem somewhat excessive, but as with the other consolations, Seneca's motivations and audiences may have been quite varied. To his mother he presents reasoned and intellectual demands that she approach the period of separation with virtue and appropriate behavior (exile on Corsica was not simply an enforced holiday—many exiles were executed, died, or never returned for other reasons). To other readers he presents a mother who is less secure and more vulnerable after the loss of her son's care, and also presents himself as enduring exile with good grace and eager to return to Rome.

It would be easy (and has been easy for scholars) to criticize *Consolation to Polybius* for excessive flattery, given the significance it attributes to Emperor Claudius as a source of comfort to his freedman Polybius on the death of a brother. And it is obvious that, as Claudius' chief secretary, Polybius could wield some influence on the emperor who had exiled Seneca. But the consolatory letter is a strong challenge to Polybius to live Stoic ideals and to approach death and grief as he approached life and duty. It is not impossible to be a good friend to another person and to seek good things for oneself at the same time, all while striving toward a rigorous, and perhaps unreachable, set of ideals.

Further Reading

I offer below a short bibliography of further reading, should readers wish to begin to explore some of the issues raised in the Introduction and in the dialogues. Those with an asterisk are useful introductions to Seneca or Stoicism.

Bartsch, S., and D. Wray. 2009. *Seneca and the Self.* Cambridge: Cambridge University Press.

*Brennan, T. 2005. *The Stoic Life: Emotions, Duties, & Fate.* Oxford: Oxford University Press.

Coleman, R. 1974. "The Artful Moralist: A Study of Seneca's Epistolary Style." *Classical Quarterly* 68: 276–89.

Currie, H. M. (1966). "The Younger Seneca's Style: Some Observations." *Bulletin of the Institute of Classical Studies* 13: 83–84.

Edwards, C. (1997). "Self-scrutiny and Self-transformation in Seneca's *Letters*." *Greece and Rome* 44: 23–28.

Gill, C. (1988). "Personhood and Personality: The Four Personae Theory in Cicero, *De Officiis* I." *Oxford Studies in Ancient Philosophy* 6: 169–99.

Graver, M. 2007. *Stoicism and Emotion*. Chicago: University of Chicago Press.

*Griffin, M. 1992. *Seneca: A Philosopher in Politics,* 2nd edition. Oxford: Oxford University Press.

*Inwood, B. (ed.). 2003. *The Cambridge Companion to the Stoics*. Cambridge: Cambridge University Press.

Inwood, B. 2005. *Seneca: Stoic Philosophy at Rome*. Oxford: Oxford University Press.

Long, A. A., and D. N. Sedley (eds.). 1987. *The Hellenistic Philosophers*, 2 vols. Cambridge: Cambridge University Press.

Pembroke, S. 1971. *Oikeiosis*, in *Problems in Stoicism*, edited by A. A. Long, 114–49. London: Bloomsbury Academic.

Rist, J. M. 1989. "Seneca and Stoic Orthodoxy." *Aufstieg und Niedergang der Römischen Welt*, II 36.3, 1993–2012.

Sellars, J. 2003. *The Art of Living: The Stoics on the Nature and Function of Philosophy*. Burlington, VT: Ashgate Pub. Ltd.

*Sellars, J. 2006. *Stoicism*. Berkeley, CA: University of California Press.

* Veyne, P. 2003. *Seneca: The Life of a Stoic*. Translated by D. Sullivan. New York: Routledge.

On Providence

(De Providentia)

1.1. You have asked me, Lucilius, why, if Providence controls the universe, many bad things happen to good people. This question would be more properly answered in a work in which I demonstrate that Providence rules over everything and that god takes an interest in us. But I will make things easier, since it seems right to you that a little part be chopped off from the whole question, I mean, to make only this one counterargument while leaving the larger complaint untouched. I shall speak in defense of the gods.

1.2. It is unnecessary for the matter at hand to show that a creation as great as the universe doesn't carry on without some oversight and that the conjunction and movement of the stars do not belong to accidental forces. I don't need to show that what chance sets in motion is often disordered and quickly crashes, that the heavens' great speed is maintained uninterrupted because of the commanding power of an eternal law and carries such diversity of things on land and in the sea, such diversity of the most brilliant stars, shining brightly in an ordered way. I don't need to show that this ordered structure is not made of wandering atoms. And I don't need to show that things joined randomly don't fit together with so much skill that land, because it's heaviest, rests immovable and watches the flight of the heavens rushing around it, or that seas soften the land in its hollows and don't increase their level though rivers flow into them, or that enormous things are born from the smallest seeds. **1.3.** Phenomena that seem confused and unpredictable are not. Rain and clouds, thunder and lightning, volcanic eruptions, earthquakes, and other things that the wild part of nature sets in motion all around the world do not happen without a reason, although they are sudden. They have their proper causes too, no less than things that are considered to be extraordinary because they are seen in odd places, such as hot spots in the middle of the sea and new spans of islands rising up in the vast ocean. **1.4.** Now, perhaps someone will see the shore exposed by the sea as it slips back into itself and then within a short period of time see the shore get covered up again. He will think that the waters are at one point drawn back and at another pushed out, regaining their earlier

1

position in a great rush because of some unperceived revolution of the earth. The sea level, however, grows steadily bit by bit and comes up higher or lower punctually to the hour and the day, according to the pull of the moon, at whose command the ocean swells. But let's hold back on such topics, especially since you are complaining about Providence, not doubting its existence.

1.5. I shall bring you back into relationship with the gods, who are best toward the best. Nature, you see, never allows good things to harm good people. Between good people and the gods there is a friendship, and virtue is the mediator. Did I say friendship? I mean, an intimacy and a similarity too, since a good person is different from a god only in the amount of time he lives. A good person is the student of god, an imitator and true offspring, whom god, a noble parent and a demanding overseer of virtues, raises in a more demanding way, just as stern fathers do. **1.6.** And so, when you see people who, although they are good and acceptable to the gods, are struggling, sweating, climbing upward on a difficult path, while bad men are immoral and swimming in pleasures, think about this: we are delighted by the self-control of our children and by our slaves' children's lack of restraint. The former are held in check by a harsher discipline, but we encourage the bold behavior of the latter. The same thing ought to be clear to you about god: god does not make a good person his favorite—he tests, hardens, and prepares a good person for himself.

2.1. "Why do many difficult situations happen to good men?" Nothing bad can happen to a good man: opposites don't mix. Many rivers, the great quantity of fallen precipitation, and the great potency of medicinal springs do not change the taste of the ocean—they don't even dilute it. In the same way, the attacks of adverse circumstances don't change a brave man's spirit. He stands his ground and colors whatever happens with his own perspective, because he has power over every external circumstance. **2.2.** I'm not saying that he doesn't feel these things, but that he rises up to meet their attack and conquers them, although in every other respect he is peaceful and calm. The good person thinks that difficult circumstances are tests. What person, as long as he is a man and attentive to what is noble, does not desire honest hard work and is not ready for dangerous duty? Isn't retirement a punishment for a hard-working man? **2.3.** We see that prize-fighters, who care about strength, compete with all of the strongest men and require those who are getting them ready for a fight to use their whole strength against them. They allow themselves to be struck and hurt and, if they do not find single partners a match, they open themselves up to many at once. **2.4.** Without an adversary, virtue withers; how great virtue is, and how potent, is clear at the moment it shows what it can do through endurance. You should know, of course, that good people need to adopt the same practice, so that they do not fear harsh and difficult circumstances or complain about their fate, so that they interpret any event favorably and make it favorable. It doesn't matter what you endure, but how you endure it.

2.5. You see how differently fathers and mothers treat their children, don't you? Fathers demand that their children be woken up to get to their studies on time, do not allow them to laze around, even on festival days, and extract sweat from them—and sometimes tears. But mothers coddle them, want to keep them close by, to always keep them from sadness, tears, and hard work. **2.6.** God has a father's spirit toward good people—that is, he loves them with a powerful love and says, "Let them be harassed by work, suffering, and loss, so that they can acquire true strength. They are growing soft, fattened through inactivity, and are not only tired out by hard work, but even by moving their own weight." Prosperity that has never seen trouble can't endure any attack. But for a man who constantly battles his misfortunes, toughness carries him through his injuries and he doesn't yield to any badness. No, even if he has fallen, he fights from his knees. **2.7.** Are you surprised that god, who loves good people very much and who wants them to be as good and noble as possible, puts them in situations that can train them? I at least am not surprised that the gods seize the opportunity to see great men struggling with some disaster.

2.8. We take pleasure now and then, if a stout-hearted young man takes down a beast with a hunting spear as it rushes him, or if he endures the attack of a lion without fear. The nobler he who does the deed is, the more pleasing the sight. But these childish diversions and inconsequential human pleasures are not the sort of things that draw the attention of the gods. **2.9.** Here is a worthwhile sight, of which god takes notice, because he is attentive to his own work. Here is a prizefight worthy of god: a brave man, matched in battle with bad fortune, especially if he is the one who issues the challenge. I can't see, really, what on earth Juppiter would think more beautiful, if he wished to give it his attention, than watching Cato still standing straight and tall among the ruins of the Republic, even though his political faction had been splintered several times. **2.10.** He says, "Although everything has submitted to the will of one man, although the land is guarded by the legions and the sea by the fleet, and although Caesar's soldiers are at the gates, there is a way out for Cato: with one hand he can pave the way for liberty. This sword, unstained and free of guilt even in civil war, will at last do something good and noble. It will give the liberty to Cato that it could not give to his country. My dear spirit, do what you've long planned to do, rip yourself away from human concerns. Petreius and Juba have already engaged in battle and lie dead by each other's hand.[1] Theirs was a brave and distinguished acceptance of fate, but not appropriate to my own greatness. It is as shameful for Cato to seek death from someone else as it is for him to seek life."

2.11. It seems clear to me that the gods watched with great delight while that great man, that intensely passionate self-avenger, made plans for others' safety and arranged for the escape of his retreating troops—all while, on that last night, he spent time with his books, then placed the sword against his revered body, and then with his hand dragged out his own life along with his inner organs; a most holy life that was not worthy to be defiled by a blade. **2.12.** I want to believe that the wound was poorly done and not immediately effective for this reason: it wasn't enough for the immortal gods to watch Cato die once. His virtue was kept from leaving and was summoned back to the fight so that it could show its quality in a more difficult situation: for a great spirit, you see, death is not so much encountered as sought out. How could the gods not watch their own foster-son escaping through such a noble and memorable death? Death offers up as a gift to the gods people whose dying moments are praised even by those who fear them.

3.1. As this speech unfolds I shall show how things that seem bad are not. For now I'll say this: The things that you call hopelessly difficult, which are unfavorable and ill-omened, are first of all beneficial for those to whom they happen. Second, they are beneficial for humanity as a whole, for whom the gods have a greater concern

---

1. Marcus Petreius (110–46 BCE) played an important role in several battles from 63 BCE (during the Catilinarian Conspiracy) until 46 BCE when, defeated after marching against Caesar in support of Pompey, he fled to Africa with the Numidian king Juba. They died at each other's hands in April 46 BCE.

than for individuals. Third, these things are just events for those who accept them willingly—those who are unwilling are worthy of misfortune. To these points I will add that these events are fated to occur: they happen to good people by the same law through which good people exist. I will persuade you never to pity a good person. You see, a good person can be *called* pitiable, but can't actually *be* pitiable.

3.2. It seems to me that what I suggested first is the most difficult argument to make—that is, to show how the things that cause fear and trembling are beneficial to those who experience them. "Is it beneficial to be thrown into exile or driven into extreme poverty? Is it beneficial to bury your children or spouse, to suffer humiliating public disgrace, to be physically disabled?" If you are surprised that these things are beneficial to someone, you will be surprised to learn that some patients are healed using knives and flames, no less than by hunger and thirst. Consider this: as a medical treatment, bones are filed down and cut off and veins are pulled out and limbs are amputated when they would be deadly for the rest of the body if they stayed attached. If you think about it this way, then you will also allow yourself to agree that some painful and difficult things *are* in fact beneficial to those who experience them just as certain things that are praised and sought after are detrimental to those who enjoy them, for example, overindulgence and drunkenness and other things that kill pleasantly.

3.3. Among the many magnificent sayings of our Demetrius[2] is this one, which I just read (I can even still hear it in my head): "Nothing seems less fortunate to me than a man to whom no adversity ever happened." Such a man, you see, wasn't allowed to test his strength. Although everything had turned out for him according to his prayers, even before his prayers were made, nevertheless the gods rendered a negative judgment on him: he was judged unworthy to overcome Fortune, which shuns any weakling as if saying, "What? Am I supposed to fight this adversary? He'll lower his weapons right away! There's no need to exert my whole strength against him since I can make him run away with only a casual threat. He can't stand the sight of me. Find another with whom I can have a real battle. It's shameful to step into the ring with a man who is ready to be defeated." **3.4.** A gladiator thinks it reflects badly on his reputation

---

2. Demetrius the Cynic.

to be matched against an inferior opponent and knows that a man who fights without danger wins without glory. Fortune has the same opinion: she seeks out the bravest opponents and passes over others in disgust. She assaults a very steadfast and self-controlled person so she can exert her full force. She used fire against Mucius,[3] poverty against Fabricius,[4] exile against Rutilius,[5] torture against Regulus, poison against Socrates, and death against Cato. A person can't be a great role model without enduring misfortune.

3.5. Was Mucius unfortunate because he put his right hand into the enemy's fire and took away from himself the penalty of his error? Or because he made a king flee with a burned hand when he couldn't with his hand holding a weapon? What then? Would he have been more fortunate if he had warmed his hand under his girlfriend's clothes? **3.6.** Was Fabricius unfortunate because he plowed his farm as often as he could find time away from state affairs? Or because he waged a war against affluence as much as one against Pyrrhus? Was he unfortunate because for dinner at his own hearth the old war hero ate the roots and herbs that he harvested while clearing his fields? What then? Would he have been more fortunate if he had eaten imported fish and exotic birds, if he had stimulated the weak appetite of a nauseated stomach with shellfish from the Adriatic or Etruscan seas, or if he displayed the finest wild game—brought down only after the death of hunters—ringed with a huge pile of fruit? **3.7.** Was Rutilius unfortunate because those who condemned him will be trying to justify their actions for eternity? Or because he calmly and peacefully allowed himself to be taken from his homeland rather than allow the punishment of exile to be taken from him? Was he unfortunate because he alone refused the dictator Sulla and, although ordered to return, not only backed away from the summons but even fled farther from Italy? "Let those at Rome," he says, "whom your 'fortune'

---

3. Gaius Mucius Scaevola (early fifth century BCE) is a frequently cited example of courage in the face of pain. Captured by Lars Porsenna when the Etruscan king was laying siege to Rome, Mucius placed his left hand in fire to display Roman courage.
4. Gaius Fabricius Luscinus, a third-century BCE Roman politician and general, is a frequently cited example of incorruptibility, who negotiated a peace treaty with King Pyrrhus in 280 BCE after the disastrous Battle of Heraclea. He was also known for his severe lifestyle.
5. Publius Rutilius Rufus was consul in 105 BCE, and was charged and convicted falsely for extortion in 92 BCE and forced into exile.

controls see the forum flooded with blood and the heads of senators rising above the *Lacus Servilius*[6] (it was like a *spoliarium* for the Sullan proscriptions).[7] Let them see the gangs of thugs roaming throughout the city and many thousands of Roman citizens slaughtered in one place after a guarantee of safety—or rather, because of that guarantee. Let those who are not able to be in exile see these things!" **3.8.** Well then, was Lucius Sulla fortunate because his passage was secured by swords whenever he went to the forum? Or because he allowed the heads of former consuls to be displayed and kept a public record through the state treasurer's office of the profit from the slaughter?[8] And he did all of these things, the same man who sponsored the *Lex Cornelia* against murder! **3.9.** And let us think too about Regulus.[9] Did Fortune harm him because she made him into an example of trust and endurance? Spikes pierced his skin and however he positioned his tired body he lay on a wound. His eyelids were kept open so that he could not sleep. But the worse his torments, the greater his glory. Do you want to know how unashamed he was to set his life as the price of his virtue? Bring him to life again and send him to the Senate. He will give them the same advice as before.

3.10. So, perhaps you think that Maecenas was more fortunate than these people, a man who, perturbed by his desires and weeping because his wife as good as divorced him every day, had to fall

---

6. Not strictly a "lake" in modern terms: there were three famous wells or fountains in the Forum Romanum: *Lacus Servilius*, *Lacus Curtius*, and *Lacus Juturnae*. The heads were likely stuck on the surrounding wall.

7. The *spoliarium* was a part of the Colosseum complex where the bodies of dead gladiators would be taken to be stripped of their armor and displayed. The Sullan proscriptions, enacted after Cornelius Sulla came to be sole ruler in 82 BCE, were public lists of people (considered enemies of the state, and often of Sulla or his supporters) whose life and/or property could be seized with impunity. Rewards were offered for the death or capture of any person on the list.

8. That is, during the proscriptions.

9. Regulus is often used by Roman writers as an example of virtue, especially of endurance against suffering and courage. Although not a Stoic, he frequently used to embody Stoic virtues. To honor an oath made to the Carthaginians after his capture in 255 BCE, Regulus returned to imprisonment after a failed negotiation at Rome (in which he counseled against agreeing to his captors' demands in spite of the fact that he would return to Carthage to face execution). According to some sources, on his return to Carthage—in addition to other tortures—his eyelids were cut off, and he died from sleep deprivation.

asleep to the sound of music playing softly in the distance? Although he numbed himself with strong wine, distracted himself with the sound of fountains, and blanketed his troubled mind with countless delights, he was as awake on his featherbed as that man on a cross. But for the latter there is some comfort in enduring terrible things for a noble cause and he looks away from his suffering toward its purpose. Maecenas, withered by his sensual pleasures and struggling under too much lucky prosperity, was tormented more by the cause of his suffering than by the things he actually went through. **3.11.** The human race is not so tied up in vice that we can't be sure if more would wish to be born a Regulus than a Maecenas, given the choice. Or if there *were* someone who dared to claim he would prefer to be born a Maecenas, he (though he'd never say it) likewise would prefer more to have been born a Terentia.[10]

3.12. Do you think that Socrates was badly treated because he considered the hemlock brewed up by order of the state nothing other than a cure for mortality? Or because he debated about the nature of death up until the moment of his own? Did he suffer badly because his blood grew cold and, as the chill crept over him, his pulse grew weaker? **3.13.** We ought to envy him much more than those who are served their drinks in crystal, or have wine mixed with snow served in a gold vessel by a promiscuous slave whose manliness is gone or in question[11] and who has learned to endure everything. These people will force themselves to throw up whatever they drank, sad and tasting their own bile. But Socrates, happy and willing, will drink his poison to the last drop.

3.14. As far as Cato is concerned, I've said enough, and the consensus is that he experienced the highest degree of prosperity and happiness. The universe chose him because he was someone with whom she who is fearsome could compete. She says, "The hatred of powerful people is hard to bear: let Cato be hated by Pompey, Caesar, and Crassus at the same time. In an election it is hardship to lose to worse men than yourself; let Cato be beaten by Vatinius. It is

---

10. That is, if one would choose to be like Maecenas on the basis of his life of pleasure, one would then prefer to be Maecenas' wife, Terentia, who was an even more notorious pleasure-seeker. See also n. 11 on effeminacy.

11. That is, a eunuch or an effeminate man; the word carried a strong (negative) implication of sexual passivity for a Roman audience.

hard to bear being in the middle of a civil war; let him make war in every land for a good cause, with an abundance of resolve and a lack of success. It is hard to bear killing oneself; let him do it. What will I gain from this? That all understand this: the things I considered Cato worthy to experience are not bad things."

4.1. Prosperity comes also to the common man and from common abilities. But it is characteristic of the great man to subdue and control the disasters and horrors of mortal life. To be continually prosperous and live a life without distress in the spirit is to be ignorant of the other half of the world. **4.2.** You are an important person, a great man. But how do I know that, if Fortune has not given you the capability to prove your virtue? You competed at Olympia, but you were the only contestant. You have a crown of wild olive, but you weren't really the winner. If you win an election, I won't congratulate you as the best man, but as the man elected to the office of consul or praetor: the position makes you more than you are. **4.3.** Likewise I can also say to a good man, if he hasn't had some really difficult experiences in which he could show the strength of his spirit, "In my opinion you are pitiable because you were never pitiable. You lived your life unchallenged. Nobody will know what you can do, you won't even know it yourself." To know oneself, there must be a test. No one can learn what he is capable of without making the attempt. And so, some have stepped forward, even when misfortune was far off, and have sought out the opportunity to make their virtue shine just when it was about to fade away.

4.4. I'm telling you, great men sometimes enjoy it when things are tough, just as courageous warriors enjoy war. I overheard a *murmillo*[12] called Triumphus, during the reign of Tiberius Caesar, complaining about the infrequency of gladiatorial games: "A beautiful era has ended!" Virtue is greedy for danger and thinks about where it is headed, not what it will suffer, since what it suffers is part of its glory too. Soldiers boast about their wounds and happily show off blood when bleeding for a noble cause. Although the man who returns from the battle unharmed has achieved as much (by returning at all), we pay more attention to the one who returns wounded. **4.5.** God, I tell you, has regard for those whom he wants to be the most noble-spirited each time he provides them with raw material for doing

---

12. The *murmillo* was a category of heavily armed gladiator, with a distinctive crested helmet.

something bravely and with determination. To this end, it is essential to experience difficult circumstances: one recognizes a real helmsman in a vicious storm, a real soldier in battle. How can I know how much spirit you would show against poverty if you are drowning in wealth? How can I know how much unwavering determination you have against rumor, damaged reputation, and the hatred of the people if you grow old hearing applause, if you are followed around by unassailable public approval that is brought on by a certain bias in the people's thinking? How do I know if you would endure losing a loved one with a peaceful spirit if all your children are still before your eyes? I have heard you offering sympathy to others. I would have admired you if at the time you had been consoling yourself or if you had stopped yourself from grieving.

4.6. Please don't be terrified of the things the gods bring to challenge our spirits, as prods to move us forward. Disaster is an opportunity for virtue. There is some merit in the suggestion that people are pitiable when they grow numb from excessive prosperity, when serenity holds them back as if they were becalmed on a still sea. Whatever happens will come as a surprise to them. **4.7.** Dire circumstances are harder to endure for those who haven't experienced them before and the yoke is heavy on a tender neck. A new recruit gets pale at the thought of an injury, but a veteran has the guts to look at his own bloody wounds—and he knows that he has often survived them. And so, God hardens, inspects, and tests those he approves of and loves. Those whom he seems to pamper and spare, he is keeping safe and soft from bad things about to come. You are wrong if you think anyone is exempt from trouble. The prosperous man will get his own fair share later. Anyone like that hasn't avoided trouble—it's just been deferred.

4.8. Why does god afflict each of the best with either bad health, or grief, or other painful things? For the same reason that on military campaigns high-risk duties are assigned to the bravest. A general sends his elite troops to attack the enemy on night raids, or to scout a path, or to remove an enemy outpost. None of those who go on such missions say, "The general doesn't have a good opinion of me," but, "He thinks highly of me." Likewise, commanded to endure things that bring tears to fearful and spineless men, good people say, "We seem to be worthy in god's eyes; we are people from whom he can find out how much the human spirit can endure."

4.9. Flee from pleasures, flee from the incapacitating prosperity that weakens the spirit and (unless something happens to remind the spirit about human mortality) makes it sag as if drunk and passed out all the time. The brush of a cool breeze is dangerous for a man protected from the winter winds by proper windows, whose feet are kept comfortable with warmed blankets, regularly replaced, and given dinner in rooms with heating in the walls and the floor. **4.10.** Although everything that goes beyond proper measure is harmful, the lack of control prosperity brings is the most dangerous: it affects the mind, drawing it to useless thoughts and clouding our judgment about truth and falsehood. Wouldn't it be better to maintain a constant lack of prosperity, with the help of virtue, than to be destroyed by constant excess? Death for a hungry man is a gentler thing: men burst from stuffing their stomachs.

4.11. And so, the gods follow the same strategy in the case of good people that teachers follow with good students: they require more work from those for whom they have higher hopes. Or maybe you think the Spartans hated their children when they tested natural ability with public trials of pain?[13] Fathers themselves urged their sons to endure the blows of whips with courage and asked them, lacerated and half-conscious, to continue offering up their wounded bodies for more wounds. **4.12.** Is it so surprising then that God sets harsh tests for noble souls? There is no gentle proof of virtue. Fortune whips us and lacerates us: let us endure. It is not brutality, it is a test, and we grow stronger whenever we take it. The toughest part of the body is the one that is used the most. We need to offer ourselves up, so that Fortune herself can train us to resist Fortune; bit by bit, we will become matches for her and constant exposure to danger will lead us to disdain danger. **4.13.** This is how sailors' bodies are hardened against the sea, farmers' hands are calloused, soldiers' arms are strong enough for throwing javelins, runners' legs are swift. In each case, what is exercised the most is the toughest. The spirit reaches the point of disdain for bad things by enduring them. If you consider what hard work bestows on nations

---

13. The Romans were fascinated by the Spartans. The *diamastigosis* (a ritual in which young men would attempt to grab cheese from the altar after running through whips) at the Temple of Artemis Orthia at Sparta became a spectacle during the late Republic and early Empire to which Romans would travel.

that are poor—I mean nations that are stronger because of poverty—
you will recognize what endurance can effect in us too.

4.14. Think of all the peoples who resist the *Pax Romana*,[14] like
the Germans and the nomadic tribes that move around the Danube.
Unceasing winter, dreary skies, and harsh, unfertile soil sustain them.
They keep off the rain with bundled grass and tree branches, play on
frozen lakes, and hunt wild game for food. **4.15.** Do they seem pitiable
to you? Nothing is pitiable that has become second nature through
long habit. Bit by bit, you see, what they began out of necessity has
become a pleasure for them. There are no grand houses or dwelling
places except where their weariness puts them at the end of the day.
Their food is basic and gathered by hand, the weather harsh, their
bodies are not fully clothed. But what seems a disaster to you is a way
of life for so many people. **4.16.** Why are you surprised, then, that
good men suffer in order to grow strong? A tree is not firm and strong
unless it is struck often by the wind: that hardship keeps it trim and
firmly rooted. Trees that grow in sheltered, sunny areas are weak. It is
a benefit for good men, then, to be subjected to terrible events so that
they can be unafraid and to endure with a brave spirit things that are
not bad unless they are experienced badly.

5.1. One could also argue that it is beneficial for everyone that
each of the best be a soldier, in a manner of speaking, and a doer of
deeds. It is god's intention to show that for the wise man the appetites
and fears of the crowd are neither good nor bad. For instance, it is
quite clear that something is good if god only allots it to good men
and that something is bad if god imposes it on bad men only. **5.2.**
Blindness would be an appallingly bad thing if only those who ought
to be blinded lose their sight, so let Appius and Metellus[15] lose their
sight. Wealth is not a good thing, so let even Elius the pimp be wealthy
in order that men can see money in a whorehouse *and* can dedicate it
to a temple. There's no better way for god to show how disgraceful the
things we desire are than by giving them to the worst kind of people
and taking them from the best.

---

14. The "Roman Peace," a term usually applied to the time after the rule of Augustus
(r. 27 BCE–14 CE) until Marcus Aurelius (r. 161–180 CE), when there was a period
of relative peace inside the borders of the Roman Empire.
15. Both are frequently cited examples of Republican heroes.

5.3. "But it's unfair for a good man to suffer a debilitating illness or to be horribly injured or to be imprisoned, while bad men walk away, soft and safe from bodily harm." So what? Is it fair for strong men to take up arms, to spend the night on campaign, and to stand watch on the walls, bandaged, while castrated men and the shamelessly corrupt are safe in the city? So what? Is it fair for honored virgin priestesses to be roused in the night to perform sacrifices while the impure enjoy a night's deep sleep?[16] **5.4.** Hard work stimulates the best people. The Senate often discusses matters for the entire day, during the time when the lowest of the low is relaxing on the playing field or lurking in a tavern or whiling away the day at a party. The same thing happens in our great Republic. Good men labor and cover expenses at their own expense, quite willingly. They are not compelled to do so by Fortune— they follow beside Fortune, keeping pace with her. And they would have gone ahead of her if they'd known what their future would be.

5.5. I can recall hearing about this very courageous statement of that great hero Demetrius: "I can complain about you, o gods, for this reason alone, that you did not make your will known to me earlier: I would have come long ago and on my own to the place where I now find myself summoned. Do you want to take away my children? It was for you that I raised them. Do you want to take away some part of my body? Take it. It's not like it's a big deal—I will give up my whole body soon enough in death. Do you want my life's breath? Why should I linger any longer, if you want to take back what you gave? You will take whatever you seek and I am willing anyway. So, why am I complaining? Because I would have preferred to give it to you myself than to have to hand it over under duress. Was it really necessary to take it? You could have had it given to you. But as it is you can't exactly take it from me, since you can't snatch away something no one is trying to hold on to." **5.6.** I am not compelled at all, I suffer nothing unwillingly. I am not god's slave, but cooperate fully, all the more so because I know that everything happens according to an unchanging and eternally valid law. **5.7.** Fates lead us and determine from the first hour of our birth how much time is left for each of us. Cause depends on cause and a long progression of events brings about public and private matters. For that reason, all things must be endured

---

16. That is, the Vestal Virgins, whose duties included keeping the sacred fire burning in the Temple of Vesta at Rome.

with courage because they do not *happen*, as we think, but *arrive*. The thing you might be happy about or cry about was decided long ago and, although life seems to be separated into a great variety of individual things, it all comes down to one thing in the end: we who are about to perish are given things that are about to perish. **5.8.** So, why be indignant? Why complain? We were made for this. Let nature use its physical bodies as it wishes. Let us, joyful and courageous in the face of everything, consider that nothing that is ours will perish.

What is characteristic behavior for a good man? To offer himself to Fate. It is a great comfort to be snatched away along with the rest of creation. Whatever it is that commands us to live and die in a particular way also constrains the gods with that same inevitability. A relentless flow carries human and divine alike. The founder and master of all things composed fate certainly, but also follows it—obeying always what he once commanded. **5.9.** "But why was god so unfair in sharing out fate that he decreed poverty and injury and harsh deaths for good men?" An artisan cannot transform his materials—they are what they are. Some things can't be separated from other things—they are combined and have become indivisible. People with weak constitutions, who are prone to sleepiness (or to a waking state that is almost the same as sleep), are made up of passive elements. You need stronger stuff to make a man worth talking about. For that kind of man the path will not be smooth and flat—it is right for him to go up and down, to be whirled about in the current and to sail under control through the rough patches. He ought to chart a course straight at Fortune. Many difficult and harsh things will happen, but of the sort that he can soften and level out himself. Fire tempers gold, misfortune brave men. **5.10.** When you see how high virtue must climb, then you will see that its path is not a safe one:[17]

> The road is hard at first, and although from a night's rest refreshed,
> The horses strain. The highest point is at midday
> And there I look upon the earth and sea.
> Even my heart trembles with terrible fear.
> The end of the path goes down steeply and maintaining
> control is hard.

---

17. The following lines are taken from Ovid's *Metamorphoses* 2.63ff, when Phaethon, son of Apollo, convinces the Sun God to let him drive the chariot of the sun. The effort ends in disaster and Phaethon's death.

> At that point Tethys, who catches me in her spreading waves,
> Fears from below that I might crash into her headfirst.

5.11. When he had heard these words Phaethon, that noble boy, said, "I like it, I'm going. It will be worth it for me to travel the path, even if I fall." Apollo did not stop trying to fill his eager spirit with fear, saying,

> Even if you keep the path, not driven from it by any error,
> You will nevertheless pass through the horns of the hostile Bull,
> The Haemonian bow, and the raging mouth of the Lion.[18]

After these words Phaethon said, "Yoke the chariot: I am motivated to go for the reasons you think will scare me off. I want to stand where the Sun God himself feels fear." Insignificant and sluggish men follow the safe paths: virtue travels on the peaks.

    6.1. "Still, why does god allow something bad to happen to good men?" He doesn't *allow* that! He removes all bad things from them, wickedness and shameful actions and impure thoughts and plans motivated by greed and blind lust and covetousness. He watches over them and claims them for himself! Does anyone require god to also safeguard wise men's luggage? They themselves release god from this concern, since they do not concern themselves with external things. **6.2.** Democritus threw away his riches, judging them to be a burden for a good mind. Why wonder, then, that god allows something to happen to a good man that a good man sometimes wants to happen? Good men lose their sons—and don't they sometimes even kill them?[19] Good men are sent into exile—and won't they themselves at some point leave their homeland, never to return? Good men are killed—and don't they sometimes even kill themselves? **6.3.** Why do they endure hardship? So they can teach others to endure: they were born to be role models. Imagine god saying, then, "What reason do you have to complain about me, if you are pleased by what's right? I have handed around counterfeit goods to others and I have let their empty spirits play as if in a long, false dream. I have covered them with gold and

---

18. The constellations Taurus, Sagittarius (Haemonian because of the association of the centaur Chiron with Thessaly, whose mythical king was named Haemon), and Leo.
19. This must be a reference to Titus Manlius Imperiosus Torquatus, a fourth-century BCE general who ordered his son's execution in accordance with military discipline for leaving his post.

silver and ivory, but there is no wealth inside. **6.4.** The ones you think are prosperous and happy, if you look not at where they are running but at where they are hiding, are pitiable, disgusting, and filthy, dressed up to look like the walls of their houses: elegant, on the outside. This is not a lasting and secure prosperity; it is a thin veneer. And so, they shine and dupe others as long as they are allowed to stand up and to be shown off in a light of their own choosing. But when something happens to demolish the facade and reveal the inside, then it becomes clear how deep their pile of filth is, covered by a gleaming outside that didn't belong to them anyway. **6.5.** I give you reliable things that will endure, that become better and stronger the more someone turns them over and inspects them from all sides. I have allowed you to scorn things that should be feared, to disdain desires. You do not shine on the outside; your goodness faces inwards. Thus the universe, scorning what is outside itself, is happy to look upon itself. I have set every good within you. It is the source of your prosperity and happiness to not need prosperity and happiness. **6.6.** And you say, 'But many tragic and horrible things happen that are hard to endure.' Since I cannot lead you away from such things, I have fortified your spirits against them all. Be courageous and endure! This is how you can surpass a god, because while a god is beyond suffering, you can rise above it. Disdain your poverty: no one is as poor as when he was born. Disdain pain: either it will die or you will. Disdain death: it will either give you an end or a new beginning. Disdain Fortune: I have given her no weapon that can harm your spirit.

6.7. "I have seen to it above all that no one can restrain you if you are unwilling. The exit is plain to see: if you don't want to fight, you are allowed to flee. For this reason, of all the things that I wanted you to have to face, I made nothing easier to do than dying. I set life on a downward slope: as it rolls on, all you need to do is pay attention and you will see how short and sweet the road to freedom is. I did not arrange your exit from this world to be as long as your entrance. Fortune would have held great power over you if it took a man as long to die as it did to be born. **6.8.** Let every moment, every place teach you how easy it would be to renounce Nature and throw her gift in her face. Among the altars and solemnity of the sacrifices, while you pray for life, learn also about death. The enormous bodies of bulls topple from one slight wound and the blow of a human hand lays low these immensely strong animals. The neck joint can be cut by a thin knife. When that small joint, which holds together head and body, is cut, that massive creature tumbles in a heap.

6.9. "Your spirit does not hide deep inside, nor does it have to be dug out with a knife. You don't need to deeply wound to hit a vital spot. Death is very near. I didn't settle on a particular place for such a blow. You can do it anywhere on the body you like. This thing called death, through which the breath leaves the body, is so quick it can't be felt. Whether you choke to death, or drown, or smash open your head falling on the hard ground, or suffocate in a fire, whatever happens, it's fast. Why are you so mortified? You fear for such a long time something that happens so quickly!"

On the Resolute Nature of the Wise Man

(*De Constantia Sapientis*)

1.1. I might say, Serenus, and not without reason, that there is as much of a difference between Stoics and other philosophers who lay claim to wisdom as there is between women and men: each group contributes to life in a human community to the same degree, but one is born to take orders, the other to give them. The other wise men are doctors for the sick in a coaxing and coddling way—doing, I suppose, as friendly family doctors do: not giving the best or quickest treatments, but the acceptable ones. Stoics, marching on a manly path, aren't worried that the road seems pleasant for travelers, but that it grabs us immediately and brings us up to that lofty height so far beyond any weapon's reach that it stands towering above Fortune.

1.2. "But the roads we are called to take are steep and full of danger." So what?! Can you get to a mountaintop on flat ground? At any rate, the path is not at all as sheer as some believe. Only the initial portion has rocks and outcroppings and looks like it's obstructed, just as many cliffs (when you look at them from far away) seem sheer and without break, because distance deceives the eye. But then, as you get nearer, the very same things that a trick of the eye had jumbled into one open out bit by bit: in the areas that appeared vertical and impassable from a distance a smooth trail comes into view.

1.3. Not too long ago you took it badly when talk turned to Cato, intolerant of injustice as you are. His own age had understood him so little that it had ranked him—a better man than Pompey and Caesar—inferior to Vatinius. For you it seemed totally outrageous that, as he was about to speak against legislation in the forum, his toga was ripped from him and that, dragged by a rabble-rousing partisan mob from the *rostra* all the way to the Fabian Arch,[1] he endured vile names, spit, and every other insult from the crazed crowd. **2.1.** At the time, I responded that you had a good reason to be irritated on behalf of the Republic, which first Publius Clodius then Vatinius and every scum kept enslaving. They didn't understand, because they were ruined by

---

1. If the Fabian Arch was near the Regia, as it seems to have been (there are no remains), this was a distance of about 150 meters.

blind lust, that they were selling themselves while they were selling the state. But as for Cato, I recommended that you not worry for his sake. I said that a wise man can't be insulted or injured,[2] and that with Cato, more to the point, the gods had given us a more reliable model of a wise man than they had given earlier generations with Ulysses and Hercules. Our Stoics considered these heroes to be wise men, since they were unconquered by their labors, despised their desires, and conquered all their fears. **2.2** Cato didn't fight with wild beasts: that is work for hunters and country folk. He didn't battle monsters with fire and the sword, and he wasn't born into times when it could be believed that the heavens rested on the shoulders of one man. But, when old beliefs were abolished and his generation was led to the depths of corruption, he—battling the crooked ambition of others, the many-headed monster, and their massive passion for power (the whole world split into three could not satisfy it)—he stood alone against the sins of a degenerate citizen body sinking under its own filth. He supported the toppling Republic as much as one person could have, until, alienated, he embraced the fall of a state that had been propped up for so long. So, at one and the same moment two things it was sacrilege to separate were snuffed out: Cato did not live longer than liberty, nor liberty longer than Cato. **2.3.** Do you think he could be injured by the crowd because they had ripped away from him the office of praetor or his toga, or because they had splattered that sanctified head with spit? The wise man is wholly safe, and he cannot be touched by any insult or injury.

3.1. I can see you starting to boil over. You're ready to shout, "These are the sorts of comments that take away from the power of your teachings! You promise great things, the kind of things that can't even be hoped for, much less believed. Then, with your extraordinary arguments, you Stoics deny that the wise man is poor. But you do not deny that he often lacks a slave, a roof, and food. You deny that the wise man is insane. But you do not deny that he can act crazy and says totally crazy things and dares to do whatever the compulsion

---

2. Throughout, the word "injury" translates *iniuria*, which can mean any unjust action that damages a person (not just physically, but also extending to reputation, etc.) or a person's property. So, we must not think in terms of harm, but in terms of what is lost as a result of harm. Seneca's argument rests on the Latin meaning of this word, and without understanding "injury" properly, most modern readers would reject out of hand the arguments he will make in this dialogue.

of an illness makes him do. You deny that he can be a slave. But, just the same, you don't go on to deny that he can be sold and do what he's ordered and provide for a master the services of a slave! So, although you keep your noses in the air, you stoop to the same level as the other philosophers by playing with the names of things. **3.2.** There is a similar kind of trick in this argument too, I suspect, which at first glance seems noble and marvelous—that is, that a wise man won't receive injury or insult. But there's a huge difference whether you put the wise man beyond insult or beyond injury. If you say that he'll endure it with an even spirit, that's nothing special. He's discovered a common thing, something one learns by experiencing injury: endurance. But if you deny that he can be injured, and I mean that no one will try to do it to him, I'll drop everything and become a Stoic!"

3.3. Now look, I haven't tried to set up the wise man with a sham of honorific terms, but to set him in the sort of place where no injury is permitted. "Come on! Will there be no one who would provoke him, or who would try?" There's nothing in the world so sacred that it might not encounter sacrilege. But the divine is no less divine because people, even though they won't reach it, try to strike out at the amazing thing set very far beyond their reach. It isn't that which is not *struck* that is invulnerable, but that which is not *harmed*. With this distinction in mind, I'll present the wise man to you.

3.4. Is there any doubt that strength that has not been defeated is more tried and true than strength that has never even been given a challenge? There's always a question about untested strength, but— and rightly so—strength that has beaten back every attack is thought most tried and true. Understand that, in the same way, the wise man's nature is better if no injury harms him than if no injury ever happens to him. For example, I would say that a mighty warrior is the one whom wars do not overcome, whom a charging enemy does not terrify, and who does not rest idly among a lazy populace. **3.5.** So, I tell you this: a wise man isn't subject to any injury. It doesn't matter how many weapons are thrown at him since his defenses can't be breached. Certain rocks are indestructibly hard: adamantine can't be cut or scratched or worn down but repels every attack. Other rocks aren't damaged by fire but, even though directly in the flames, maintain their stiffness and shape. Some rock-faces, jutting out into the water, break the sea and show no traces of its savagery although they've been battered for years. In the same way, the wise man's spirit stands firm and gathers to itself so much strength that it is as safe from injury as the things I just described.

4.1. "What are you saying, that no one would try to injure the wise man?" Yes, yes, someone will try, but the injury won't *touch* him. The wise man, you see, is too far removed from the reach of inferior men for a hostile attack to exert its force on him. Even when those in positions of power threaten to harm him, even though they are appointed with *imperium* and have many servants, all their attacks fall as far short of Wisdom as missiles shot from bows or ballistae at the heavens. Although the missiles fly out of sight, they turn and fall far short of the target. **4.2.** What, do you think that when King Darius, the fool, darkened the daylight with a multitude of arrows any of the arrows struck the sun? Do you think that the sea can be bound by chains dropped into the deeps? Heavenly things can't be held by human hands and nothing divine is harmed by people who destroy temples and pull down sacred images. In the same way, if anything violent, insolent, or arrogant happens to a wise man, it happens without real effect.

4.3. "Even so, it would be preferable if no one would wish to try to do injury." You want something the human race finds difficult: harmlessness! The fact that injury might not occur only matters for people who intend to do harm, not for someone who can't feel harm even if someone tries. And anyway, I think that serenity in the midst of harmful things shows the strength wisdom has more clearly, just as the greatest proof that a general with a big army is powerful is that he is completely safe in hostile territory.

5.1. Now, let's distinguish injury from insult, if you would like to, Serenus. The former is more serious in nature, the latter less serious— and by that I mean serious only to pampered people. People aren't harmed by insults, they're offended by them. Even so, the weakness and insincerity of the spirit is such that certain people think nothing is more distressing than an insult. As a result, you can find slaves who prefer to be beaten with whips than to be slapped in the face, and who think that sticks and stones, even death, are more tolerable than insulting words. **5.2.** Things have reached such a degree of foolishness that we are not only distressed by actual physical pain but even by the expectation of pain, like children. Shadows, ugly faces, and distorted bodies make them afraid, but bad names, rude gestures, and the other things they run away from (in a kind of foolish rush) make them cry.

5.3. The objective of injury is this: to do something bad to someone. But wisdom leaves no room for badness. Shameful behavior is the only badness wisdom recognizes, but shameful behavior can't coexist with virtue and decency. Therefore, if there is no injury without badness, and if nothing is bad without shameful behavior, and if shameful behavior can't happen where there is decency, injury can't happen to the wise man. For if injury is the experience of something bad and if the wise man experiences nothing bad, no injury can reach the wise man. **5.4.** All injury takes something away from its victim. To be more precise, no one is able to receive injury without some kind of reduction, either of personal honor, or of the body, or of physical property beyond our body. Now, the wise man has nothing to lose, since he deposits all he owns inside himself. He entrusts nothing to Fortune and keeps his possessions secure, because he is content to possess only virtue.

Virtue has no need for what Fortune brings and for that reason can't be augmented or diminished. What is perfect has no room for any addition, and Fortune can only take away what she gave. Fortune doesn't give virtue, and so Fortune doesn't take it away. Virtue is free, inviolable, immovable, unshakeable, and so hardened against misfortune that it isn't even able to be bent, much less broken. It stares down devices of torture. It does not change expression at all if harsh or pleasant things are shown to it. **5.5.** Therefore, the wise man won't lose anything that he could truly feel he has lost, since he only truly possesses virtue. And from this he can never be separated. Everything else he sees as if it were on loan. Who can be distressed by having something taken away when it wasn't his in the first place? Now, if injury can't harm anything a wise man possesses, since these things are safe while his virtue is safe, then injury can't happen to the wise man.

5.6. Demetrius, who was called Poliorcetes, took the city of Megara. Stilbon the philosopher was asked by him whether he had lost anything. "Nothing," he said. "All that belongs to me is with me." But his entire fortune had become booty, and the enemy had taken his daughters, his homeland had come under the power of a foreigner, and the new king, surrounded by the might of his conquering army, was questioning Stilbon from a throne! **5.7.** But Stilbon shrugged off Demetrius' victory and testified that he, although his city was captured, was not only unconquered but even uninjured. You see, he was still in possession of all his true possessions, against which no force could be aimed. He didn't think that the property that had been scattered and snatched away belonged to him. For that reason he had loved it all but not as if it were a possession. Our ownership over all that flows to us from outside ourselves is very uncertain.

6.1. So then, think whether a thief or an unscrupulous lawyer or an antagonistic neighbor or some wealthy man wielding the power child-less old age brings can cause injury to this man Stilbon, from whom war and enemies and a famous conqueror, that exemplar of the glorious skill of devastating cities, couldn't take away a thing. **6.2.** Amid the glint of swords on every side, the mayhem wrought by soldiers bent on pillage, the flames and blood and the carnage of a city captured, the clamor of temples crashing down upon their own gods—amid all this, one man alone was peaceful. Now, there's no reason for you to think that I've spoken rashly. If you don't trust me, I'll give you proof. One can scarcely believe, for example, that so much determination or so much nobility of spirit can be found in one man. But here is Stilbon, who comes among us to say, **6.3.** "There's no reason for you to doubt that a person can lift himself above human concerns, or that he can look without anxiety upon suffering, loss, open sores, wounds, and the great disturbances of nature howling around him, enduring adversity calmly and favorable circumstances with restraint. There's no reason to doubt that he, not yielding to adversity and not depending on favorable circumstances, can remain unchanged though surrounded by change and can think that nothing is his possession except his self, and only the better part of his self at that. **6.4.** I'm here to prove this to you: that while walls topple with the blow of a siege engine under the command of this sacker of cities Demetrius, while high towers are suddenly brought low by sapping tunnels and hidden ditches, and while a ramp is built to reach the height of the highest fortifications, no machine or stratagem can be found to shake a spirit that is well grounded. **6.5.** I have just crept from the ruins of my house and, with the glow of fire and flame all around, I fled through carnage. I don't know what has happened to my daughters, whether theirs is a worse fate than most. Old and all alone, aware that everyone around me is hostile, nevertheless I claim that what is mine is whole and undamaged. I possess now whatever was mine before. **6.6.** There's no reason for you to believe that I am the conquered and you are the conqueror. No, your fortune has conquered my fortune. Where my perishable goods are—that is, all the property that can change owners—I don't know. As for my possessions, they are with me and always will be with me. **6.7.** Those rich men over there have lost their inheritance. Those men over there who are motivated by lust have lost the objects of their desire—their whores—whom they loved at a great cost to their self-respect. Those ambitious men over there have lost the *curia* and the forum and the places where vice has free play in public affairs. The bankers have lost their record-books, through which their cheerful greed creates the illusion of wealth. I, however, have kept everything whole and undiminished. So, ask your question of those men who are weeping and wailing, or with swords drawn are interposing their naked bodies to protect their treasure, or are fleeing from the enemy with loaded pockets."

6.8. So, Serenus, you should understand that this perfect man, full of human and divine virtues, lost nothing. His possessions were protected by solid and insurmountable fortifications. You couldn't compare these walls to the walls of Babylon, which Alexander the Great entered, or the walls of Carthage and Numantia, both of which were captured by one man,[3] or the Capitoline Hill—even those walls bear the mark of the enemy.[4] The walls that protect the wise man from flame and assault, in contrast, are secure. They have no entrance, they are very high, they are immune to attacks, and they are equal to the gods.

7.1. There's no reason for you to say, as you usually do, that this wise man of ours doesn't exist. We aren't making up a glorious, but empty, paragon of human ability. And we aren't imagining some great but false conception. No, in fact, we have in the past produced the sort of person we describe, and we will do so again (although perhaps only once in a long interval of years). You see, great things that are beyond the norm happen only rarely. But, as for Marcus Cato himself—our discussion began with him—I think that he might surpass even our exemplar.

7.2. Logically, what causes harm ought to be stronger than what is harmed. But wickedness is not stronger than virtue. For this reason the wise man cannot be harmed. Injury isn't attempted against good men except by bad men (good men keep peace with each other, but bad men are as violent toward each other as they are toward good men). Now, if one cannot be harmed unless weaker, if the bad man

---

3. Publius Cornelius Scipio Aemilianus Africanus captured Carthage in 146 BCE and Numantia in 133 BCE.
4. During the Gauls' sack of Rome in 390 BCE the Capitoline Hill served as the last defense.

is weaker than the good man, and if wise men shouldn't fear injury except at the hands of a stronger person, then injury can't happen to a wise man. And I don't need to remind you at this point that no one is good unless he is wise.

7.3. "If Socrates was condemned unjustly, then he was injured." Well, at this point we need to realize that it's possible for someone to commit an injury against me and also for me not to receive it. It's like this: if someone puts an item he took from my country house in my city house, he has committed a theft, but I haven't had anything stolen from me. **7.4.** It's possible for a person to become a criminal even though he hasn't done a crime. If a man sleeps with his own wife thinking she's some other man's wife, he's an adulterer even though she isn't an adulteress. And if someone gave me poison, but it lost its potency when mixed with food, he has made himself liable for the crime of giving poison even if he didn't injure me. A mugger isn't any less a mugger if his weapon gets caught up in his victim's clothes. As far as culpability is concerned, all crimes are completed before their effect is complete. **7.5.** Other things are like this, bound together in such a way that the first can happen without the second taking place, but not the second without the first. I'll try to make this clear. Here, look: I can move my feet in such a way that I do not run, but I can't run without moving my feet. I am able to *not* swim, even if I'm in the water, but for me to swim I absolutely must be in water. **7.6.** What we're talking about is in the same category of action. If I receive an injury, it is necessary that injury was committed. But if an injury has been committed, it isn't necessary that I have received it. You see, many things can happen that might displace the injury. Just as some chance event is able to deflect a threatening fist or knock a flying missile off course, something can block any sort of injury and intercept it in midflight. The result is that the injuries, even though they are committed, are not received.

8.1. To continue: justice can't suffer an injustice, because contraries cannot coincide, and injury isn't able to happen except through injustice. Therefore, injury isn't able to happen to a wise man. There's no reason to be surprised that no one can do the wise man an injury: no one can do him a favor either. The wise man lacks nothing that he could receive from another as a service or gift, and a bad man isn't able to give anything appropriate for a wise man. This is because one must have before one can give, but the bad man has nothing that the wise man would be happy to get.

8.2. So, it isn't possible for anyone to harm or benefit the wise man, since divine things don't want to be helped and aren't able to be harmed and since the wise man lives right next to the gods, similar to a god except in his mortality. As he struggles forward toward nobility, self-regulation, and fearlessness, toward things that flow along evenly and agreeably, that are free from anxiety and beneficial, that by nature are in the public interest and that promote health for himself and others, he won't crave or miss terribly anything earthly. **8.3.** If a man relying on reason walks a path through the ups and downs of human life with a godlike spirit, there is no spot he can take an injury. Do you think I'm only talking about injuries from men? I mean not even injuries from Fortune, which, whenever it contends with Virtue, always leaves the loser. If we accept death, that ultimate event (beyond which laws gone wild and the most brutal rulers have no further threat to make, in the midst of which Fortune has absolutely no authority), if we receive death with an even and tranquil spirit, and if we realize that death is not bad, and so is not an injury either, we shall much more easily endure other things like loss and pain, public disgrace, exile, loss of friends and family, or separation from them. These things, even if they were to come at him all at once, do not overcome the wise man. Still less is he distressed by assaults coming one at a time. If he can endure the injuries of Fortune with an even temper, how much more easily can he endure the injuries of powerful men, who he knows are Fortune's instruments too? **9.1.** So, a wise man endures all things in the same way he endures severe winter cold and storms and fever and illness and other things that can happen. As for people, he doesn't form so high an opinion of anyone that he thinks that a person has acted with the judgment only a wise man possesses. The thoughts of all others are not sound judgments, but tricks and traps and uncontrolled passions of the spirit, which he treats the same way he treats chance events. You know, chance rages all around us, especially against what is commonplace.

9.2. Think about this, too: the raw materials for injury are most widely available in the things that carry some risk for us, such as when someone is paid to be an accuser, or when a false accusation is made, or when the hostility of powerful people is provoked against us, or whatever other kinds of corruption happen among people in politics. There is also a more common kind of injury, such as when someone's profit or a long-anticipated reward is snatched away, or when the inheritance a gold-digger spent a long time and lots of effort trying to get is given to someone else, or when the favor of a rich family is taken away. These are the things a wise man escapes because he doesn't know how to live based on hopes or fears.

9.3. Here's something else to consider: no one receives injury unless he has a disturbed mind and is disturbed at the thought of injury. But a man who is free from error, who is in control of himself, content and tranquil, lacks disturbance. Now, if an injury reaches the first man, he is reactive and pushes back. But the wise man lacks anger, which is provoked when a person thinks he has been injured. The wise man can lack anger when he remains uninjured[5] and understands that there's no such thing as injury for him. These are the reasons the wise man is so upbeat and happy, so constantly full of joy. In fact, he's so *not* disheartened in the face of the unpleasantness of the world, and of human beings in general, that attempted injury is even useful for him! Through it he puts himself and his virtue to the test.

9.4. Let's all agree about what I've suggested, please, and focus with sympathetic spirits and ears while the wise man is made exempt from injury. There is no diminishment at all of your impudence, your self-serving desires, or your immoral recklessness and pride because of this exemption. *Your* faults still count for something—I'm only looking to make the wise man free of their effect. I'm not working through this problem so you'll be denied the chance to do injury to anyone. I'm doing it so that the wise man can cast all injuries far away and protect himself with endurance and nobility of spirit. **9.5.** In the same way, many have won at the games by tiring out the hands of their opponents through unremitting endurance. You need to think of the wise man as one of the kind of men who, by long and faithful practice, have acquired the inner strength to endure and outlast every aggressive force.

10.1. Since we have worked our way through the first part of the question, let's pass now to the second part, in which I will present arguments against the possibility of insult, some of them specific Stoic arguments, and many also used by others. Insult is less significant than injury, something we can complain about more than punish. Even the law has not thought it deserving of any penalty. **10.2.** The degradation of a spirit diminishing itself because of a disrespectful word or action prompts this reaction. "He didn't give me an appointment

---

5. A standard Stoic definition of anger is the desire to exact vengeance for a wrong done (e.g., an injury or insult).

today, although he gave one to other people," and "He turned away from a conversation with me, nose in the air," or "He laughed at me in public," and, "He gave me the worst seat at dinner, not the place of honor," and other thoughts of this type. What could I call them except the complaints of a squeamish spirit? The pampered and the prosperous generally indulge in such thoughts, since a man over whom worse things loom doesn't have the time to pay attention to insults.

10.3. During times of excessive rest, intellects that are weak by nature, womanly, and given to pleasure because they haven't experienced a real injury are affected by such things, the majority of which come from the interpreter's own weakness. A person affected by an insult shows that he has no practical knowledge or self-assurance, since he decides right away that he has been disrespected. This mental pain comes from the submission of a spirit that is suppressing and demeaning itself. But the wise man isn't disrespected by anyone. He understands his own importance and doesn't grant power over himself to anyone else. Not only does he overcome all those things that I would describe as irritations rather than afflictions of the spirit, he doesn't even feel them.

10.4. There are other things that strike the wise man, even if they don't topple him, such as bodily pain and feebleness or the loss of friends and children, and the terrible misfortune of a country raging with the fires of war. I don't deny that the wise man feels these things. After all, I'm not claiming he's made of stone and steel. It isn't virtue to have suffered through what you can't even feel. So, what's my point? My point is that the wise man is struck by certain blows, but overcomes them once he's been struck, heals them, and subdues them. Minor things like insults he doesn't even feel and doesn't exercise his usual virtue of endurance against them. He either doesn't pay attention to them or thinks they're good for a giggle.

11.1. And anyway, since it's arrogant, rude people who give the most insults (I mean, people who deal poorly with prosperity) the wise man has a way to spurn their conceited attitudes: the spirit's finest virtue of all, magnanimity. Magnanimity skips over those sorts of things as if they were worthless illusions and the phantom visions of dreams, lacking any substance or reality. **11.2.** At the same time, the wise man thinks that all of those people are too inferior for their insolence to give any real disrespect to what is so very much more sublime.

They say the word "insult" (*contumelia*) comes from the word "contempt" (*contemptus*), since no one singles out another for such an injury without showing contempt. But no one's contempt can affect a more important or better man, even if he does something that contemptuous people usually do. For instance, small children strike their parents' faces and toddlers muss up their mothers' hair. They scratch and drool and get naked in front of their families and don't refrain from using naughty words. But we don't call any of these things insulting. Why? Because the child doing them isn't able to be contemptuous. **11.3.** This is the same reason why the impertinent wittiness of slaves directed at their masters is funny, and why (provided it starts with the master) their nerve with guests is permissible. The more despicable the slave is, the more their freedom of speech is incredibly wild. Some even buy sharp-tongued slaves for this purpose, encourage them and give them a teacher so they can pour out abuse with practice. And we don't call these insults; we call them witty jokes! How crazy to be delighted at one time and offended at another by the same act. How crazy to call something a grievous insult when it's said by a social equal but a clever joke when it's said by a slave!

12.1. The spirit with which we deal with children is the spirit the wise man has toward all who are childish even into adulthood and old age. Or have these people not developed at all? Their spirits are distressed and their confusion grows more serious as they age. They differ from children only in the size and shape of their bodies but are otherwise no less unfocused and unsure, pursuing pleasure indiscriminately, anxious or calm not because of their temperament, but because of their terror. **12.2.** One might say that there's no difference at all between those people and children. Children are greedy for knucklebone dice, sweet-nut treats, and pennies. Those people are greedy for gold and silver and mirrors. Children act like important officials and dress up in the *toga praetexta* and the *fasces* and play-act tribunals. Those people play the same games for real on the *Campus Martius*, in the forum, and in the *curia*. Children erect little houses, sand castles, on the shore. Those people (as if they were doing something really important) turn a house that was devised as a source of safety for the body into a source of danger by making walls and roofs higher and higher. The delusion, then, for children and for grown-up children is more or less the same but about different matters and on a larger scale. **12.3.** So, it's not without good reason that the wise man thinks insults from these people are like witty jokes, and also sometimes warns them, like he would warn children, with a bad thing or a punishment. He doesn't do it because he actually received injury, but because they committed one and so that they stop committing them. This is how animals are tamed, with blows. We aren't angry with them when they refuse a rider, but we assert control so that their pain conquers their stubbornness. So, you'll see that the objection raised against us ("Why, if a wise man does not receive injury or insult, does he punish those who give them?") has been countered: he's not avenging *himself*, he's correcting *them*.

13.1. Why is it that you find it incredible for a wise man to have this steadfastness of spirit when you can see it in other men (if not for exactly the same reason)? What kind of doctor, for example, would become angry with a mentally unstable person? What kind of doctor takes offense at the verbal abuse of a feverish man denied cool water? **13.2.** The wise man approaches everyone with the same spirit that the doctor has toward his patients. The doctor does not find it undignified to touch patients' private parts if they need treatment, or to examine their feces and fluids, or to put up with the abuse of patients raging during a fever. And the wise man knows that all those people who, looking healthy, march around in their purple-hemmed togas are actually quite ill. He doesn't see them as anything other than sick people lacking a sense of restraint. So he doesn't get angry at all if, in their illness, they do something aggressively insulting against their doctor.

13.3. He also thinks the things they do to honor him are inadequate in the same way he judges their titles and achievements of no use. If a beggar pays him some respect, it won't make him feel good, and he won't think it's an insult if the least-significant citizens don't give him the proper response when he greets them. In exactly the same way, he won't look up if many rich men look up at him (he knows, you see, that rich men are not at all different from beggars and are even more pitiable, since beggars need little, but rich men need a lot). Likewise, he wouldn't be affected if the king of the Medes or King Attalus of Asia were to walk on by, in silence and with a superior expression on his face, after the wise man greeted him. The wise man knows that the king's position is no more enviable than the position of someone who happens to be in charge of the physically and mentally ill in a large household. **13.4.** Should I be upset if the people who conduct business near the Temple of Castor, buying and selling worthless slaves, their shops stuffed full of slaves in the worst condition, don't return my greeting? I don't think so. What good thing does a man possess if he's master of no one but bad people? So, just as the wise man ignores the kindness and unkindness of such men, so also he ignores a king. "You have Parthians and Medes and Bactrians under your rule, but you only control them through fear. Because of them you are not allowed to unstring your bow. They are the most frightening kind of enemies: open to bribes and always on the lookout for a new master."

13.5. Therefore, insults will never affect him since, though people think they differ among themselves, the wise man thinks people are all the same. Their foolishness is equal. If he lowers himself to the point where he's affected by injury or insult, he'll never be able to be free of anxiety. But freedom from anxiety is a good thing, and characteristic of the wise man. He'll never, by thinking that an insult had an effect, be guilty of giving honor to an insolent person, since it follows from this that he would be glad to be well thought of by the same man whose insult he took badly.

14.1. Some people are affected by a derangement so great that they think they can be insulted by a woman! What does it matter how wealthy they think she is because she has many litter-bearers, how overladen her ears are with jewelry, and how spacious a sedan-chair she has? She is the same thoughtless animal and, unless knowledge and a great deal of culture comes her way, a wild one, unable to control impulses. Some men are irritated when they are bumped by the hairdresser, and say that the intractability of a doorman or the arrogant superiority of a *nomenclator* or the disdain of a personal servant is an insult. How much laughter must bubble up in these situations, how much delight at the confusion of other people's erroneous beliefs must fill the spirit, for the person who is aware of his own contentment!

14.2. "What then, doesn't a wise man arrive at doors that a bully of a doorkeeper is guarding?" If some essential business calls him there, he'll of course endure it. And he'll soothe the bully—whoever he is—just like he would soothe a vicious dog, by throwing scraps. He won't consider it below his dignity to spend some money to enter the house, since he also expects to pay a toll to cross certain bridges. So, he'll pay the man who's doing the toll-collecting for the morning *salutatio*, since he understands very well that when something is for sale it gets bought with money. A man has a puny spirit if he is pleased with himself because he spoke his mind to a slave doorkeeper, or because he broke his stick on the doorkeeper's back, or because he pushed his way to the doorkeeper's master and asked for the slave to be beaten! When you put up a fuss, you make yourself into an opponent. And in order to win the fight, you have to have brought yourself to the same level as your opponent.

14.3. "But what will a wise man do if he's struck by a hand?" Just what Cato did when he was struck in the mouth. He didn't blow up, or avenge the injury. He didn't even forgive it. Instead, he denied that any injury was done. With a greater spirit than if he had just ignored it, he simply did not acknowledge the injury happened. **14.4.** We won't stick to this thread of thought long. After all, who doesn't know that the things commonly believed to be good or bad by everyone else don't seem the same to the wise man? He doesn't pay attention to what men consider filthy or contemptible; he doesn't go where the crowd goes. Instead, just as the stars set their course contrary to the revolution of the earth, the wise man sets his path contrary to the opinion of everyone else. **15.1.** So, stop saying, "Will the wise man, then, take no injury if he is beaten or if his eye is poked out? Will he take no insult if he is herded through the forum with foul words from vulgar people? What if he is commanded, at dinner with the king, to sit at the least important table and eat with slaves assigned to the most degrading kinds of tasks? What if he's made to endure anything else that can be devised to be offensive to his freeborn dignity?" **15.2.** In whatever way these things increase in number or in size, they are always the same in nature. If the small things don't affect him, the bigger ones won't either. If a few things don't affect him, many won't either.

Now, you've come to a conclusion about the expansive spirit of the wise man based on your own mental weakness. When you think about how much *you* could endure, you set the limit of a wise man's endurance just a bit farther on from that. But the wise man's virtue sets him in a different place in the world altogether, and he has nothing in common with you. **15.3.** Seek out harsh things, things hard to tolerate, things that eyes and ears should recoil from. He won't be crushed by all of them taken together: the man who resists them one by one is the same sort of man who will resist them all at once. Someone who says that this or that is tolerable for a wise man and that this or that is intolerable, or who keeps magnanimity within defined boundaries, has it all wrong. Fortune conquers us unless we conquer it completely, in its entirety.

15.4. So you don't think that this toughness is strictly a Stoic idea, Epicurus, whom you allege as the sponsor of your inaction and who you suppose advocates soft living and idleness and things that are pleasurable, says, "Rarely does Fortune hinder the wise man." This is *so* close to a manly statement! Don't you want to speak more strongly and take Fortune out of the picture altogether? **15.5.** This wise man's house is humble, without decoration, without commotion, without pomp. It isn't guarded by doorkeepers directing visitors with a contempt that can be bought. But through his doorway, empty and free of doorkeepers, Fortune does not enter. She knows there's no use going where she has no power. **16.1.** Now, if even Epicurus, who most of all indulged the body, made a stand against injury, how can it seem unbelievable or beyond the limit of human nature for us Stoics? He said that injuries are tolerable for the wise man; we say that such events aren't even really injuries. **16.2.** Now, there's no reason for you to say that this is inconsistent with Nature.[6] We don't deny that it is a misfortune to be beaten and to be pushed around, or to lose a limb. We deny that all of these things are *real injuries*. We don't exclude the sensation of pain, we exclude the name "injury" because injury cannot be granted without impairing virtue. We'll see which of the two (Epicurus or the Stoics) speaks more truly. At any rate, both think alike in disregarding injury.

What is the difference between the two then, you ask? It's the kind of difference there is between very brave gladiators, one of whom staunches his wounds and stands his ground while the other, glancing at the noisy crowd, signals that he has not even been wounded and allows no interference. **16.3.** There's no reason to think that we differ in a big way. Both traditions advise what we are talking about, the one thing that matters to you: to scorn both injury and insults, which I'd call shadows and hints of injuries. One doesn't need to be a wise man to scorn these things, just as a sane man can say to himself, "Are these things happening to me deservedly or not? If I deserve them, it's no insult; it's justice. If I don't, it's a matter of shame for the one doing an unjust thing." **16.4.** And what is it, this thing we call insult? Let's say someone makes jokes about my bald head and my weak eyes and my spindly legs and my size. How is it an insult to hear what is quite true for all to see? In front of one person we laugh at some joke,

---

6. The primary Stoic principle is that the wise man acts according to Nature. Seneca is suggesting here that being impervious to injury is not, as it seems to some, contrary to human nature.

but in front of more than that we get indignant, and we don't allow others the freedom of speech to say the things we usually say about ourselves. We are delighted with moderate jokes, but we get angry when they get out of control!

17.1. Chrysippus tells how a certain person was offended because someone had called him a "sea-monsterette." We saw Fidus Cornelius, the son-in-law of Ovidius Naso, weeping in the senate house because Corbulo had called him a "plucked ostrich." Against other damning words, ones attacking his character and lifestyle, he kept a steady resolve on his face, but against this incredibly silly one he burst into tears! A spirit's mental weakness really is *that* bad when reason has left it. **17.2.** What about how we're offended if someone imitates our voice or how we walk, or if someone apes some defect of our body or language? As if more people are going to notice these things because someone imitates them than because we do them ourselves! Some people don't want to hear about how old and gray they are, but other people pray to stay alive that long. The taunt "Poor-boy!" really gets to some people, although anyone who hides his poverty is really just insulting himself.

You take away material for jokes from insolent and rude people if you take the initiative and move on it first. No one becomes a joke if he laughs at himself. **17.3.** It's public knowledge that Vatinius, a man born to be ridiculed and hated, was a clever and witty joker. He used to say lots of things about his feet and scarred cheeks. This is the way he escaped the clever wit of his enemies (he had more enemies than illnesses!), especially Cicero. If *he* was able to do this, a man who had forgotten his sense of shame in the stream of abuse, why can't a man who has gained some success through liberal education and the cultivation of wisdom? **17.4.** And anyway, it is revenge of a sort to take away the pleasure of an insult from the ones who made it. They usually say, I think, "Poor me! He just doesn't get it!" That's how much enjoying an insult depends on the feelings and indignation of the target. In the end, someone like that will one day meet his equal—someone will pop up who'll get revenge for both of you.

18.1. Gaius Caesar, among the other vices that he had in abundance, had a nasty sense of humor. He had this strange desire to make everyone the victim of a particular insulting slur. He himself was a very rich source for ridicule: his pale coloration (testimony to his insanity) was repulsive, his eyes projected a fierce focus, although hidden under a forehead as wrinkled as an old lady's, and his head was malformed and bald, with stray bits of hair on top. His neck was riddled with coarse hair, his legs were skinny, and his feet were enormous. It would be a huge task for me to report each and every way he insulted his parents, his grandparents, and men of every rank. But I shall mention the people who finally killed him. **18.2.** Caligula considered Asiaticus Valerius among his closest friends. He was also a fierce man and not one to take nasty jokes with a calm spirit. But at a dinner party—that is, in public—the emperor tossed out in a loud voice how Valerius' wife was in bed. Good heavens! How awful for a husband to hear such a thing and for an emperor to know it. How awful for an emperor to have reached such a degree of wantonness that he could describe his adulterous act *and critique* the woman, not just to a man who was an ex-consul and a friend, but also the husband! **18.3.** Chaerea, a military tribune, didn't speak the way he fought: his voice had a delicate sound to it and, unless you knew what kind of man he was, it could make you wonder. When he asked for the password, Caligula would sometimes give him "Venus" or "Priapus," accusing the soldier of one or the other kind of effeminacy. And Caligula himself in silk robes, Greek sandals, and gold jewelry! As a result, Chaerea was forced to stab Caligula with his sword so he wouldn't have to ask for a password anymore! Of all the conspirators *he* raised the first hand, *he* chopped Caligula's neck in two with one blow. Only then was there a great rush from all sides of swords taking vengeance for public and private injuries. But the first was from a man who least seemed to be a man. **18.4.** All the same, Caligula used to think everything was an insult to himself. Those most eager to give offense are least able to take it. He got angry at Herrenius Macro because he greeted him as Gaius, and a *primipilaris* got into trouble because he said "Caligula." This was the name he used to be called because he was born in a military camp and raised among the legions; it was the most common name for the soldiers to use. But now that he had earned actor's boots, he considered being called "Bootie" a disgraceful insult.[7]

18.5. This, therefore, will be a source of consolation for us, that (even if our easy-going nature dismisses thoughts of vengeance) there will be someone in the future who will make a smart-mouthed, arrogant jerk pay. Such moral failings never stop with only one man or only one insult. **18.6.** Let's examine the examples of men whose

---

7. Caligula means "little (military) boot."

tolerance we praise, like Socrates, who took the jibes of the comedians, publicly circulated and even performed, in good humor and laughed no less than when he was doused with dirty water by his wife Xanthippe.[8] Antisthenes[9] was taunted because of his mother (she was a barbarian and a Thracian), but he replied that even the mother of the gods[10] was from Mt. Ida.

19.1. We shouldn't start a fight or an argument—we should walk away. Whatever comes out of the mouths of thoughtless people (only the thoughtless give such insults) should be ignored and the honors and insults of the crowd should be considered of similar value. **19.2.** We shouldn't be sad about the latter and happy about the former or else we will refuse to do many necessary things. As long as a womanish worry about hearing something that might hurt our feelings tortures us, we won't get involved in private or in public business because, even if some of it is good for us, we're afraid of or sick of insults. Sometimes too, when we're angry at powerful people, we'll show emotion through unrestrained free speech. But it isn't freedom to be intolerant: we are deluding ourselves. It *is* freedom to place the spirit above injuries, for the spirit to make itself the only source of joyful things and for it to separate out what is external to itself, so that we don't have to lead a life of discontent, afraid of everyone's laughter and everyone's words. You see, if anyone can be insulting, is there anyone who cannot?

19.3. Now the wise man and the man on the road to wisdom use different remedies. Those who aren't perfect and still act guided by public opinion must consider that they themselves ought to pass their time among injuries and insults. Everything is easier to bear when you expect it. The more respectable a man's family, reputation, or wealth, the more bravely he should conduct himself, remembering that the units that stand in the front line behave nobly. Let him withstand insults and vulgar words and public disgrace and other disreputable events just as he would the enemy's battle cry and weapons thrown from a good distance, rattling harmlessly around his helmet. Let him endure injuries as he would endure wounds. Some pierce his armor and some reach his chest, but he isn't beaten down and doesn't even

---

8. Xanthippe is variously portrayed in our sources as a devoted and tolerant wife or a terrible nag.

9. Antisthenes was a student of Socrates.

10. That is, Rhea, mother of the Olympian gods who were fathered by Kronos.

yield one pace. Even if you're in a bad situation and hemmed in by a hostile force, it's still a disgrace to give ground. Take up the soldier's duty given to you by Nature. Do you want to know what that duty is? It's a *hero's* duty. **19.4.** The wise man's remedy is different, I mean opposite, to this one. You see, while you are in the thick of battle, he has already won.

Don't resist your own good. Nurse this hope in your spirit while you are arriving at the truth. Accept better teachings willingly and help yourself with belief and prayer. It's in the common interest of all humanity for there to be something unconquered and for there to be someone over whom Fortune has no power.

Consolation to Marcia

(*Ad Marciam De Consolatione*)

1.1. Were I not sure, Marcia, that you had pulled as far away from the weakness a woman's spirit shows as you have from other faults, and that your character and habits are as highly respected as those of an ancient role model, I wouldn't dare to take issue with your grief, since men are willing to attach and cling to their grief too. And I wouldn't begin to hope that I could make you stop blaming your fortune—it's a bad time, you're a hostile judge, and the crime was detestable. But your strength of spirit and your virtue, both validated by this great test, have given me the faith to try.

1.2. Everyone knows how you behaved toward your father. You loved him no less than you loved your children, except that you didn't want him to live longer than you. Or maybe you did—I don't know—since great love and duty are allowed to act contrary to normally good ways of thinking. You opposed the death of your father, A. Cremutius Cordus,[1] as much as you could. After you realized that only the one avenue of escape from slavery among Sejanus' underlings lay open to him, you gave in to a plan you didn't like, you wept in secret, and you swallowed your sadness, although you did not put on a cheerful face. And you did all of this in an age when people thought being a loyal family member meant only not being *disloyal*. **1.3.** But when times changed, and you had the chance, you restored your father's talented writings for our benefit—this was why he was killed—and you freed him from true death. That is, you re-established as a public monument the books that very courageous man wrote with his own blood. You've done a very good thing for the study of Rome, since the majority of his books were burned. And you've done a very good thing for the future, since it will receive an unbiased, true account that cost its author his life. You've also done a very good thing for your father, since his memory is strong and will

---

1. A famous historian, Aulus Cremutius Cordus, was ordered to commit suicide in 25 CE, during the reign of Tiberius. His writings, which seem to have favored Brutus and Cassius (and so under the law of *maiestas* were considered damaging to the person and position of the emperor), were burned at the order of the Senate.

remain strong as long as it's thought rewarding to understand Roman history, as long as anyone exists who wants to look back at the deeds of our ancestors, and as long as anyone wants to know what it is to be a Roman man, what it is to be an unbroken man (although everyone's necks were yoked and controlled by Sejanus), and what it is to be a man with a free will, a free spirit, and a free hand. **1.4.** My goodness, the state would have suffered a huge loss if you hadn't rescued a man sent into oblivion for two of the most beautiful reasons possible: an ability with words and freedom of speech. He is being read and he is held in high esteem. He does not need to fear becoming old now that he's in the hands and hearts of men. But soon even the wickedness of his butchers, the only thing about them that deserves to be remembered, will be silenced.

1.5. Your greatness of spirit kept me from taking into account your gender or your face, which has been marked by the continuous sadness of so many years, and was marked as soon as sadness found you. Look, I'm not trying to sneak something past you or thinking that I can rob you of your emotions. I have brought back memories of old, bad events and shown you the scar from your equally old wound so you'll understand that the current injury can also be healed. So, let others approach this gently and speak charming words. I have decided to engage your sorrow in combat. I will subdue those exhausted eyes, if it can be done. (If I may say so, they weep more from habit than from loss.) And I'll do it whether you approve of the therapy or not, even if you hold on tight to the sorrow you are keeping alive in your son's place. **1.6.** What end will there be to sorrow otherwise? Everything has been tried, without effect: the consolations friends offer have been used up, as has the influence of important men and your male relatives. Philosophy is a good you inherited from your father, but it has not had lasting effect—only bringing solace as a brief diversion—and your ears have been deaf to it. You are the only one on whom even time, the natural remedy, has used up its power—and time calms the worst of our troubles.

1.7. Three years have passed now, and during that time your grief has been as fresh as the first surge. Your grief renews itself and grows stronger every day. Because of the delay, grief has become the rule. It has got to the point that you think it would be shameful to stop. All vices creep deep into our hearts unless they are crushed at the start, and it's the same with sadness and misery: things that treat themselves savagely feed on bitterness in the end and sorrow becomes a perverted pleasure of an unhappy spirit. **1.8.** I would have wanted to resort to this cure in the early days of your grief: it still would have been possible to confine its power at the inception. The battle against an entrenched foe is more violent, but healing a wound is easier when it is fresh. (When a wound has gotten infected it's usually cauterized or opened up all the way again to be probed.) Now, I can't offer an indulgent or gentle treatment for such an established grief. It must be shattered.

2.1. I know that everyone who wants to give advice starts with instructions and ends with role models. But it's useful sometimes to change the custom since things need to be done differently in different situations. Some people are convinced by reason and others need to have famous names set before them—I mean an authority that doesn't let their spirits free while they stare amazed at its brilliance. **2.2.** I'll set before you two women of this age as excellent role models. One was a woman who gave herself over to an enduring grief. The other was a woman who, although affected by an equivalent situation and a greater loss, didn't make herself a slave to bad things for a long time, but swiftly settled her spirit back again in its place. **2.3.** Octavia and Livia, the sister and wife of Augustus respectively, both lost their sons while young men, each with a solid hope of them becoming *princeps* in the future.[2] Octavia lost Marcellus, on whom Augustus his uncle and father-in-law[3]—had turned his favor and laid the burdens of the Empire. He was a young man with an active spirit and a powerful talent, but was temperate and self-controlled in a way that was worth admiring in someone of his age and wealth. He had endurance for hard work, was a stranger to pleasures, and was ready to bear whatever his uncle would have wanted to lay as a burden on him and, if I can say it, wanted to build on him. In him Augustus made a good choice for a foundation that would not collapse under any weight.

2.4. Octavia didn't stop weeping and mourning for the rest of her life. And she didn't allow any words offering healthy advice or even allow herself to be cheered up. Her whole spirit was focused on this one thing: she remained for the rest of her life what she was at his

---

2. Octavia's son Marcus Claudius Marcellus (42–23 BCE) died after an illness at the age of 19. Livia's son was Nero Claudius Drusus Germanicus (38 BCE–9 CE), who died on campaign in Germany. Both were marked by Augustus as possible successors.
3. Augustus had married his only child, Julia, to Marcellus in 25 BCE.

funeral. I don't mean that she didn't dare to lift herself up out of grief, but that she refused to be lifted. She decided that letting go of her tears would be like letting go of her son again. **2.5.** Octavia didn't want to have an *imago* of her dearest son, and no mention of him happened in her presence. She hated all other mothers, and especially Livia, since it seemed like the success promised to her son had been transferred to Livia's. In the shadows, with solitude for a best friend and avoiding even her brother, Octavia rejected all the songs composed to perpetuate Marcellus' memory and the other works of literature that honored him. She closed her ears to every comfort and hid herself away entirely, withdrawing from her usual duties and despising her brother's ever-shining good fortune. Besieged by children and grandchildren, she still didn't lay down her mourning clothes. This was quite insulting to her family, since she seemed to herself utterly bereft although they were all alive.

3.1. Livia lost her son Drusus, who was going to be a great *princeps* and was already a great general. He had penetrated deeply into Germany and had set up Roman standards where they barely even knew there were people called Romans. He passed away on campaign, but the enemy showed him honor while he was sick, giving respect and declaring a peace, and they didn't presume to ask for any advantage. Enormous grief, felt by citizens, provincials, and all of Italy, accompanied this death: he died in the service of the state. His funeral procession, with towns and settlements emptied for this sorrowful duty, was almost exactly like a triumph proceeding all the way into Rome. **3.2.** She, his mother, had not been allowed to receive her son's last kiss and the final words from his mouth as he died. On the long journey to Rome she was moved by all the many funeral pyres burning throughout Italy, as if she were losing him again each time she saw one. Nevertheless, as soon as she placed him in the tomb, she laid him and her sorrow down and didn't mourn more than was noble or fair, since Caesar Augustus was alive. She didn't stop glorifying the name of her son Drusus, setting images of him everywhere, in public and in private, speaking of him or hearing about him very eagerly. She lived with his memory: no one who turns memory into sadness can hold onto and revisit it. **3.3.** So, choose which role model you think is more commendable. If you want to follow the first one, Octavia, you should remove yourself from the living. You should turn from others' children and your own and the one you're missing too. Mothers will treat you as ill-omened when you run into them; you'll reject noble and honest pleasures as if they weren't appropriate for your lot in life. You'll see the light of day and hate it, and you'll see the days of your life as the enemy because they don't hurry up as fast as possible . . . and end. Most abhorrent of all (and most unlike your spirit, which is known for making the better choice), you'll show that you don't want to live, but aren't able to die. **3.4.** But if you model yourself after that greatest of women, Livia, but with more moderation and more gentleness, you won't be in distress and you won't rip yourself apart with grief. What a bad thing—what madness!—it is to punish yourself because you are unfortunate and in this way add to your bad fortune. Also, you will in this case show the nobility and reverence of the character you've shown during your whole life. There is also self-control in grief. And you'll put the young man himself in a better place, if he lives on in his mother's mind as happy and as joyful as he was when he was alive. And he's especially deserving of it because he, always on people's tongues and minds, always made you happy.

4.1. I won't give you commands that require too much bravery to follow, so that I am asking you to endure something human in an inhuman way or to dry a mother's eyes on the same day the funeral takes place. But I will take you to court, and this will be the issue before us: whether sorrow should be deep or be eternal.

4.2. I don't doubt that Julia Augusta,[4] who was a close friend of yours, is a more pleasing role model for you. She's calling you to take her advice. She went to Areus, her husband's philosopher, for advice in the early stages of her deep-rooted grief, when sadness is at its most uncontrollable and vicious.[5] She admitted that this was very beneficial. In fact, he was more beneficial than the Roman people whom she didn't want to burden with her own sadness. He was more beneficial than Augustus, who was reeling from the loss of a second heir[6] and unable to respond to the grief of his family. Areus was even more beneficial than her son Tiberius, whose loving duty during that

---

4. That is, Livia. One provision of Augustus' will was that Livia be adopted into the *gens Julia* in order, presumably, to secure the succession for her son by Tiberius Claudius Nero (85–33 BCE), her first husband.

5. Areus is generally thought to be Arius Didymus, a philosopher who was close to members of Augustus' court. He seems to have been best known in antiquity for collecting and summarizing the precepts of different philosophical schools.

6. That is, after Marcellus.

difficult funeral, when nations wept, made her feel as if the only difference was in the number of sons she had. **4.3.** I think this was the
approach he took with her and that this was how he began to speak
to a woman who held her own opinions very tightly, "Until today,
Julia, as far as I am aware (and I am a very faithful companion to your
husband, someone who knows not only what the public opinions are
about you but also all of the secret motivations of your spirits), you've
made sure that there would be no reason for someone to find fault
with you. I've observed this in big things, and also in little things: you
have not done anything you wouldn't have wanted known publicly—
rumor is a very unrestrained judge of nobles. **4.4.** I think nothing is
more beautiful than for those who are in the highest positions to offer
forgiveness for many things, but to seek it for none. So, you should
behave as you usually behave in this case too, and not do something
you might want to have turned out otherwise. **5.1.** I ask you, I
beg you, don't be difficult and rude to your friends. There's no reason
for you to ignore the fact that none of them know how to act, whether
to talk about Drusus in your presence or not, in case they hurt you by
forgetting about that brilliant boy or by mentioning him. **5.2.** When
we go away from you and meet together, we talk all about what he did
and said with as much respect as he deserved. In your company our
silence about him is profound. So you're missing a very great pleasure,
to hear your son praised, something I don't doubt you, even at the cost
of your life (if it were in your power), would want to last for all time.
5.3. This is why you should expose yourself to—no, better yet,
invite—conversation about him, and lend willing ears to the reputation and memory of your son. Others in this sort of difficult situation
think that listening to words of consolation is a bad thing. Don't, as
they do, think that it's a heavy burden. **5.4.** In reality, however, you've
brooded over the negative side of things; forgetting the better things,
you look at how your fortune is worse. You don't turn your mind to
time you spent with your son in conversation; you don't remember his
childlike and sweet charm or the growth of his studies. You keep only
that last picture of things in your head, and you add to it whatever you
can, as if it were not horrible enough by itself. Please, don't desire to
be thought of as the least fortunate woman ever—that would be a very
perverse glory. **5.5.** At the same time, you should consider that it's not
really a big accomplishment to be brave when things are going well,
when life is moving forward smoothly. A calm sea and a following

wind don't show how skilled a helmsman is. You need some adversity to test a spirit. **5.6.** So, don't collapse, but instead take on a wider stance and hold up whatever burden crashes down from above, even if you're terrified at first by the sound. Fortune envies nothing more than a calm spirit." After these words he showed her the son who remained unharmed and her dead son's children.

6.1. Areus sat beside *you*, Marcia, talking about *your* problems: change the person and he was consoling you! But think, Marcia, that what was ripped from you was more than any mother ever has lost—I'm not flattering you or lessening the disaster you've experienced. If the fates can be conquered by tears, bring them on! **6.2.** Let's spend every day grieving, and use up the night in sleepless sorrow. Let's pound our torn chests with our hands and let them loose on our faces too. Let's let grief get to work if its range of wild behaviors will be useful. But if nothing that has been lost can be recovered by any amount of wailing, if our lot in life is fixed for eternity and can't be changed by any misery, and if death keeps hold of what it took away, then end this wasted sorrow. **6.3.** For this reason we should determine our own heading and not let any force take us away in the other direction. A totally useless helmsman loses control of the helm to the waves, or leaves the sails flapping in the wind and hands over his ship to the storm. But even if the ship wrecks, a helmsman should be praised if he is holding tight to the rudder, with a wide stance, when the sea takes him.

7.1. "But it's natural to miss your loved ones." Who would deny it, as long as it's not excessive? Pain and a tightening in even the bravest of spirits are inevitable when the ones we love the most leave, as well as when they die. But public opinion adds more to grief than what Nature requires. **7.2.** Consider how full, and yet how brief, the sorrow of dumb animals is. You can hear cows low for one or two days, and a mare's crazy wandering about lasts no longer. Wild animals, when they have followed their cubs' tracks all over the forest and returned many times to their devastated lair, smother their eagerness over a short period of time. Birds circle their empty nests with great cries, but soon peacefully resume their flight. No animal misses its babies for long except humankind, which stays present to its sorrow. But sorrow doesn't affect us for as long as we feel it, just for as long as we decide it should.

7.3. So that you'll understand that it's not according to Nature to be broken by grieving, the same loss wounds women more than men, barbarians more than peaceful and cultured peoples, and the uneducated more than the educated. But things that get their power from Nature have the same force against all: it seems that what is variable is not natural. **7.4.** Fire will burn citizens of every city of any age, as well as both men and women. A sword will prove its power to cut on any body. Why? Because force was given to them by Nature, which does not discriminate. People feel poverty, grief, and ambition differently, in the way their experience conditions them. The customary opinion—opinion causes fear about things that shouldn't be feared—makes people helpless and weak. **8.1.** Now, natural things don't decrease over time. But a long day can reduce sorrow. Sorrow is very tenacious, coming back again every day and bubbling up in spite of the remedies we apply. Nevertheless, its fierce strength fades with time, which is so very effective at blunting sorrow's effects.

8.2. You still have, even now, Marcia, an enormous sadness and it already seems to have grown a callous. It's not as strong as it was at the beginning, but it's persistent and stubborn. Even so, time will remove this much too, bit by bit. Whenever you use your spirit it will loosen. **8.3.** At the moment you are guarding your heart. But there is a big difference between allowing yourself to mourn and making yourself mourn. It would correspond to the nobility of your character if you were to make an end to your grief rather than waiting for it to end, waiting for the day when your grief will cease even if you don't want it to. Give it up yourself!

9.1. "So why do we show such stubbornness in weeping for our loved ones, if weeping did not happen through the will of Nature?" Because we do not think ahead to any bad event before it happens. Instead, as if immune and taking an easier path than others, we aren't made aware through the misfortunes of others that their misfortunes are ours too. **9.2.** So many funeral processions go past our houses, but we don't think about death. So many funerals are bitterly sad, yet we still make plans to give our little boys their man's toga or to have them finish their military service or to divide the family property. We see the sudden destitution of rich men all the time, but it never occurs to us that our own wealth teeters in the balance too. So, it's inevitable that we fall harder: we're attacked as if we didn't expect it. But anticipated attacks hit us with less force. **9.3.** Aren't you willing to see that you're standing exposed to every attack and that the projectiles that have pierced others are whizzing past all around you? It's as if you were attacking a city wall wearing minimal armor, or someplace fortified with many enemy troops and hard to reach. Expect to be wounded! Assume that those rocks flying over your head, and the arrows and spears too, were aimed at your body. Whenever someone at your side or behind you falls, shout, "You won't trick me, Fortune! You won't take me unaware and careless! I know what you're preparing for me. Even though you hit someone else, you were trying to hit me!"

9.4. Who ever looked at his property thinking he was going to lose it? Who among you ever dared to think about exile, abject poverty, or grief? Who, if he were told to think about it, would not reject it as an ill-omened thought and ask for these things to be deflected on to his enemies' heads or even the head of the one who dared to tell him to think about it? "I didn't think it would happen to me." **9.5.** Is there anything that you think won't happen to you that you know is happening to many people, or that you see has happened to many people? Here's an outstanding verse that didn't deserve to have come from the common stage:

"What can happen to anyone can happen to someone!"[7]

Has that man over there lost his children? You could lose yours too. Has that man been condemned? Your innocence is under attack too. This is the error that tricks us and weakens us, while we suffer what we never foresaw we could suffer. The man who foresees his future takes away the force of his later bad fortune in the present.

10.1. Whatever it is, Marcia, that shines about us on the outside (children, public office, wealth, *atria* full of clients, and an entry hall packed with another crowd of clients who can't get in, a famous name, a noble or beautiful spouse, and the other things that fall to us by uncertain and unstable chance), it's provided for our use by someone else. None of those things is given as a gift. Our stage has been designed and set with props and scenery that will return to the owner of the troupe. Some of these are returned on the first day, some on the second—only a few props last to the curtain. **10.2.** So, there's no reason for us to feel superior, as if we are living among things we own: they are on loan. We have the usufructuary rights, but the duration of our access is determined by the grantor. We should have what was given to us for an undisclosed amount of time ready at hand and, when

---

7. A quote from Publilius Syrus (see *On Serenity* 10.3).

asked, we should give everything back without arguing. It's the worst kind of borrower who insults the lender.

10.3. We should, therefore, love our dear ones, those whom we pray will outlive us (by order of birth) as well as those who would very rightly offer their own prayer for us to outlive them. And we should love them as if their permanence was never promised to us—no, better, as if not even a day with them was promised. We should remind our spirits all the time that they love things that will leave—no, better, things that are already leaving. You possess whatever is given by Fortune without a guarantor. **10.4.** Take pleasure from your children, and give them your time in return for that pleasure. Drink down every joy to the dregs, without delay. There are no promises about tomorrow evening—wait, I've granted an adjournment that's too long—there are no promises about the next hour! We must hurry—it's right on our heels! This companion at your side will soon be lost, and your company will soon be scattered when the battle is sounded. Everything is ready for looting. You poor people don't know how to live on the run.

10.5. If you are grieving for a dead child, the crime lies in the moment of his birth: death was decreed for him while he was being born. He was born under this law, and this fate followed him from the womb.

10.6. We've fallen under Fortune's power and it is harsh and invincible. Under her rule we'll suffer what we deserve and what we don't. She'll abuse our bodies violently, spitefully, and cruelly. She'll burn some with fire, either as a punishment or as a cure. She'll chain others—an enemy first, then a fellow citizen. She will toss some people about naked on unknown seas, and after they've wrestled the sea she won't deposit them on a sandy shore, but in the belly of some enormous beast. And she'll keep others stuck for a long time between life and death, emaciated by various kinds of diseases. Just like a fickle and lustful mistress who doesn't care about her people, she will wander about with her punishments and her gifts.

11.1. Why should we weep about parts of our life? We can weep over the whole thing. New problems will make us weep before we have wept enough over the old ones. So, you ought to show self-control, you women who behave without control, and you must gather the power of the human heart against many sorrows. Why have you forgotten about our common, well, your own, mortality? You were born a mortal and you gave birth to mortals. Did you hope that from such weak material—you are a decaying and changing body, constantly attacked by disease—to give birth to something enduringly eternal? **11.2.** Your son has died—that is, he has dashed off to the same end to which everything and everyone you think is more fortunate than him are rushing. This crowd fighting in the courts of the forum, or applauding in the theater, or praying in the temple, it's heading to that end even if at unequal speeds. And what you love, what you adore—and what you despise—everything will end equally in ashes. **11.3.** This, of course, is what the famous Pythian oracle "Know Thyself" means. What is a human being? A vessel that can be broken by any bump or fall. There's no need for a big storm to break you—you'll be shattered by whatever you smash into. What is a human being? A weak and fragile body, naked, naturally helpless, depending on the resources of others, thrown to all the insults of Fortune. When the human being exercises its limbs it is food for beasts and a victim for anything. We're woven from changing and weak materials, sleek featured on the outside only, unable to endure cold, heat, or hard work, bound for decay from mold or rest. We fear our own food, too little of which kills us and too much of which bursts us. Anxiously guarding our safety, we keep a precariously loose grip on our life's breath—a sudden panic or an unexpected loud noise can knock it out of us. Corrupt and useless, we always nourish our own anxieties. **11.4.** Why are we surprised that the body can die, when death is only one rattling gasp away? Or is it too big an effort to understand that it will die? Smell and taste, sleep and wakefulness, drink and food, and whatever it can't live without, all bring about death. Wherever it goes it senses its vulnerability immediately. It can't endure every kind of weather. Rotting, diseased, and sickened by strange and different water, by air and breezes it's not used to, and by the tiniest of reasons and ailments, it comes to think such grand thoughts, forgetting its conditions of life. It begins life with tears, but this contemptible animal makes such a big fuss all the rest of its life. **11.5.** A man turns over immortal and eternal things in his spirit and makes plans for his grandchildren and great-grandchildren. But while he is planning a long way ahead death crushes him. What we call old age is just the turning of very few years.

12.1. Your sorrow, if it's reasonable to begin with, is it looking to its own misfortune or to the misfortune of the one who died? Are you feeling grief for the loss of your son because you didn't find any pleasure in him or because you might have found greater ones if he had lived? **12.2.** If you say that you found no pleasure in him, you're making your loss more tolerable: people don't miss the things that didn't please them or bring them joy. If you admit that you found great pleasure in him, it's not right for you to complain about what has been taken away. Instead, you should be thankful for what you did have. There are a sufficient number of wonderful things that have come from the labor of raising him, unless perhaps there's no reward for those who raise children other than the act itself. Even those who lovingly raise puppies and birds and other impractical little pets to delight the spirit get some pleasure from seeing and touching them, and from their charming loyalty. So, although his dedication didn't benefit you, his devotion didn't protect you, and his wisdom didn't guide you, the fact that you had him and that you loved him is a reward. **12.3.** "But his life could have been longer and richer!" But it's been better for you than if he'd never been born at all since, if we can set aside the question of whether it's better to have been happy for a short time or never, it's certainly better to have good things that will go away someday than to have nothing. Would you prefer to have an immoral son who can only be a son in name, or a son with the kind of nature yours had: wise and lovingly dutiful beyond his years, a husband and father early on, quickly focused on all kinds of public service and made a priest at a young age? He did everything quickly. Almost no one finds great blessings that also last. Happiness and prosperity don't endure and stay with us until death unless they are slow-growing. The immortal gods, although they wouldn't give you a son for a long time, gave you the kind of son one has after a long time, just more quickly. **12.4.** Good grief! You can't say that you were specially chosen by the gods to not be allowed to enjoy your son! Take a good look at all the people you know, and the many you don't. People everywhere have suffered worse than you. Great generals have felt loss like yours, and so have *principes*. Our myths don't even leave the gods untouched by loss. I think that is because our load will be lightened when we hear that loss happens in the divine realm too. Look around, then, at everyone. You won't be able to name a single household so miserable that it can't find comfort through a deeper misery than theirs. **12.5.** But, my goodness, I don't have such a low opinion of your character that I'd think you could feel less sorrow for your misfortune if I produced a huge list of people who felt grief. A crowd of miserable people is a rotten kind of comfort. I will, however, mention a few—not so you understand this happens all the time to mortals (it'd be silly to collect role models for mortality), but so you understand there have been many people who have softened harsh blows by enduring them peacefully.

12.6. I'll start with the happiest person. Lucius Sulla lost a son, but the loss didn't affect his cunning and harsh prowess against enemy and citizen alike. And it didn't make it seem like he'd taken his *cognomen*, Felix, unfairly.[8] He took the *cognomen* after his son had died, not fearing the hatred of men, who contributed too much to the bad man's happiness, or the jealousy of the gods, whose fault it is that Sulla was so *felix*. But what sort of man Sulla was is not the question up for debate. Even his enemies would say that he took up arms well, and laid them down well.[9] This is the question: there's no very bad fortune that does not also come to the happiest of people. **13.1.** Greece can't admire too much the father who, when the death of his son was announced as he was performing a sacrifice, simply asked the flute player to be silent and took his chaplet[10] off, then finished the rest of the ritual. Pulvillus the *pontifex*,[11] while holding the doorpost as he dedicated the Temple on the Capitoline,[12] heard that his son was dead. He pretended that he hadn't heard the news, completing the ritual words of the pontifical song without a groan to interrupt the prayer.[13] He prayed to Juppiter in his son's name. **13.2.** Do you think that his grief ought to have an end, when the very first he heard of it didn't pull him, a father, from public sacrifices and a favorable public prayer? Good grief! He was worthy of leading a remarkable dedication ritual and of holding the most significant priesthood, since he did not cease to worship the gods even when they were angry. But when the same man returned home, his eyes filled with tears and he cried out in grief. And when he had completed the mourning

---

8. Lucius Sulla took the *cognomen* Felix "the Happy" or "the Blessed" after he celebrated a triumph (81 BCE) for military success in the Mithradatic Wars.

9. After enacting a series of reforms and carrying out a severe proscription of fellow citizens, Sulla laid aside his dictatorial powers and restored power to the Senate.

10. In both Greek and Roman religion, the person performing a sacrifice generally wore a crown woven of some significant material (e.g., olive branches, wheat, gold, etc.).

11. Probably Marcus Horatius Pulvillus, who consecrated the Temple of Juppiter on the Capitoline in 507 BCE, either in his capacity as consul as some sources indicate, or as *pontifex maximus*.

12. Presumably this is a detail from the ritual of the consecration of the physical space for a temple, which was a different ceremony from the selection of the place and the boundaries of the temple precinct.

13. Roman ritual practice was centered around the complete, accurate, and sometimes painstakingly careful enactment of proper ceremonies and speech formulae.

custom required, he put on the same expression he had worn on the Capitoline back on his face. **13.3.** Paulus, around the time when he led the defeated King Perses in his triumphal procession,[14] gave two sons to be adopted[15] and held funerals for the two he had kept for himself. What kind of sons do you think he kept when Scipio[16] was one of the two he gave for adoption? The Roman people watched Paulus' triumphal chariot, empty of children, but full of emotion. And he still gave a public speech, thanking the gods for granting his prayer. He had prayed, you see, that if there had to be some envy from his enormous victory, the negative consequences would fall on him rather than the state. **13.4.** Can you see what a courageous spirit the man had? He expressed joy for his losing a child! Who would have felt such a great change of circumstance more than he: in the same moment he lost his consolation and his support. But Perses didn't get to see Paulus unhappy.

14.1. Now, why should I drag you through countless examples of great men, searching for miserable people, as if it weren't more difficult to find happier people? How many households are there that have made it to the end with everyone alive, or in which there was not some trouble? Choose any year at all and mention either of its magistrates, Lucius Bibulus,[17] if you like, or Julius Caesar. You will see that the two shared a common fortune as well as a bitter hatred. **14.2.** The two sons of Lucius Bibulus, a better man than he was brave, were killed at the same time after being mocked by Egyptian soldiers. As a result, the reason for their deaths was no less worthy of tears than the bereavement itself. But Bibulus, who would later stay at home for the entire year of his consulship because of his hatred for his co-consul, performed his usual duties on the day after he heard about the double funeral.[18] Who was ever able to give less than one

---

14. Lucius Aemilius Paulus Macedonicus (d. 160 BCE) defeated Perses, king of Macedonia, in 168 BCE in a decisive battle at Pydna.

15. It was common among noble families for those with many children to have some adopted into the families of relatives and closely associated families, even as adults.

16. Publius Cornelius Scipio Aemilianus (185–129 BCE), a great general and statesman.

17. Marcus Calpurnius Bibulus (d. 48 BCE; Lucius was his son) was consul with Caesar in 59 BCE. He was opposed to Caesar's legislation and purposes, but after the mob broke the symbols of his power (his *fasces*), he withdrew his active opposition and tried to set procedural obstacles for Caesar's legislation, without result.

18. In 51 BCE, when the sons died, Bibulus was proconsul in Syria. This was a time of great unrest in the region, with Parthia threatening (and attempting) invasion.

day to mourn two sons? The man who later mourned the consulship for a year ended his mourning for his sons so quickly! **14.3.** When Julius Caesar crossed to Britannia and his prosperity could not even be limited by the sea, he heard that his daughter[19] had died, taking the fate of the state with her. It was clear that Pompey wasn't about to endure with a calm spirit the fact that another statesman was Great and it was clear that he would set a limit to Caesar's successes, which seemed hard for him even though he grew in power with them too. Nevertheless, within three days he took up his assigned command and conquered his sorrow as quickly as he conquered everything else. **15.1.** Why should I tell you about the losses of other Caesars? Fortune, it seems to me, does violence to them in this case so they can benefit humanity: they are proof that not even those who are said to be born from and to give birth to gods have power over their own fortune, as they do over the fortunes of others. **15.2.** The divine Augustus, after his sons, his grandsons, and a whole crowd of Caesars had died, strengthened his deserted household through adoption. But he endured the loss as bravely as if it was his business and in his best interest that no one complain about the gods. **15.3.** Tiberius Caesar lost a biological son[20] and an adopted son,[21] but even so he gave the eulogy from the *rostra* and stood near the visible body (although a veil had been interposed so the eyes of the *pontifex* would be blocked from seeing a dead body). And while the Roman people wept he wore the same expression. He offered himself to Sejanus, standing at his side, as proof of how resolutely he was able to lose his loved ones.[22] **15.4.** You see, then, how big it is, this list of the greatest men whom loss, which lays every person low, has overcome. And so many blessings of the spirit and so many public and private honors were piled on them! But of course this storm

---

19. Julia apparently died in childbirth in 54 BCE. Gnaeus Pompey (the Great) was her fourth husband and the marriage ensured, while she was alive, the political union of the two men, Caesar and Pompey.

20. Drusus Julius Caesar (13 BCE–23 CE).

21. Germanicus Julius Caesar, his nephew (16 BCE–19 CE).

22. Lucius Sejanus was suspected of poisoning Drusus in order to gain power, which he did after 23 CE while Tiberius withdrew into seclusion and left the governance of the state in his hands. In 31 CE Tiberius tricked Sejanus into being present in the Senate while his execution order was read aloud; Sejanus was tried and executed shortly thereafter.

crosses the globe and razes everything without distinction, acting as if it owned everything. Ask each man to settle his account. Everyone who is born owes this debt of death.

16.1. I know what you're saying. "You've forgotten that you're consoling a woman, giving examples of male role models." But who said that nature treated women unkindly as far as natural ability is concerned and reduced the number of virtues available to them? Women's physical vitality is equal to men's, and they have just as much ability, if they want it, to be noble. They suffer sorrow and hard work equally, if they become habituated to them. **16.2.** And exactly which city, gods above, are we talking about? The one in which Lucretia and Brutus cast off kingship from our heads: we owe freedom to Brutus, and we owe Brutus to Lucretia.[23] We're talking about the city in which Cloelia is almost included in the list of male heroes because of her daring in braving the river and the enemy.[24] An equestrian statue[25] of Cloelia on the *Via Sacra*, a very high-traffic area, rebukes our young men sitting on their pillows for traveling in that manner in a city where the women are honored with equestrian statues too. **16.3.** Now, if you want me to give role models of women who felt the loss of their loved ones bravely, I won't list them house by house—I'll give you two examples from the same family. The first is the daughter of Scipio, mother of the Gracchi. She gave funeral honors to her twelve children. For ten of them it was easily done: people didn't know that she'd given birth or that she'd lost the babies. But she also saw Tiberius and Gaius killed and laid in the tomb, sons who, you'll admit, were great men even if you deny they were good. Nevertheless, when people tried to console her and said sympathetic things she replied, "Never say that I, who gave birth to the Gracchi brothers, am unfortunate." **16.4.** Cornelia, daughter of Livius Drusus, lost a noble young man of considerable

---

23. Sextus, the son of Lucius Tarquinius Superbus, the last of the ancient Roman kings, raped Lucretia, the wife of a distant relative. Lucretia subsequently killed herself to protect her honor. Lucius Junius Brutus, although not motivated only by Lucretia's death, killed Tarquinius in 509 CE during the unrest that followed Lucretia's suicide, after which the Republic was born.

24. Cloelia escaped being hostage of the Etruscan king Porsenna, leading other young women with her. She later returned to Porsenna in exchange for the lives of other women and children.

25. Equestrian statues usually honored significant military commanders.

talent[26] following in the footsteps of the Gracchi to an unknown killer. He was killed in his own home before his many bills could be seen into law. Still, she endured the bitter and unavenged death of her son with as much courageous spirit as he had set forth his legislation. **16.5.** Will you return to a right relationship with Fortune now, Marcia? If Fortune aimed her weapons at the Scipiones[27] and at the mothers and daughters of the Scipiones (from which family she raised up Caesars), should she have held back from you? Life is dangerously full of different kinds of misfortunes, because of which no one can enjoy a long peace and barely even short periods of truce. You gave birth to four children, Marcia. They say that no spear thrown into a packed battle line falls to the ground. Is it really surprising that so many children could have been able to avoid jealousy or harm?

16.6. "But Fortune was harder on me because she not only threw down my child but also raised him up." You would never call an even share with a more powerful person an injury. Fortune left you two daughters and their children—and the son you mourn so much (have you forgotten an earlier loss?) is not totally gone. He gave you two granddaughters. They will be great burdens if you take his death badly, but great comfort if you take it well. Get to this point: whenever you see them, be reminded of your son, not your sorrow. **16.7.** When trees have been damaged, uprooted by strong winds or splintered and broken by a sudden gust, farmers care for the shoots left behind and sow seeds from the old tree or make plantings right away. In no time at all, since time moves just as quickly toward growth as it does to destruction, trees have grown to be more bountiful than what was lost. **16.8.** Put the daughters of your son Metilius in his place, fill the emptiness, and lighten one sorrow with two comforts. The nature of mortals is that nothing pleases us more than what is missing. It's harder for mortals to deal with what remains because of our longing for what was taken. But if you want

---

26. Marcus Livius Drusus was killed in 91 BCE while *tribune of the plebs.* A visionary legislator, he had been pursuing reforms aimed at alleviating significant issues for the plebeian, equestrian, and senatorial classes. But when he proposed granting citizenship to all Italians, he met staunch (and fatal) opposition. His death precipitated the Social War of 91–88 BCE.

27. The extended family (or clan) of Scipio were extremely influential in the Roman Republic. Many Scipiones were chief actors in the major political and military events of this period.

to value how much Fortune has done for you, how much Fortune has spared you, you'll see that you have more than two solaces: consider your grandchildren and your two daughters. Marcia, you need to say, "I might be upset if Fortune gave according to a person's character, and if bad things never happened to good people. But in reality, I see that good and bad people are all battered and tossed in the same way without distinction.

17.1. "But it's a serious blow to lose the young man you have raised, who had already become his mother's and father's delight and refuge." Who's denying it? But it is human. You were born for this, to lose and be lost, to hope and to fear, to disturb yourself and others, to fear death and to pray for it, and—worst of all—to never know what will happen to you. **17.2.** If someone had said to a traveler going to Syracuse, "Imagine every inconvenience and every delight of the trip that's coming, then set sail in the proper frame of mind. This is what you can admire: you'll see first of all the island itself, cut off from Italy by a strait, though it's thought to have once been connected to the mainland—it was pushed away suddenly by the sea, and 'Sicily was sliced away from Italy's shore.'[28] Then you will see—it'll still be possible to slip past that very greedy whirlpool—the famous mythical Charybdis, calm, without a south wind but swallowing ships with its wide and deep mouth if one ever blows too strongly. **17.3.** You'll see the Arethusa, the spring made famous by songs, very low with a brilliantly clear pool and flowing with very cold water.[29] Maybe the source that gives out the water is located there or maybe it flows from an underground river moving untouched under a great distance of ocean, preserved from mixing with worse water.[30] **17.4.** You'll see the calmest port of all those that occur naturally to protect ships or that are manmade. The port is so safe that even the fury of the greatest storms does not affect it. You'll see the place where the power of the Athenians was broken, where that famous prison, carved so deeply down into the rock, held countless

---

28. Seneca is quoting Vergil, *Aeneid* 3.418, the prophecy given to Aeneas of his journey to Latium (via Sicily).

29. Arethusa's spring was an abundant freshwater spring located on the island Ortigia in the mouth of the port of Syracuse, very close to sea level on the shore.

30. There is a legend that Arethusa, a nymph who lived near Olympia, was pursued by the river god Alpheus and fled, transformed into an underground stream, to Ortigia.

Athenian captives.[31] You'll see the enormous city itself, occupying territory wider than the boundaries of many cities.[32] Winter is very mild and not a day goes by without some sunshine. **17.5.** But when you've seen all this, the heavy and unhealthy summer weather will ruin all the positive aspects. Syracuse is also the home of Dionysius the tyrant, who brought death for liberty, justice, and the rule of law. He desires sole power even after Plato, and life even after exile.[33] He will burn some, beat others, and order others to have their heads chopped off for the slightest offense. He'll summon males and females for his lusts, and in the disgusting range of his unchecked power it won't be quite enough to have intercourse with two at the same time. You have heard what will excite you and what will terrify you. Now, go or stay." **17.6.** If anyone had said after this information that he wanted to go to Syracuse, would he have had enough just cause to blame anyone but himself, since he had not found these things out by accident, but had gone knowingly and deliberately?

Nature says to us all, "I'm not deceiving anyone. If you have sons, you might have handsome ones and you might have ugly ones. Maybe you'll have many—any one of them could as much save his country as betray it. **17.7.** There's no reason for you to lose hope that they might become men of such distinction that no one will dare to slander them. But keep in mind that they might become men of such disgrace that they will be like slander itself. There's nothing stopping them from being at your funeral and giving your eulogy, but prepare yourself to be the one who places a child, or a young man, or an old man on the pyre. But age has nothing to do with it, since any funeral in which a parent follows the casket is a harsh one." If you raise children after hearing these rules laid down, you free the gods from jealous hatred—they didn't promise you any certainty.

---

31. The expedition to Sicily in 415 BCE, undertaken at a critical point in the war and under adverse circumstances, ended in 413 BCE in disaster, with the Athenian ground and sea forces utterly defeated in spite of the fact that it was described as the largest fleet to set sail since the Trojan War. Surviving ground forces, numbering only in the thousands, were jailed in the quarries near Syracuse and finally sold into slavery.
32. Cicero, in describing Syracuse, delimits four distinct cities within the metropolis.
33. Dionysius II (397–343 BCE) was an extravagantly cruel and hedonistic ruler, ruling Syracuse twice, from 367–357 BCE, and at the end of his life from 346–344 BCE. Plato is thought to have been invited to Dionysius' court to advise him at the beginning of his reign, without effect. Dionysius' period of exile was spent in Italy.

18.1. Compare your entrance into life to this image I just used, when I explained what could delight or offend as if you were thinking about whether to visit Syracuse. Imagine that I am giving advice to you as you're being born. **18.2.** You're about to enter a city that all people share, that encompasses everything, but is bound by fixed and eternal laws, revolving among the tireless duties of the heavens. You'll see uncountable stars shining there, and everything full of the light of one star, the sun, marking the span of day and night with its daily course and dividing the summer and winter more evenly with its annual one. You'll see the nightly progression of the moon, sharing a soft and reflected light from her brother, hanging over the earth, hidden at one point and full at another, changing by growing and diminishing, always different from the last and the next. **18.3.** You'll see the five stars[34] going their different paths and straining in the opposite direction to the rush of the universe. The fortunes of the people hang from their slightest movements—the most and least significant things are shaped from this, as a favorable or unfavorable star ascends. You will marvel at clouds piled high and at the rain, at the flashing lightning and the crash of thunder in the sky. **18.4.** When your eyes are full of the spectacle of the heavens, you'll drop your eyes to the earth where another beauty of nature, but of a different sort, will draw your attention. Over here you will see plains, stretching into the boundless distance. Over there, the peaks of mountains rising, high and snow-capped, into the sky. You'll see rivers flowing down, and streams that spill from their sources west and east. You'll see woodland, its upper canopy swaying, and great forests with animals inside and the dissonant harmony of birds. **18.5.** There will be different sites for cities, and nations separated by difficult terrain. Some of them will be up in the high mountains, others surrounded by and in fear of rivers, lakes, and valleys. There will be wheat fields and wild uncultivated fruit trees, rivers softly meandering among meadows, beautiful coves and shores that form a harbor. There will be islands sprinkled upon the vast sea, which by their placement mark out the oceans. **18.6.** Shall I mention the glitter of stones and gems and gold mixed with sand rushing down mountain streams? Shall I mention the terrifying tongues of flame in the middle of the land and sometimes the sea?[35] Or the ocean, which chains the lands together,

34. The five visible planets: Mercury, Venus, Mars, Jupiter, and Saturn.
35. Presumably volcanoes.

cutting an otherwise unbroken connection of nations with three great gulfs and churning with unfettered freedom?[36] **18.7.** You'll see animals there bigger than any on land, swimming in unsettled waters that move without wind. Some, very big, swim guided by another,[37] others are swift and more nimble than ships rowed at full speed, and others suck in water and blow it out, producing great danger for ships that sail by. You'll see ships sailing to find unknown lands, and find nothing that human daring has not attempted. You'll watch and participate in new struggles and you'll learn and teach skills—some will prepare you for life, some will enhance your life, and others will regulate it. **18.8.** But there'll be thousands of sicknesses of the body and of the spirit, and there'll be wars, theft, poison, shipwrecks, storms in the sky and in the body, bitter longing for your dearest loved ones, and death that will either be (who knows?) easy or an excruciating punishment. Think carefully and completely about what you want to do. If you want to reach these things, you will need to leave through them too. You'll answer that you want to live. Well, of course! But, wait, maybe you won't approach something that can cause you sorrow through loss. Live if you want, then. "But no one actually asked me!" Our parents were asked about us and, although they knew the conditions of life, *they* brought us into it.

19.1. Now, turning to comforts, let's look first to see what has to be cured and then how. Longing for a person who was loved arouses grief. It seems that this in itself is bearable, since we don't cry when living people are, or are going to be, away, even though the pleasure of their company was taken away along with their presence. Therefore, it's our perception of things that tortures us and every thing that is bad is as bad as we have decided it is. The cure is in our power: let's decide that the dead are just absent, and let's trick ourselves. We were the ones who sent them away—or better yet, we sent them ahead and are following along behind. **19.2.** This also arouses grief: "There won't be anyone to defend me or save me from contempt!" I'll offer an unprovable but still true comfort that in our city losing a

---

36. In antiquity, geographers tended to view the world as encircled by the ocean, with the Mediterranean Sea, the Black Sea, and the Red Sea more or less surrounded by land.

37. The Elder Pliny proposed in *Natural History* 9.186 that the *musculus marinus* (what this is is not entirely clear) guided whales.

child gives you more friends than it takes away. Having no children brings so much influence to an old person that some people pretend to hate their children and cut them out of their will, bereaving themselves! And to think that having no heir used to ruin an old person's influence. **19.3.** I know what you'd say. "My losses aren't arousing my grief. A parent isn't worth consoling if she bears the loss of her son in the same way she bears the loss of a possession or has time to think about anything except her son." Why then are you grieving, Marcia? Is it because your son died or because he didn't live a long time? If because he died, you ought to have grieved all along, because you always knew he was going to die. **19.4.** Reflect on the fact that a dead person can't experience any bad thing, that stories are what make death and the underworld terrible for us. There's no darkness to threaten the dead, there's no prison or burning river, no river of forgetfulness, no judgment or criminals. Even in that expansive freedom provided by death there are no second-time tyrants. The poets play with these ideas and rile us up with empty terrors.

19.5. Death is a release from sorrows and a boundary beyond which our bad fortune does not pass. This boundary restores us to that serene place in which we lay before we were born. If anyone pities the dead, he should also pity those not yet born. Death is neither good nor bad, because only a thing can be good or bad. But death is nothing at all and takes everything back to nothing—it doesn't pass us on to any Fortune. Bad things and good things must work themselves out on matter. Fortune has no hold over what Nature has sent away, and someone who is no one cannot be pitied. **19.6.** Your son has broken through the boundaries that define our slavery, and has been welcomed by a great eternal peace. He isn't attacked by fears of poverty, concern for wealth, or the urgings of desire gnawing at the spirit with pleasure's teeth. Envy of another's prosperity and happiness won't touch him, and envy for his own won't weigh him down. His modest ears aren't being struck by any insults. He doesn't see public or private disasters. He isn't anxious about the future, hanging in suspense for an outcome that's always waiting for something better to come along. Finally, he's in a place from which he can't be expelled and where there is no fear.

20.1. People who don't praise death as Nature's best invention and look forward to it are unaware of their own bad fortune. If it ends a time of prosperity or drives back disaster, if it makes an end of the weariness of an old man who's had too long a life or takes a thriving young man while he's hoping for better things, or if it calls back a child before life gets too hard—whatever the circumstance, death is an end for all, a cure for many, and a prayer come true for some. And death treats no one better than those it comes to before it is invoked. **20.2.** Death emancipates even though the master is unwilling, loosens the chains of captives and leads prisoners of unrestrained power out of their cells. For exiles, as they turn their eyes and spirits back again and again to their homeland, death shows that it makes no difference where they are buried. When Fortune has unfavorably distributed the common share and has given some men to others even though all are born with equivalent rights, death makes everything equal. After death no one acts under another's power and no one feels of lower status: death is open to all. Death is what your father, Marcia, desired. Death is, in my opinion, what stops my birth from being a punishment, what keeps me from falling when troubles are looming, and what makes it possible for me to keep my spirit safe and in control of itself. I have something to call upon for help. **20.3.** I can see crosses over there, all different—different makers have different designs. Some hang the victim head down, others drive a spike through the victim's pelvis, others stretch out a victim's arms on a forked transverse beam. I can see stretching lines and I can see whips, and machines designed cleverly for every single part of the body. But I see death too. There are blood-soaked enemies and arrogant citizens, and I see death beside them. It's not a burden to be a slave where it's possible to cross into freedom with one step, if you're tired of the master. You are dear to me, life, because of the gift of death.

20.4. Think about how good a suitable and timely death is, how harmful it is for many to have lived too long. If Gnaeus Pompeius, the glory and support of the Republic, had been taken at Neapolis[38] by illness, he would without a doubt have died a *princeps* of the Roman people.[39] But it turned out that his fall from the pinnacle of success happened a short while later. He saw his own legions slaughtered in front of him. He, the general himself, survived that battle, in which the Senate was in the first battle line. How unlucky the survivors are! He saw his assassin on an Egyptian shore, and handed over his body to a

---

38. Modern Naples, Italy.

39. It is clear from other sources that Pompey was seriously ill in Naples in 50 BCE, the year before Julius Caesar crossed the Rubicon to challenge his power and, eventually, secure his rule over the Republic.

slave, a body that had been sacrosanct for his conquerors. But even if he had remained unharmed he would have been ashamed of his safety. What could be more reprehensible for Pompey than for his life to be the gift of a king? **20.5.** If Marcus Cicero had died instead of avoiding Catiline's daggers, which were aimed at the state also, if he had died after the state had been set free, or if his daughter's funeral had followed his own, he would even then have been able to die happy.[40] He wouldn't have seen swords unsheathed to kill civilians and property divided up among the killers so that life and property would be destroyed. He wouldn't have seen the property of consuls sold at auction,[41] or slaughter performed for pay, or theft, war, rape—the product of many Catilines. **20.6.** If Marcus Cato had been drowned in the sea when he was returning from Cyprus where he set the king's inheritance in order,[42] or when he reached Rome with the money[43] that bankrolled the civil war, wouldn't that have been much better for him? At least he could have known for sure that no one would dare to commit a sin in front of Cato. But in reality, the addition of a very few years forced a man born for his own freedom and for the freedom of the state to flee Caesar and follow Pompey.[44] Therefore, untimely death didn't bring bad things to your son, it removed the need to endure every bad thing.

21.1. "But he *did* die far too early and before this time." Imagine first that he survived and then make him live as long as a man can. How old? We're born to live for such a short time and to give up our place to the ones coming behind us—we look out on a temporary dwelling. Am I talking about our lives, which the ages sweep along, unbelievably swift? Count up the generations a city has survived—

---

40. Cicero was a principal actor in suppressing the rebellion in 63 BCE known as the Catiline Conspiracy. He encountered serious political retribution several years later, suffering exile from 58–57 BCE. Tullia died after childbirth in 45 BCE, and it is clear from his letters to his friends that her death was a crushing emotional blow.

41. This refers either to the proscriptions under Octavian and Antony, or to the sale of Pompey's properties described by Cicero in *Phillipics* 8.9.

42. After a little over twenty years of dispute, Cato was sent in 58 BCE to oversee the annexation of Cyprus to Roman control, and away from the possibly illegitimate heirs of Ptolemy Alexander II, who had died in 80 BCE (according to Roman sources) bequeathing all his possessions to Rome.

43. Cato returned to Rome from Cyprus in 56 BCE with 7,000 talents.

44. That is, into death. Cato committed suicide in 46 BCE to avoid being under Caesar's power.

you'll see how short a time even those who boast about their age have stood. All human things are brief and fragile, taking up no space at all in infinite time. **21.2.** We can place the earth with its cities and peoples, rivers and surrounding ocean in a tiny point if we compare it to the universe. Our life is even smaller than a point, if we compare it to all of time, which is greater than the measure of the universe, since the universe repeats itself within the same physical space.[45] So, what difference does it make to extend something that will be pretty much nothing at all no matter what you add to it? We only live for a long time if the time we have is enough. **21.3.** Now, you can tell me about men who are alive and men whose names are proverbial for old age, and you can say they are 110 years old. But when you turn your mind to consider all of time, there will be no difference between a very long life and a very short one if you have compared the amount of time a man was alive with the amount that he wasn't. **21.4.** In the end, Metilius died a timely death. He lived as long as he ought to have lived, and there was nothing for him beyond that point. Old age is not the same for all people or even for animals. Some animals grow weary of life within fourteen years—their longest lifespan is as long as the first part of a human's. A different scope for living was given to each. No one dies too quickly, since we aren't going to live longer than we are alive. **21.5.** An end is determined for each of us. It will always stay where it was placed and no care or kindness will push it further back. Think of it this way: you lost your son according to plan. He found his death and "crossed the finish line of his life's race."[46]

21.6. So, there's no reason for you to carry around the idea that he could have lived longer. His life wasn't cut short and chance events don't interfere with time. What was promised to each is fulfilled: the fates make their own path and neither subtract nor add to what was promised once. Prayers and studies have no effect—each person will receive the number of days prescribed on that very first day. From the first moment we saw the light of day we walked the path of death and

---

45. Seneca is referring to the Stoic understanding of the cosmos, in which all matter (and time is not considered matter) proceeds forward in time to a final conflagration, then renews the cycle from the beginning.

46. Quoted from Vergil, *Aeneid* 10.472, the moment before the young hero Pallas is killed by Turnus, as Juppiter warns Hercules of the inevitability of death for mortals and his inability to intercede.

came closer to our own death. The very same years that were added to his young age were taken from the total years of his life. **21.7.** We all make this mistake: we don't think that anyone is headed toward death except those who are bent with old age, although every stage of life, newborn and young adult alike, is headed that way. The fates have their work to do. They take away our ability to feel our death (so that it's easier for it to sneak up on us), and hide death under the name "life." Childhood comes from infancy, puberty from childhood, and old age from youth. Our profits, if you count them up properly, are actually losses.

22.1. Are you complaining, Marcia, that your son did not live as long as he could have? How do you know whether it would have been good for him to live longer or whether this death was planned for his benefit? Can you, right now, find anyone whose property and situation are so well established that there's no reason to be afraid while time marches on? Human affairs sway and flow; no part of our life is as exposed and weak as what we enjoy. This is why the happiest and most prosperous should choose death, since in this unpredictable and confused world nothing is certain except what has already happened. **22.2.** Who told you that your son's body, which was very handsome and protected by decorum's vigilance in a city of greedy eyes, could evade every illness so that his beauty could reach old age without being lessened? Think about the many, many ways a spirit can fail. Great talent doesn't carry through to old age whatever hope for success it had created in youth. It's often deflected, or extravagant living infects it (all the more shamefully later in life) and begins to corrupt what began beautifully. Or it ends up in taverns focused on its stomach, concerned most of all about what it should eat and what it should drink. **22.3.** Add to that fires, earthquakes, shipwrecks, and the scars left by doctors taking out bone fragments, putting their whole hand into body cavities and causing extraordinary pain when treating the private parts. And there's exile, too (your son was not less harmless than Rutilius), prison (he was not wiser than Socrates), and self-inflicted wounds (he was not holier than Cato). When you have scanned the list of possibilities you'll understand that things have worked out best of all for those whom Nature has quickly taken back into safety since something like the list above might have been the price of continued life. Nothing is as tricky as human life, or as insidious. Good grief, no one would have accepted life if we hadn't been ignorant when it was given. So, if the best thing is to not be born at all, the second best, I think, is to be returned quickly to wholeness after living for a short time.

22.4. Remember that very difficult time in your life, when Sejanus turned your father over to his client Satrius Secundus as a reward. He was angry at him because he had spoken his mind once or twice—he couldn't sit by in silence while Sejanus was imposed on our necks, like a yoke, much less while he imposed himself. A statue was being voted for him, to be placed in the Theater of Pompey, which Caesar was rebuilding after a fire. Cordus exclaimed that the theater was really ruined now. **22.5.** What? Should he not have made the outburst when Sejanus was placed on the ashes of Gnaeus Pompey, a traitorous soldier made holy on the monument raised to the greatest of generals? I suppose the death-warrant he signed was holy too, and those vicious dogs he kept around him. They were only gentle with him and savage with everyone else, feeding on human blood. And they began to bark around Cordus even as the order was given. **22.6.** What should he have done? If he wanted to live, he would have had to beg Sejanus. If he wanted to die, he would have had to ask his daughter. Both would have been adamantly opposed. He decided to deceive his daughter. So, after taking a bath that would reduce his strength, he retired to his room as if he was going to eat. After dismissing the slaves, he tossed some of the food out the window, so it would look like he had eaten. He didn't eat dinner, pretending that he'd had enough in his room. On the second and third day he did the same thing. On the fourth, his body's weakness betrayed him. So, giving you a hug, he said, "Dearest daughter, in my whole life I've hidden only this from you. I've started on the road to death, and I'm just about halfway there. You should not, and cannot, call me back." And so he ordered all the lights to be put out and hid himself in darkness. **22.7.** When his plan became public knowledge people were happy because the prey was escaping from the greedy wolves' jaws. Cordus' accusers, prompted by Sejanus, appeared before the tribunal of consuls and complained that Cordus was dying and asked that the consuls intervene to stop what those same accusers had forced him to do. This is how much Cordus seemed to be escaping them.[47] It

---

47. It was customary for those making a successful prosecution to have a percentage share of the convicted criminal's property, which would be confiscated for the state.

was an important question: would a defendant lose the right to die? While the question was argued, while the accusers were making a second appeal, he had already set himself free. **22.8.** Do you see, Marcia, how many reversals can happen all of a sudden in bad times? Are you crying because one of your loved ones had to die? Crying was almost forbidden then!

23.1. Beyond the realization that the future is entirely uncertain, except that it's quite certain to get worse, the path to the gods is easiest for spirits quickly released from earthly bonds. This is because they are light, with the least impurity. Before the spirits can harden and take the world's impurities in too deeply, they fly back, free and lighter, to their birthplace and wash off any encrusted dirt. **23.2.** Great spirits don't tend to linger in the body. They're trying to leave, to burst free, and they endure the body's constraints poorly because they are used to wandering everywhere and looking down on human affairs from high above. This is why Plato cries out that the whole spirit of the wise man stretches toward death, wants it, contemplates it, and tries to be carried by this desire into what is outside. **23.3.** Well, Marcia? When you saw that your son was wise beyond his years, that his spirit had conquered every desire, when you saw that his spirit was whole and without fault, seeking riches without greed, political office without blind ambition, and pleasure without extravagance, when you saw this, did you think that it would be possible for you to keep him unscathed for long? Whatever reaches fulfillment is near its conclusion. Virtue perfected takes itself out of our sight: what comes to maturity first cannot expect to last until the end. **23.4.** The brighter a fire burns the quicker it's extinguished—a fire lasts longer when it's started with dense and hard material and shines from the middle of heavy smoke. The factors that provide bad fuel provide prolonged burning. Human potential is the same: the brighter it is the briefer it is. When there is no room for getting bigger, a collapse is imminent. **23.5.** Fabianus says (and our parents saw this too) that there was a boy at Rome who was as tall as a large man, but he died quickly. Every wise person had predicted that he would die before long, because he couldn't have been able to reach the age his body had already jumped to. That's the way it is: excessive maturity is a sure sign of imminent death, and the end finds you where growth stops.

24.1. Begin to value Metilius according to his virtues not his years: he lived long enough. Fatherless, he was left in the care of guardians[48] until he was fourteen years old, but always under the care of his mother. Although he had his own household, he did not want to leave yours but he remained in your company when boys can barely stand being with their fathers. When he was a young man he did not want to leave you, even though in size, beauty, and pure strength of body he was born for the military life. **24.2.** Think, Marcia, how rarely women who live in different houses see their children. Consider how many years mothers lose and spend in worry when their children are on campaign and you'll understand how much time you have *not* lost. He never left your sight and he completed his studies under your eyes with a talent that rivaled and would have equaled his grandfather's, if his sense of shame had not held him back. Shame often silently suppresses the progress of many. **24.3.** He was a young man of exceptional beauty, and in a great crowd of women who had corrupted men he offered them no hope of getting him. When the shocking character of some women led them to try, he blushed as if he had done something wrong, which they enjoyed. His own character was so holy that although just a boy, he was thought worthy of a priesthood.[49] Without a doubt, this was through his mother's influence, but not even a mother can help a bad candidate. **24.4.** As you contemplate these virtues, hold onto to your son as if he were in your lap. He has more time for you now—he has nothing else to do and nowhere to go. He will never cause you worry, never cause you grief. The one sorrow that you could have suffered from so good a child is what you have suffered—the rest is safe from chance events and full of pleasure as long as you know how to enjoy your son and understand what was most precious about him. **24.5.** It's only the image of your son—not a true likeness—that has perished. Your actual son is now eternal and in a better state of being, stripped of burdens that were not his own and authentic. These things you see around us—bones, tendons, and stretched skin; a face; hands for doing things; and all the other things that make our bodies—these things are chains and shadows for our spirits. They overwhelm the spirit, suffocate it, infect

---

48. Under most conditions, a widow would not have had independent legal status at Rome in this period.

49. Priesthoods were often elected positions, but increasingly under the empire appointed. Ritual in nature, holding priestly office was a source of influence, especially the office of *pontifex maximus*, which following the example of Julius Caesar was usually held by the emperor.

it, and force it away from what is truly its own: the spirit is pushed into lies. Every struggle is a battle against this heavy body, so that the spirit won't be dragged down and settle in. It pushes to reach the place it was sent from. And in that place there is lasting peace for the spirit. **25.1.** This is why there's no reason for you to run off to your son's tomb. The worst part of him is lying there, and what was the most trouble: bones and ashes that are no more a part of *him* than his clothes and the other things that go on a body. He is whole and has left no part of himself on the earth. He has fled and is gone. He spent a little time above us, purifying himself and knocking away the adhered faults and dirt of this mortal life. Then lifted up to the higher regions he is running with other happy spirits. A sacred gathering has picked him up, Scipios and Catos; your father is there too, Marcia, among those who disdained life and were freed by poison.

25.2. Your father, although everything is related to everything else there, has found his grandson rejoicing in the dawn light and is teaching him the orbits of the nearby stars—he's happy to induct him into the arcane mysteries of Nature, not through guesswork but through real experience of everything. A guide is a nice thing for a guest in an unknown city to have. In the same way, having someone from the family to act as interpreter is good for a person delving into the causes of heavenly things. Your father asks him to direct his gaze to the earth too, since it's pleasant to look down from above on what was left behind. **25.3.** So, Marcia, behave as though your father and your son were watching you, not the men you knew but now more divine by far and set in the highest place. Blush when you think about anything ordinary or vulgar and when you weep because your loved ones have been changed into something better. They have gone away into the free and open spaces of eternity. Oceans apart do not block them and neither do high mountains, impassable valleys, or the unpredictable flow of the Syrtes. There, everything is flat—effortlessly swift and speedy, they have intermingled with stars.

26.1. So, imagine your father is speaking from heaven's high stronghold—his words carried as much weight for you as your son's. Imagine that he's speaking, not with the ability he had when he lamented the civil war and indicted for eternity those who began the proscriptions, but with an ability that is as dignified as he is sublime. **26.2.** "Why, daughter, has this illness possessed you for so long? Why do you remain in such a state of ignorance that you think life hasn't been fair to your son, because he has returned himself to his ancestors undamaged while the condition of his house is undamaged? Don't you understand how many violent storms Fortune uses to cause disorder? Don't you know that she does not offer herself kindly or easily to anyone except those who have little to do with her? Shall I list by name the kings who would have been very blessed if death had taken them sooner, away from the bad things that were awaiting them, or the Roman generals who would have no less significance if you were to take away some of the years from their ages? What about those very noble men, brilliantly noble, who peacefully stretched out their necks straight to be struck by a soldier's sword? **26.3.** Think again about your grandfather and me. Your grandfather came under a death sentence pronounced by foreign murderers. I have given nothing over me to anyone and by denying food I seem to have proven that I have as great a spirit as I wrote about. We dead have all come together as one and we see, without the deep darkness that surrounds you, that nothing is worth praying for, that nothing is heavenly, and that nothing is glorious. We see that it is all completely abject, distressing, anxiety ridden, and only a small part of the light we see. **26.4.** Should I tell you that there are no armies here raging against each other in violence, no navies smashed by other navies, and no parricides (either those who've done it or those who've thought about it)? There is no forum here echoing all day with the sound of the courts. Nothing is hidden for us: thoughts and hearts are openly known, and the life and future actions of every coming generation are public knowledge. **26.5.** I enjoyed setting down in writing the deeds of one age in one part of the world, deeds done in a short period of time. I now see many, many ages and the sum of years in sequence—however many there are left. I can see kingdoms coming to their own and kingdoms about to be destroyed, the collapse of great cities, and the always new boundaries of the seas. **26.6.** If the fate we share can be a comfort for your longing, nothing will be left standing where it is standing now—the passage of time will flatten everything and lead it to ruin. It won't only play with human beings (we're a small portion of what chance has power over, aren't we?), but places and regions and sections of the universe. It will press mountains down and in other places push new ones up into the sky. It will drink up the oceans, change the course of rivers, and break up the relations and connections of nations by bursting our economic ties. Some cities will be sunk into huge chasms, shaken by earthquakes and airborne diseases will come up from below. The passage of time will bury every habitation there is and will kill every animal by burying the earth with water. Time will burn up every mortal thing with limitless fire. And when the time comes for the conflagration of the universe, when the universe becomes new again, all of these things will destroy themselves with their own strength: stars will collide with stars and whatever shines now in its proper place will burn bright, all matter ablaze in one flame. **26.7.** We happy lives who have found eternity, as everything is toppled when god thinks it's the right time to build the universe again, we shall be changed into our basic elements, a tiny portion of an enormous destruction.

"Your son, Marcia, who now knows these things, is blessed!"

On the Happy Life

(De Vita Beata)

1.1. Gallio, my dear brother, all men wish to live a happy life, but they can't really see what it is that makes a life happy. And it's not easy to live a happy life. The more enthusiastically a man pursues this goal, the farther he falls from the path if he stumbles because his own speed takes him farther away if he deviates from the path. So, first of all, we ought to discuss what it is we're after in this discussion. Then we should examine the fastest way we can reach this goal and how we'll know *en route*—if we're going the right way in the first place— how far we've come each day and how much closer we are to where our innate desire is driving us.

1.2. Of course, as long as we're drifting about, not following one leader but the babble and jarring noises of people calling us to go in different directions, our life will be wasted in wandering. And life is brief enough even if we work hard day and night for a healthy mind! So, we have to discern both where we are going and how we will get there—and we shouldn't forget to find someone who has already traveled where we are headed. The conditions on this trip aren't the same as on other kinds of trips. On other trips, clearly marked roads and locals with advice keep us from losing our way, but on this trip the most well-traveled and well-known path is the most misleading. **1.3.** So, nothing is more important than avoiding the tendency to follow the herd that has gone before us, moving forward where most go instead of going where *we* should go. There's nothing that can get us in worse and bigger trouble than paying attention to public opinion and thinking that what meets the approval of the majority is best. With so many examples to follow we won't be living according to reason but according to convention.

1.4. We're all in such a rush, piling one upon another in a heap. You can see in the lives of those around you what happens in a crushing mob when the crowd presses in on itself: no one falls without dragging someone else down too, and the front of the mob leads the back to their death. No one makes a mistake in isolation, but the mistake becomes the cause of another person's error too. You see, to devote yourself to those who are in front is harmful, and as long as each

70

person prefers to believe others rather than reach their own conclusions, no proper conclusions can be reached about life, just opinions. An error handed down from person to person engulfs us and rolls us under. We are dying because of others' examples of living. We will be healthy if we can only separate ourselves from the crowd. **1.5.** The reality is that the mob takes a stand against reason while it defends its own badness. So, the same thing happens that happens when voters elect the magistrates: those who voted for one politician are surprised, after public opinion has driven their capricious support to another candidate, that the first politician actually won. We endorse the same thing we later criticize. This is the end result of any decision in which the majority rules. **2.1.** When we're discussing the happy life, there's no reason for you to speak like such people when the election was close: "*My* side had more votes." That's exactly what's worse about it. Life isn't so well ordered that the best things are the ones that please the most people. Sure proof of the worst choice? Whatever the mob supports. **2.2.** So, let's try to find out what is in reality the best, not what is most conventional, and what may set us up to hold onto a lasting prosperity and happiness, not what is valued by the crowd (which is very bad at explaining the truth).

When I say "the crowd" I mean socialites as much as slaves. I don't look at color of the clothes that cover the body and I don't judge a man with my eyes. I have a better and more reliable way to discern wrong from right: let the spirit discover a spirit's goodness. The spirit, if it ever has space to take a deep breath and retreat into itself, will force itself to speak the truth. **2.3.** "Whatever I have done up to this point I would rather undo. When I think over what I've said I am envious of people who can't talk. I think that whatever I wanted is what enemies would curse me with. And the things I feared—oh god!—how much less scary they were than what I thought I wanted! I made enemies of many people, and became friends again after making up—if, that is, friendship can exist between bad men. But I'm not even a friend to myself yet. I give my all to stand out from the crowd and make myself known as a man of some talent. What else have I done than set myself up as a target and shown malicious people what they should bite into? **2.4.** Do you see those people who praise persuasive speaking, who follow the money, who flatter others to ingratiate themselves, and who worship power? All of them either are my enemies or—it amounts to the same thing—could be my enemies. The crowd is as much a bunch of admirers as it is a bunch of jealous people. Shouldn't I look for some true good, something I can feel but not show? The things that catch the eye, that the crowd gathers around, that one fool shows to another, mouths gaping wide open—they sparkle nicely on the outside, but inside they're unpleasant."

3.1. So let's try to find some good thing, not good in appearance, but solid and steady and more beautiful on the inside. This is what we must unearth. And it's not far off—it will be found—you only need to know where to dig. In fact, we pass by things right next to us as if we're in the dark, bumping our shins against the very things we long for. **3.2.** I'll not mention the opinions of other writers so that I don't have to drag you through all of them—it would take a long time to list them and then refute them. Here's ours. Now, when I say ours, I'm not adhering to any single teaching of the Stoic masters: I have the right to form an opinion too. So, I shall follow this teacher's teaching, and take part of that one's too. Perhaps I'll even say, if I'm summoned to the witness stand with all the rest, "Here's what I can add to the discussion." But I won't dispute any of what earlier Stoic teachers have claimed. Meanwhile, as all Stoics agree, I take my cue from Nature. It is wisdom to not deviate from Nature and to follow her laws and examples.

3.3. A happy life conforms to its own nature, and can only be attained if the mind is healthy (and I mean in a state of constant health), if it is courageous and forceful, has stunning endurance, is prepared and is concerned for the body and what matters to the body—but not in an anxious way. Finally, the mind must be conscientious about the other things that make life better without being seduced by any of them, able to use the gifts Fortune gives without being a slave to them. **3.4.** You know, even if I don't say it out loud, that lasting peace and freedom come after we've pushed aside the things that excite us or frighten us. You see, after we've cast off pleasures and sorrows, an enormous joy creeps in their place, one that is unshakeable and constant. Pleasures and sorrows are inconsequential, fragile, and harmful because wickedness is inherent in them. And then we have peace and harmony in our spirits and grace matched by graciousness, because all savage behavior comes out of weakness.

4.1. There's another way we can define our good thing. That is, the same idea can be expressed in different words. An army is still an army whether it's spread out or packed into a narrow space, whether it's in weak-center formation or deployed in tight ranks. However it is deployed, its power is the same and its determination to hold its position is the same. Similarly, the definition of the highest good can sometimes be extensive and prolonged, and at other times compressed and succinct. **4.2.** So, it's basically the same thing to say, "The highest good is a spirit that disregards its circumstances and is happy with virtue," or "The highest good is an indomitable force of the spirit, experienced in life, calm in action, deeply compassionate and concerned for those it interacts with." It's also possible to define it this way: "Let us call a man happy for whom there is no good or bad except a good or bad spirit, who cultivates noble character, who is content to pursue virtue, who is neither boosted up nor beaten down by his circumstances, and who knows there is no good better than what he can give to himself, a man whose true pleasure is disdaining pleasures." **4.3.** It's also possible, if you want to take things a little farther, to alter the outward appearance of the definition while keeping its inner power whole and untainted. What's stopping us, for example, from saying that the happy life is a free spirit, upright, fearless and unshakeable, beyond fear and beyond desire? A spirit for which the only good is nobility, the only bad depravity, and everything else a worthless bunch of things that don't take way from or add to the happy life, but come and go without affecting the highest good in any way, negative or positive?

4.4. It's inevitable for a soul with such a foundation to have constant cheerfulness and profound happiness, from a deep source, as would anyone who finds joy in what he has and desires nothing more. Wouldn't these easily be worth their weight compared to frivolous and insignificant things or the short-lived sensations of this bag of bones? The day you conquer pleasure, you conquer pain and sorrow. Surely you can see how bad and damaging a slavery it is when pleasures and pains—very unpredictable and wild masters—take turns controlling a person. Therefore, break free for freedom. **4.5.** Only disregard for Fortune gives freedom. A truly priceless good will rise up within you: the stillness and elevation of a spirit with a secure foundation and, when error has been removed, the great and unshakeable joy that comes from the knowledge of the truth, and cheerfulness. A man will find pleasure in these qualities not as goods themselves, but because they come from the good within him.

5.1. Since I haven't begun this argument in a very strict fashion, it's even possible to say that a man is happy if, because of his gift of reason, he doesn't desire or fear. I say "because of reason" because rocks don't feel fear and sadness, and sheep don't either. When a thing can't understand happiness, no one can say that it is truly happy. **5.2.** People whose dull nature and lack of self-awareness make them like sheep and animals belong in the same category as sheep and animals. There's no difference between these people and those animals, since there is no faculty of reason in the latter and the faculty of reason in the former is warped by its own badness and they become clever at doing the wrong thing. No one, you see, can be called happy if he has rejected truth. **5.3.** So, a happy life is rooted in and unalterably based on correct and precise judgment. Then the mind is pure and released from all bad things. It has escaped life-threatening wounds, and even scratches. It will defend its position and claim its foundation for itself, even from angry and hostile Fortune.

5.4. Now, as far as pleasure is concerned, it surges around us on all sides, flowing through the streets, weakening the spirit with its smooth talk, and doing one thing after another to arouse us, in whole or in part. Even so, what mortal being with any trace of humanity left wants to be stimulated day and night, exerting the body but rejecting the spirit? **6.1.** Someone will say, "The spirit also has its own pleasures." Certainly, yes, let it, and let it be a connoisseur of indulgence and pleasures. Let it stuff itself with all the things the senses usually enjoy, then look back at what it's done. And, remembering those faded pleasures, let it dance through memories of the past and be impatient for the future. Let it make a list of hopes and, while the body lazes around stuffed from the current meal, let it plan out the future. To me this seems a very pitiable thing, since it's crazy to choose bad things over good. No one is happy unless they're sane, and a sane man doesn't look to the future instead of to what's best. **6.2.** So, the happy man has good judgment. The happy man is content with the present—whatever it is like—and is friendly toward his own affairs. The happy man is one for whom reason guarantees the character of his life.

7.1. Even those who say that the highest good is in the belly understand that they've set the highest good in a low and dirty place. They deny that pleasure and virtue are separate things, and say that no one lives nobly in such a way that he does not also live with delight, or with delight in such a way that he does not also live nobly. I personally don't see how things so different can be connected so intimately. What grounds are there, I ask you, to *not* separate pleasure from virtue? Clearly, since in respect to goods everything starts from virtue, the things you love and chase after come from the same roots too. But if these things were not separate, we would not see (but we do see!) that some things are pleasant but immoral, and others are very noble but difficult, and must be achieved through pain and sorrow. **7.2.** In addition, pleasure can be found in the filthiest life, but virtue does not allow life to be bad. Some unhappy people are not without pleasures, or rather they are unhappy because of their pleasures. This wouldn't happen if pleasure didn't mix itself in with virtue[1]—virtue often lacks pleasure, but never needs it.

7.3. Why are you putting things that are different, or better, that are opposites, together? Virtue is something high, illustrious, kingly, unconquerable, and tireless. Pleasure is base, slavish, feeble, and quickly gone. You can find it living in brothels and bars. But you'll find Virtue in temples, in the forum, in the *curia*, and standing in front of the city's defensive walls covered in dust, with calloused hands. Pleasure you'll more often find skulking about, keeping to the shadows around the public baths and the sweat houses and the places that worry about the authorities. It is soft, feeble, and soaked in strong wine and perfumed oil, a sickly pale or painted lady. **7.4.** The highest good is immortal, it doesn't know how to die—you cannot fill up on it or regret it. An upright spirit never changes itself, never hates itself, and doesn't change anything else, because it has the best. But pleasure dies at the moment it is felt. There isn't much room for it, so it fills you up quickly and gets tired, withering away after the first rush. When something's nature is to be in motion, it can never be steady and fixed. Thus pleasure can't provide anything substantial because it comes and goes in a hurry, used up with the first use. It pushes forward to where it ceases to be, and sees its end from its beginning. **8.1.** What should I say about the fact that there is pleasure in good things as well as in bad things, and that shameful people enjoy their own disgrace as much as it pleases noble men to be a rare breed? The ancients exhorted us to lead the best life, not the most pleasant, so that pleasure wouldn't be in charge of our choice to pursue a correct and good desire; pleasure is the companion to choice. Nature should give us orders like a general: reason complies and seeks Nature's counsel.

---

1. In other words, if pleasure and virtue really were the same thing, there would never be any pleasure in something wicked.

8.2. To live a happy life and to follow Nature are therefore the same thing. I'll explain what this means. If we carefully and fearlessly preserve what the body gives and what is appropriate for Nature, treating them as if they are ephemeral; if we don't become slaves to them or to another person's possessions; if we classify things that please our bodies and that do not come to us through our own effort in the same way we classify auxiliary forces and skirmishers when we're on campaign (that is, they obey—they don't command); if we do all this, only then will they all be beneficial to the mind. **8.3.** Let the real man be one uncorrupted by external things, invincible, only admiring his possessions, nothing more, "trustworthy in spirit and prepared for every eventuality"[2] and the author of his life. Let his convictions not come without knowledge, or his knowledge without perseverance. Let his resolutions endure and his decisions remain unaltered. It's clear—even if I don't say it—that such a man will be calm and collected, doing what he does in a kindly and noble way. **8.4.** Let true reason return to itself, stimulated by the senses and using them as the basis for knowledge (there's no other way to begin or to make a first attack at the truth). The cosmos, and by this I mean God the ruler of the universe, encompasses everything and extends outward into what is outside itself, but also returns inward back into itself from all sides. Our mind does the same thing. When the mind, following the senses, has reached through them to what is outside, it has power over the senses as well as over itself. **8.5.** And when this happens, a person attains unified power and mastery and reason becomes reliable, undivided, and unwavering in opinions and perceptions or argument. When reason becomes coherent and agrees with itself in every way, and—in a manner of speaking—is in harmony, it has touched the highest good. **8.6.** Nothing improper or deceitful remains, nothing on which the mind might trip or fall. It will do everything in full command of itself. Nothing unexpected will happen to it, but instead whatever is done will turn out for the good, effortlessly, promptly, and without the doer's dishonesty. Inactivity and a lack of resolve are symptoms of inner conflict and indecisiveness.

---

2. Quoting Vergil, *Aeneid* 2.61. This is a difficult comparison because this line refers to Sinon, who was left behind by the Greeks to trick the Trojans into bringing the Trojan Horse into the city. Vergil's line suggests, however, that Sinon was committed to his course of action, and prepared for the consequences.

For this reason one can also say that harmony in the spirit is the highest good, since there ought to be virtue where there is full agreement and single-mindedness. Vices are antagonistic to each other.

9.1. "But you practice virtue only because you expect some pleasure from it," you say. First of all, even if virtue is going to provide pleasure, that's not why I seek it. But virtue doesn't provide pleasure. Instead, the work of virtue, although it's aiming at something else, obtains pleasure too—but it's not working toward pleasure. **9.2.** Flowers may grow in a field ploughed and sown with grain, even among the grain, but all that work was not done to get the flowers (although they're pretty). The farmer plants the grain and the flowers are a bonus. In the same way, pleasure is not the reward or the cause of virtue, but a side effect: virtue is not gratifying because it is pleasurable, but it is also pleasurable if it is gratifying. **9.3.** The highest good lies in careful judgment and in the condition of the mind at its very best. When that mind has fulfilled its purpose and surrounded itself with boundaries of its own, the highest good has been achieved and the mind desires nothing more. There is nothing outside of everything any more than there can be an end beyond the end. **9.4.** So, you're making a mistake when you ask me what it is that makes me seek virtue: you're looking for a good beyond the highest good. You ask what I seek *from* virtue. Just virtue itself. Virtue, you see, possesses nothing better and is its own reward. Or maybe this isn't grand enough for you? When I say to you, "The highest good is the spirit's unbreakable resolve, foresight, transcendence, health, freedom, harmony, and beauty," do you want something else, something better, to which these things can be ascribed? Why bring up pleasure? I am looking into the good in man, not into his gut—sheep and cows have bigger ones.

10.1. "You're confusing the argument I've made! I'm not saying that a person can live happily if he does not also at the same time live nobly—dumb animals and people who measure their own good by the food they eat can't do this. I'm saying, clearly and in public, that the life that I'm calling pleasant can't happen without virtue added in." **10.2.** But who doesn't know that those who are the most full of these pleasures of yours are some of the stupidest people around? Who doesn't know that wickedness flourishes among pleasures, and that the spirit itself can supply many corrupt pleasures? Especially, for instance, arrogance, too high an opinion of yourself, an overblown superiority complex, a blind, foolish love for your own stuff, feeling pride for insignificant and childish reasons, a clever tongue and snobbishness that takes pleasure in insults, laziness and the self-indulgence of a weak spirit drowning in delights without regard for its own dignity. **10.3.** Virtue destroys all these faults, grabs you by the ear and judges pleasures before allowing them to happen. And virtue doesn't even set much value on any of the pleasures it approves. In any case, virtue allows pleasures to happen not to enjoy them but because it enjoys exercising self-control. But in your view, self-control is harmful to the highest good since it reduces pleasure! No, you hold on to pleasure, I hold it in check; you take delight in pleasure, I make use of it; you think pleasure is the highest good, I don't think it's a good at all; you do everything because of pleasure, I do nothing.

11.1. When I said that I don't do anything for the sake of pleasure, I was making a point about your so-called wise man, who is the only one you allow to have pleasure. But I don't call a man wise if something has power over him, especially pleasure. How will a man who's busy taking pleasure be able to withstand hard work, physical danger, abject poverty, or the threats that make human life difficult? How will he endure the sight of death, the feeling of pain, the blows the world gives—and those our fiercest enemies give—if he's defeated by such a tender adversary? "He will do whatever pleasure convinces him to do." Come on, don't you see how many things pleasure can convince him to do? **11.2.** "Pleasure won't advise anything corrupt, because it is joined to virtue." Again, don't you see what sort of "greatest" good something is when it needs a guardian to actually be good? How will virtue govern pleasure, which it follows, if following is the quality of someone who obeys and leading of someone who commands? Are you putting the leader in the rear? Virtue has a really outstanding duty in your philosophy, doesn't it, to be pleasure's taste-tester!

11.3. Now, we'll see whether virtue still truly is virtue among those who have treated it so offensively: it can't be called by its proper name if it has given up its proper place. But first, concerning what we're examining now, I'll show that many people—those over whom Fortune has poured all her gifts, who you would absolutely admit are bad—are besieged by pleasures. **11.4.** Take for instance a Nomentanus and an Apicius,[3] avidly procuring the goods of land and

---

3. Both names, whether or not they refer in this case to actual people, were associated with excessive spending (Nomentanus) and excessive gourmandizing (Apicius). Nomentanus is already a byword for a spendthrift in Horace's poetry nearly a century earlier.

sea, as they say, and inspecting animals of every land laid out on their tables. Picture them on a bed of roses overlooking their private bistro, delighting their ears with the sound of voices, their eyes with visual displays, and their palates with flavors. Their bodies are stimulated entirely by these tender and soft comforts. Even the room in which they worship luxury is infused with various smells so that their noses have something to enjoy too. You would say that these men live with pleasures, and yet they do not live well because they are enjoying what is not good. **12.1.** "They are living badly," you say, "because many things that disturb the spirit and conflicting opinions that make the mind restless will find their way in." I concede the point: it's true. But, nevertheless, those foolish and unbalanced men, positioned to receive the brunt of remorse's attack, receive pleasure. As a result it has to be said that they are as far from having a bad experience as they are from having a sound mind. One must say that, like many others, they are cheerfully crazy and out of their minds with laughter. **12.2.** On the other hand the pleasures of wise men are relaxed, controlled, almost leisurely, kept private, and hardly worth noticing. As a result these pleasures come along uninvited and, although they approach on their own, aren't valued or experienced with any joy. Wise men, you see, intersperse pleasure with life the same way they intersperse play and joking with serious business. **12.3.** Therefore, those other philosophers should stop joining together things that don't belong together—I mean entangling pleasure with virtue. Through this bad mistake they pander to all the worst people. A man drenched in pleasures, always belching and drunk, thinks he's living with virtue because he knows he's living with pleasure; he has heard that pleasure cannot be separated from virtue. In the end, he advertises his vices as wisdom and reveals to the world what he should have kept hidden. **12.4.** So, they indulge to excess, not pushed to it by Epicurus but as willing prisoners of their vices. They keep their excesses hidden in the lap of philosophy and run wherever they hear pleasure is praiseworthy. That "pleasure" of Epicurus, they don't appreciate how dry and sober it really is—that's my perception of it, anyway—but they leap at the word "pleasure," seeking a sort of legal defense and camouflage for their lusts. **12.5.** They lose, then, the one good thing they had among their bad deeds, feeling shame for their transgression. They praise the things that make them blush and they boast about vice. For that reason, when a noble label is assigned to a disgraceful indolence, they can't even claim to be living like young men.[4] This is why your praise of pleasure is pernicious, because while the noble rules lie hidden within, the thing that corrupts is in plain sight.

13.1. For my own part I think—and I say this although most Stoics would be unwilling to—that Epicurus set rules that are holy and good. And they're stern ones, if you look quite closely. You see, his pleasure is pruned back to a meager little thing. The law we declare for virtue, he declares for pleasure: he commands pleasure to obey Nature. But what is enough for our nature is not nearly enough for an appetite of excessive indulgence. **13.2.** So what is really happening here? Anyone who says that indolent retirement and alternating between appetites and lusts is happiness is looking for a good authority to do a bad thing. When someone like that comes to philosophy, drawn in by that seductive word "pleasure," he isn't following the philosophical pleasure he heard about, but the one he brought along with him in the first place. And when he begins to assume his vices are similar to the rules for living well, he is handing himself over to those vices fearlessly and openly. At that point, he'll even indulge excessively in public. And so, I will not say what many Stoics say, that Epicureanism is the teacher of crimes, but I do say this: it has a bad reputation. "Undeservedly," you say? **13.3.** But how is anyone able to understand it unless invited inside? From the outside, Epicureanism allows people to make up stories and provokes a bad expectation. It's like you're a warrior wearing women's clothing: you are chaste, you have not been castrated, your body carries no dirty shame . . . but you're dressed like a party girl! So, pick out a noble slogan, another phrase to arouse the spirit. The vices have tracked down the one you have.

13.4. Whoever has decided to pursue virtue shows evidence of a noble nature. Whoever follows pleasure seems feeble, broken, worsening as a man, and headed for degeneracy unless someone shows him which pleasures belong to natural desires and which race along without limits becoming more unquenchable the more they are met—then he can know for himself. **13.5.** Come on, let virtue take the lead; the path we follow will be a safe one. Too much pleasure is harmful, but we shouldn't fear that virtue has too much of anything, since proper measure is inherent to virtue. That which struggles under

---

4. Young men in the Greco-Roman world were stereotypically prone to laziness and pleasure-seeking pursuits.

its own weight is not good. And anyway, what better thing could be imagined for those whom fate has given a rational nature than reason itself? Even if the combination of pleasure and virtue pleases you, even if pursuing the happy life in such company pleases you, let virtue take the lead. Let pleasure be *virtue's* companion and revolve around *virtue's* body like a shadow. Only a man who has no greatness in his spirit hands over virtue, a most noble lady, to be pleasure's slave-girl.

14.1. Let virtue go first; let virtue carry the battle standard. We'll have pleasure in the end, but we will be pleasure's masters and moderators. It will beg us for something, but won't make us beg. People who hand over front-line leadership to pleasure lack both virtue and pleasure. They send virtue away but do not possess pleasure: it possesses them. And their lack of pleasure tortures them or an abundance of it chokes them. They are pitiable if deserted by pleasure and more pitiable if pleasure overruns them. Like sailors grounded on the shoals near the Syrtes,[5] they are left high and dry at one point and over their heads at another. **14.2.** This situation comes from having almost no self-control and having a blind love for something. Reaching your goal is a pretty dangerous thing when you're seeking bad things instead of good. We hunt wild beasts through hard work and danger, and then are anxious about holding them in captivity (wild beasts often mangle their masters). Great pleasures behave in the same way: they end up being bad trouble, and although captured, hold their captor captive. The more and the bigger pleasures are, the smaller a man is—the crowd calls him lucky!—and he becomes a slave to many. **14.3.** I'd like to stay with the image a bit longer. A man who tracks animals to their lairs and thinks it's good "to capture beasts with a lasso" and "to surround the wide woods with his hounds"[6] in order to pick up their trails neglects more important things and renounces many duties. In the same way the man who chases after pleasure postpones everything else. At first he is indifferent to his freedom and then abandons it in favor of his stomach. He doesn't buy pleasures for himself, he sells himself for pleasure.

---

5. Syrtes refers to the irregular tides and quicksands off the coast of North Africa (near Egypt) that were famous in antiquity from at least the time of Herodotus (fifth century BCE) for causing shipwrecks.

6. Quoting Vergil, *Georgics* 1.139 and 1.140, probably from memory, given the slight verbal differences from the text that is preserved.

15.1. "Even so," he says, "why can't virtue and pleasure be mixed together and the highest good be made so that it is both noble and pleasant?" Why not? Because something can't be part of what's noble without being noble itself, and the highest good can't maintain its purity if it sees in itself something that's not as good as the rest. **15.2.** Even the joy that comes from virtue, although it is good, is not part of the absolute good, any more than cheerfulness and peacefulness (although they are caused by very beautiful things). You see, these things are good things, but they are a result of achieving the highest good; they are not the end goal. **15.3.** On the other hand, if you make pleasure and virtue partners—even if unequal ones—whatever strength there is in the latter good will be undermined by the fragility of the former. Then freedom, which remains unconquered as long as it knows there's nothing more precious, is enslaved. Freedom begins to need Fortune: this is slavery in its pure sense. An anxious, suspicious, fearful life follows, and we become terrified of failure and uncertain about change.

15.4. You don't assign virtue a strong, immovable foundation, but you order it to stand on rolling, shifting ground. What shifts as much as the anticipation of things that happen by chance? Or the vicissitudes of the body and things that afflict it? How can a man following pleasure obey god, or experience whatever happens with a happy spirit, or not complain about fate (since a virtuous man would understand his unfortunate fate in the best way) if he is shaken to the core when pleasures and pain gives him a little shove? No, not even a hero of the fatherland, or a liberator, or a friend become defender is a good man if he turns toward pleasures.

15.5. Therefore, let the highest good climb up to that place from which it cannot be removed by any violent force, where pain, anticipation, or fear cannot approach, or anything that makes the power of the highest good weaker. Only virtue can ascend to that place. The cliff face can be scaled in virtue's steps: it will stand bravely and endure whatever comes, and not just withstanding it but wanting it. It will understand that every difficult situation happens according to Nature's law—just as a good soldier will endure wounds, count up his scars, and love the general for whom he has fallen, even as he dies riddled with arrows. Virtue will have this wise, old saying in its spirit: "Follow god." **15.6.** But whoever complains and moans and groans is still forced to do what was ordered and is dragged along to the assigned tasks. How crazy it is to be dragged along rather than to follow! It's as crazy as it is foolish and ignorant to be troubled by your personal situation because you don't have something or because something rather difficult happens. And it's equally foolish to be surprised or to take it badly when these things happen to good people as much as they do to bad people—I mean illness, death, and the other unexpected things that happen in a human life. **15.7.** Whatever must be suffered because of how the universe works ought to be accepted with great courage. We are bound by this oath, like a soldier to his general,[7] to endure being mortal, to be steadfast in the face of things that aren't in our power to avoid. We are born under the rule of a king: it is freedom to obey god.

16.1. True happiness, therefore, rests on virtue. What advice will virtue offer you? First, that you not consider anything good or bad that involves neither virtue nor badness. Then, that you stand firm against badness as well as in good situations and that you imitate god in whatever way is right. **16.2.** What does virtue promise you in return for this mission? Incredible things, equal to what the gods possess: you will never be compelled to take an action, you will lack nothing, you will be free, and you will be entirely unharmed. You will be tempted, but resist; you will be forbidden nothing. Everything will happen as you think it will and nothing bad—nothing against your opinion or desire—will happen to you.

16.3. "What then," you say, "is virtue sufficient for living happily?" Why shouldn't it be, since virtue is perfect and divine? Why shouldn't it be more than enough? What could a man who is beyond the reach of all desires be lacking? What external thing is necessary for a man who keeps what is his inside himself? A man still traveling toward virtue does need Fortune's kindness, even if he has progressed a long way already, because he's still wrestling with human things . . . until, that is, he undoes the knot and all that ties him to mortality. So, what's different? It's this: some people are tightly bound, others more so, even tied down. But the man who has progressed to the summit and taken himself higher drags along lighter chains: he is not yet free, but he might as well be.

---

7. The *sacramentum* was an oath sworn when a soldier entered service, by which he placed himself entirely under the command of his general, subject to military discipline and without the normal rights of a citizen. Under Augustus the oath began to be sworn to the emperor.

17.1. So, if one of those who bark and growl at philosophy says what they usually do—"You sure talk boldly—why not live boldly too? Why do you speak politely to a superior? Why do you think money is a necessary tool? Why are you moved by loss, or shed tears after hearing about the death of a spouse or friend? Why do you maintain a good reputation? Why are you bothered by slander? **17.2.** Why do you have more cultivated fields than you can use naturally? Why do you hold dinners that break your own rule? Why is your furniture so fancy? Why do you drink wine older than you are? Why do you have gold plates? Why plant trees that only give shade? Why does your wife wear earrings worth an expensive house in her ears? Why do the boys in your slave-training halls wear nice uniforms? Why is serving at your table an art form, and the silver place settings not set carelessly but precisely positioned? Why do you have a slave trained as a master meat-carver?"—you can add if you like, "Why do you own property overseas? Why do you own more than you actually know about? Why are you so disgracefully negligent that you don't know the names of a few slaves? Or, are you so spoiled that you have more slaves than you can keep names in your head?"

17.3. In a bit, I'll keep the insults going and add more that you are thinking of. But for now I'll respond this way: I am not a wise man and—this will make you hate me more—I never will be. So, demand that I be better than bad men, not equal to the best men. This is enough for me, to erase one of my faults every day and punish my errors. **17.4.** I haven't reached full health, and I won't get there. I'm comforting my spiritual gout more than I'm curing it[8]—I am content if it comes less often and doesn't hurt as much. But compared to you, I am a sprinter even though I'm crippled. I'm not saying these things for my own sake (I'm drowning in vices), but for the man who has actually done something. **18.1.** "So," you say, "you say one thing but do another." This is exactly, you malevolent people, the enemy of each of the greatest men, what was said about Plato, and Epicurus, and Zeno. All of them, you see, weren't speaking about how they themselves *actually* lived, but about how they *ought* to live. I'm talking about virtue, not myself, and I'm disagreeing here with vices, mine first of all. When I can manage it, I'll live how I ought to live.

---

8. Gout is a kind of inflammatory arthritis, usually localized in the feet or big toe, often associated in antiquity with an excessive lifestyle.

18.2. This maliciousness of yours, even infected as it is with poison, won't scare me away from what is best. Not even that foul poison you sprinkle on others and with which you kill others will keep me from striving to praise the life I know I ought to lead, rather than the life I do lead. And it won't keep me from venerating and following virtue, even if I am far behind and barely dragging myself along. **18.3.** Of course, I shouldn't expect anything to be off-limits for the kind of malevolence that didn't think Rutilius or Cato was *sacer.*[9] Will anyone care that your people think he's too rich, when they thought Demetrius the Cynic was not poor enough? A man who was very austere and who fought against every desire of nature, who was poorer than the rest of the Cynics, because even after he had forbidden himself to possess anything, he forbade himself to ask for anything too? And they said he had too much! You see, don't you? He claimed knowledge of need, not of virtue. **19.1.** They said that Diodorus, the Epicurean philosopher, who quickly committed suicide, did not keep the doctrine of Epicurus because he cut his own throat. Some want this to seem an act of madness, others a rash act. He, meanwhile, happy and with a clean conscience, gave testimony for his own case as he was dying: he praised the calm of a life spent at anchor in port and said what you all are unwilling to hear, as if you should do it too: "I have lived and carried through to the end the path Fortune gave me."[10]

19.2. You argue about Demetrius' life and Diodorus' death. You bark at the name of men who have become great because of some especially praiseworthy thing just like dogs bark in fear at the approach of unfamiliar people. Yes, you really like it when no one can be seen to be good—it's as if one person's virtue is a condemnation of everyone else's failings. Envious, you compare their splendor with your filthiness and you just don't understand how bad you look when you

---

9. *Sacer* is a ritual term applied to things and people who are placed wholly under the power of a god. The Valerio–Horatian legislation of 450 BCE restored the sacrosanctity of the tribunes of the plebs as well as, apparently, of some other magistrates: anyone harming these officials would be *sacer* to Juppiter (and thus subject to capital punishment) because they had violated a sacrosanct official. Cato was tribune in 59 BCE and Publius Rutilius Rufus was consul in 105 BCE, charged and convicted falsely for extortion in 92 BCE.

10. Diodorus was quoting Dido in *Aeneid* 4.653, as she declares her grief and rage before killing herself. It is true that Epicurus seems mostly to oppose suicide under any circumstances.

do it. You see, if those who follow virtue are greedy, immoral, and vain, then what are *you*, when you hate even the label "virtue"? **19.3.** You deny that anyone does as he says or lives as an example of his words. How is that a surprise, when they talk about courageous and profound ideas that transcend all the storms of human life? Although they try to take themselves down from their crosses—crosses on which each and every one of you nails yourself too, with nails you yourselves provide—nevertheless they hang until dead from one pole each.[11] But those who punish themselves are tortured by as many crosses as they have desires. Slanderous people are clever in insulting others. I'd think that they had the free time to do it, except some people also spit on bystanders from their crosses. **20.1.** "Philosophers don't do as they say." But they do much of what they say and what they think of with a noble mind. If only their actions *were* equal to their words! What could be happier for them? As it is, there is no reason for you to condemn good words and hearts full of good thoughts. Discussion of pursuits that promote well-being should be praised apart from their outcomes.

20.2. What a surprise it is that philosophers haven't reached the top, although they've made the hard climb. But if you're a real man then respect men trying to achieve great things, even if they fall. It is a measure of good character—that someone is paying attention to the strength of human nature, not to his personal strength—when a man tries to climb the heights and thinks thoughts even greater than what men gifted with courageous spirit could put into action. **20.3.** A man like that says to himself, "I'll look at death with the same expression I had when I heard about it. I'll follow through on my hard work, however hard it is, supporting my body with my spirit. I'll condemn wealth whether I have it or not. I won't be sad if another person is rich and I am not, or act superior if wealth gleams all around me. I won't feel fortune coming or going. I'll consider every land my own, and my own land everyone else's. I'll live as if I know I was born for others, and I'll be grateful to the world for the following reason: how could things have worked out better? Nature has given me alone to all people, and all people to me alone. **20.4.** I'll protect whatever I have without being stingy and distribute it without being extravagant.

---

11. That is, all humans live nailed to crosses of their own making. The wise try to remove themselves from this death sentence, while pleasure-seekers simply add more nails.

I'll believe that I can possess nothing more than what has been given. I won't measure favors by counting them, or their significance, or in any other way except the receiver's respect. It'll never be a big deal for me to give if a deserving man will be the recipient. I will do nothing for the sake of my reputation, and everything for the sake of my conscience. I'll assume that whatever I do (that only I know about) has been done as if the world were watching. **20.5.** For me, the purpose of eating and drinking will be the quenching of natural desires, not the filling and emptying of my gut. I'll be pleasant to my friends, gentle and flexible with my enemies. I'll forgive before being asked to and I'll fulfill every honest request. I'll understand that the world is my homeland and the gods my protectors, that they stand over and around me, critics of my words and deeds. Whenever Nature takes my life or reason demands I let it go, I'll depart claiming that I loved a good conscience and good pursuits, that I diminished the liberty of no person and my own as little as possible." The man who promises these things, wants these things, and attempts these things is making his way toward the gods. Even if he can't reach the goal, nevertheless he will "fall daring to do great things."[12] **20.6.** Now you, by hating virtue and anyone who cultivates virtue, aren't doing anything particularly strange. Weak eyes fear the sun and nocturnal animals avoid the brightness of day. At daybreak they get confused and look all over for a hiding place and tuck themselves away in some hole or other because they fear the light. Groan away, use your empty words to insult good men, take a good bite. You'll break your teeth far more quickly than you'll break their skin.

21.1. "How can a man so zealous for philosophy live in such wealth? How can he say that wealth must be despised and yet stay so rich? How can he think that life must be despised and still keep living, that health must be despised and still take good care of himself and prefer to be very healthy? He thinks that exile is an empty word, and says, 'What's bad about moving?' And yet, if he can, he grows old in his homeland. He thinks there is no difference between a long life and a short one, but if there's no obstacle he'll extend his own life and even thrive peacefully in later life." **21.2.** The wise man says such things ought to be despised, not so he won't have them but so he won't be worried about having them. He won't shut them out but will, without

---

12. A quote from Ovid, *Metamorphoses* 2.328, which refers to Phaethon the son of the sun god Apollo. See *On Providence* 5.10 above.

a care, watch them go away. Where could Fortune deposit her wealth more safely than where she can get it back without a quarrel? **21.3.** When Marcus Cato praised Curius and Coruncanius and the genera- tion when you could be charged with a *crimen censorium*[13] for having a few small silver coins, Cato himself had four million sesterces. Without a doubt this was less than Crassus but much more than his grandfather Cato the Censor. If a comparison were to be made, Cato surpassed his grandfather's wealth by a greater margin than Crassus surpassed his. And if greater wealth had come to him, he wouldn't have turned it away. **21.4.** You see, a wise man doesn't think he's unworthy of what- ever gifts come to him by chance: he doesn't love riches, but he does prefer them. He receives them into his house, not into his spirit, and doesn't refuse possessions but controls them—what I mean is he wants his wealth to help by giving more practice for his virtue.

22.1. Can there be any doubt that there's more scope for the wise man to demonstrate his spirit living in wealth than there is living in poverty? In poverty there is one kind of virtue, to neither bend nor break. But when you're wealthy, moderation, generosity, frugality, and self-regulation all come into play. **22.2.** The wise man won't despise himself, but if he's extremely short he'll still wish he were tall. He'll be well, even if he's feeble in body and blind in one eye, but he'll prefer to be physically powerful, at the same time as he knows there's something else quite powerful inside of him.[14] He will endure bad health, and wish for good health. **22.3.** In the end, you see, even if certain things are trivial and can be subtracted without damaging the chief good, they still add something to the lasting cheerfulness that is born out of virtue. This is how riches affect the wise man and bring joy: like a good following wind affects the sailor, or a beautiful day and sunny spot in the dark days of winter. **22.4.** Besides, what wise man—I mean Stoic wise man, for whom the only good is virtue— denies that these things we call "indifferents" still have some value in them and that some are more beneficial than others? Some of them are admired somewhat, others a great deal. Make no mistake, riches are

---

13. A *crimen censorium* was a crime that could be noted by censors, who were elected to oversee the registration of citizens and property (the census), public morals, and the state treasury. The result of the *nota censoria* was public shame, as well as a possible official reduction in status.

14. That is, his strength of mind.

among the more beneficial. **22.5.** "So, then," you say, "why are you laughing at me when you rank these things the same as I do?" Do you want to know how I rank them? Because it's not the same ranking as yours. If my wealth slips away, it will take nothing with it except itself. But if yours goes away you will be stunned and it will feel like you've lost yourself. With me, wealth has *a* place. With you, it has *the* place. In a nutshell, I own my riches, but yours own you.

23.1. Therefore, stop prohibiting philosophers from having money: no one sentenced wisdom to a lifetime of poverty. A philosopher will have sufficient resources, but none taken from another or tainted with another's blood. They'll be gained without injury to any person or dirty negotiations, spent as honestly as they were got, and be a source of sadness for no one . . . except malicious and jealous people. Count it all up in a pile as you like. The money is clean, and although there might be a lot that someone might *like* to say is his, there isn't anything he can claim as his. **23.2.** The wise man won't push the kindness of Fortune away. For instance, when an inheritance is acquired through proper means, he won't boast or be ashamed. But he *will* have a reason to boast if, opening his household and all his properties to the whole state, he can say, "You can take away whatever you think is yours!" What a great man he would be, and his wealth of the best kind, if after this he thought he was just as rich! And so I tell you, if a man has opened himself to the people's scrutiny calmly and worry-free, and if no one has found anything that he could lay a hand on and claim,[15] he will be rich confidently and openly. **23.3.** The wise man doesn't let a single *denarius* through his door if it comes in badly. The same is true for great wealth, gifts of fortune, and the fruits of his virtue. He won't refuse or exclude. Why should he jealously refuse to give them a place? If they come, they will be looked after. He won't throw his wealth around, and he won't hide it—the first is what silly people do, the second what people with weak and puny spirits do, as if they're hiding some big treasure in their shirt. As I said, the wise man won't kick wealth out of his house. **23.4.** What would he say? Maybe, "Wealth, you're useless!" Or, "I don't know what to do with you, Wealth!" If he had to make

---

15. Many Roman legal procedures dealing with property, including recovery of property stolen or loaned, involved symbolically touching the person or object concerned and speaking a particular formula.

a journey on foot, he might prefer to climb on a wagon. In the same way, although he may be poor, he might wish to be rich. And so, a wise man will possess wealth but as if it were trivial and fleeting. And he won't allow it to cause trouble for anyone else, or himself. **23.5.** The wise man will give his money away. (Why are your ears pricking up? Why are you making room in your pocket?) Yes, he will give his money away—but to good men and those he can make into good men. He'll give it away, selecting with very careful consideration those most deserving, like a man who knows that he has to give an account for his expenditures as much as he has to for his income. He'll give for fair and justifiable reasons, since a bad gift is a kind of shameful loss. He'll have an accessible purse, but it won't have holes in it. A lot of money can leave his purse; none just falls out. **24.1.** It's wrong to think that giving is a simple thing. It's a very difficult business, if it's done in a serious way and not by scattering money here and there on impulse. I might be doing this man a favor or paying another man back; I might be helping one or pitying another. I might think that this man deserves it so poverty doesn't drag him down and hold him there. I might not give to certain people, even though they need it, since they'll need more even after I give them some. I'll offer to it some and force it on others. I can't afford to be casual about it: my accounts are never more carefully kept than they are for gifts.

24.2. "What!" you say, "Do you give so you can receive?" No, but so that I don't ruin anything. A gift should be given where repayment is not obligatory but is still possible. A favor should be put away like a treasure, in a deep hole—you don't dig it up unless you need it.[16] **24.3.** What a wealth of raw material the household of a rich man has for doing good! Who says that generosity is only shown to citizens? Nature commands me to be beneficial for humankind. What does it matter if those who benefit are slaves or freedmen,[17] freeborn or the son of a freedman, freed in full accordance with the law or with friends as witnesses? Wherever there is another human being there is room

---

16. As the occasional discovery of ancient coin-hoards shows, this was a common practice among some classes of people for protecting their money (there were no banks, as banks operate today).

17. Among slave societies in antiquity, Rome was very rare in offering avenues for slaves to obtain their freedom. A freed slave would become a freedman, which status gave him a limited citizenship but the right to conduct business. Usually the freedman retained very strong ties of obligation and support to the former owner.

for giving favors. And so, it is possible to distribute money within the household and to practice liberal generosity—which gets its name not from the fact that it is generosity shown to free people, but because it arises from a free spirit. This liberal generosity in a wise man never finds its way to the immoral or the undeserving, and never gets so used up that it cannot flow fully whenever it finds a deserving cause. **24.4.** So, there's no reason for you to incorrectly hear what is said nobly, valiantly, and courageously by those who devote themselves to wisdom. Hear this first of all: it's one thing to be devoted to wisdom, and quite another to have put wisdom into practice. The devotee will say to you, "I am saying excellent things, but I'm still in turmoil among many bad things. There's no reason to demand I measure up to what I say: I'm still a work in progress, shaping myself to and reaching for high ideals. If I can manage the task I have set before me, then you can demand that my deeds match my words." But the man who has reached the pinnacle of human goodness will treat you differently and say, "First of all, there's no reason for you to think you are allowed to judge your betters. In my own opinion, I have earned the displeasure of bad men, which is proof that I've done a good thing."

24.5. But—so I can give the explanation I owe you, which I don't hold back from any mortal—listen to what I'm saying and how much I value each of these things. I assert that wealth is not a good, since if it were it would make men good. And since we can't call what is found among bad men a good, I refuse to give wealth this label. Otherwise, I declare that it is worth having, useful, and a great advantage for life's journey.

25.1. Here's why you shouldn't count wealth among the goods, and how I think about it differently than you (since we both agree that it is good to have). Put me in a very elegant, luxurious home, where gold and silver plates are used every day. I won't think I'm better because of this wealth: even though it's in my house, it's outside of me. Take me from there to the Sublician Bridge[18] and throw me down among the beggars. I will not think worse of myself because I'm sitting among those who beg with hands stretched out. How does

---

18. The Sublician Bridge was the oldest bridge in Rome (rebuilt many times, because it was a wood bridge) spanning the Tiber River near the Aventine Hill. It was a favorite spot for beggars, perhaps because the bridge led to and away from the oldest and possibly busiest market in Rome (the Forum Boarium).

it really matter whether or not a man has a piece of bread when he's certain to die anyway? And yet I prefer a beautiful house over the bridge. **25.2.** Set me down in front of splendid furniture and magnificent stuff. I won't believe that I am the least bit happier because I have soft cloak, or because I can put purple cloth on all the dining couches.[19] Change my sleeping blanket, and I won't be the least bit more miserable because my weary neck is resting on a little bit of hay for a pillow or because I'm sleeping on stadium cushions that are losing their stuffing.[20] But I would rather show what kind of spirit I have dressed in a toga than shirtless. **25.3.** Let every day turn out exactly as I want, let new reasons for joy be piled up on the old ones. I still won't be happy with myself for this reason. Turn this temporary good luck around and let my spirit be bashed about here and there through loss, grief, and different kinds of physical harm. I won't, because of them, say that I'm a miserable man in the most miserable of circumstances or curse the day. I've made sure that none of my days is a dark day. And yet, I prefer to moderate joys than to suppress sorrows.

25.4. This is what Socrates himself will say to you, "Make me king of the world, let Dionysos' favorite chariot[21] carry me triumphant to Thebes from the farthest East and let kings follow my laws willingly. I shall think that I am most human when gods greet me from all sides. Then give me a fall from grace as steep as this sublime height: let me be placed captive on a foreign parade float, decorating the victory parade of a proud and ferocious conqueror. I won't behave more humbly chained on another's chariot than I would standing in my own. And yet, I prefer winning to losing. **25.5.** I'll scorn Fortune's power entirely but, if the choice is given to me, take the better things from it. Whatever comes to me will become a good, but I'd rather have the easier and more pleasant things come, and things that I can manage to make less annoying. There's no reason for you to think that any virtue comes without hard work, but some virtues need to be spurred on, others reined in. **25.6.** Just as the body needs to hold itself

---

19. The dye required to achieve this color, which was made from the mucous of specific kinds of sea snails, was very expensive and a closely regulated commodity. Purple cloth was therefore a conspicuous indicator of wealth.

20. The *tomentum* was a utilitarian stuffed pallet placed on wood or stone benches, at, for example, the Circus Maximus.

21. The god Dionysos was frequently represented returning from the East in victory on a chariot drawn by panthers or mythical beasts.

back on a downward slope, and push forward up a difficult climb, some virtues are like a downward slope and others like a hill. Is there any doubt that we climb, struggle, and fight for endurance, bravery, perseverance, and whatever other virtue stands against harsh circumstances—I mean overcomes Fortune? **25.7.** Isn't it just as obvious that generosity, moderation, and kindness are a downward slope? For the latter, we have to restrain our spirits so that they don't get out of control and fall; for the former, we have to push hard and really drive ourselves to continue. Therefore, in the case of poverty, we use the virtues that we know can fight courageously; in the case of wealth, those virtues that can stay light on their feet and balanced all the time. **25.8.** When there's a division like this, I'd rather be using the virtues that have to be practiced peacefully than the ones for which blood and sweat are part of the experience. Therefore," says that wise man, "I'm not saying one thing and doing another; I'm saying one thing and you are hearing another. Only the sound of my words reaches your ears—you are not asking what meaning they carry."

26.1. "What difference, then," you say, "is there between me, the fool, and you, the wise man, if we both want the same thing?" There's a huge difference: when a wise man has wealth it is his slave. But wealth is a fool's master. A wise man allows riches to control nothing, a fool everything. You, as if someone had promised you everlasting wealth, get used to it and depend on it. The wise man practices being a poor man precisely when he is wealthiest. **26.2.** A general never trusts the peace so much that he doesn't stay prepared for war that is imminent even if it is not actually being waged. Your beautiful house makes you arrogant (as if it can't burn down or collapse!) and your resources make you stupid (as if they can survive every danger and become too big for Fortune's power to overcome!). **26.3.** When you're relaxing you play with your wealth and you don't see the danger it holds. It's as if you're a barbarian who, under siege, is lazily watching the hard work of the besiegers and, because he doesn't know about siege engines, has no idea what the things they're building in the distance are for. This is exactly what's happening to you. You're withering among your possessions and you don't think about how many disasters are looming from every direction and even now poised to take away your precious treasure. If anyone takes the wise man's wealth, he still has all that he truly possessed before. A wise man, you see, lives happily in the present, not worrying about the future.

26.4. Socrates (or any other person who has the same composure and power in the face of human experience) says, "There is nothing that can persuade me to change the conduct of my life to meet your opinions. Bring on your usual words—I won't think that you are crying out insults, but that you're crying like very unhappy babies." **26.5.** This is what the man who has attained wisdom will say. His spirit, free from vices, orders him to criticize others—not because he hates them, but to heal them. He will add this, "Your opinion of me makes me feel bad, not for myself but for you, because in hating and harming virtue you give up all hope. You aren't hurting me—those who overturn altars don't hurt the gods either. On the other hand, bad intent and a bad plan are obvious even when they are still harmless. **26.6.** I put up with your random musings in the same way that Juppiter Optimus Maximus puts up with the absurdity of poets, some of whom give him wings, others horns. Some make him a nighttime adulterer, a brute against the gods, or unfair to humans. For others he's a boy-lover or even incestuous, or a father-killer and the usurper of his father's throne. These poets accomplish nothing except to allow men to set aside the shame of their own sin when they believe the gods are like this.[22]

26.7. Now, even though these words of yours don't harm me at all, still I offer advice for your own sake: respect Virtue, believe those who, after following Virtue for a long time, shout that they are following something important, and more closely day by day. Cultivate a relationship with Virtue as you would with the gods and with those who teach Virtue as if they were her priests. Whenever there is a reading of sacred writings, '*favete linguis*,' keep a holy silence.[23] This expression does not derive from *favor*, as in 'use favorable words,' but it commands silence so that a holy act may be completed according to the ritual, with no bad, ill-omened words interrupting. How much more necessary it is for you to be commanded to listen intently and without speaking whenever something is spoken from Virtue's prophetic texts. **26.8.** When someone, striking the *sistrum*,[24] makes

---

22. This line of reasoning is fully developed by Plato's Socrates in *Ion* and *Republic*.

23. Roman religion was very concerned with the proper completion of specific and exact rituals. Stray noises, especially words, could be considered ill-omened or could even nullify a ritual.

24. The *sistrum* was a small drum used in the worship of Isis, a mystery religion from the East.

false promises with authority, when someone skilled in slashing his own arms[25] makes blood drip to his shoulders from hands held high, when some woman crawling through the streets wails and an old man wearing linen clothes and carrying a lantern in daylight shouts out that some god is angry—when any of these things happen you run up and listen and say that he is touched by a god. You are feeding each other's stupidity.

27.1. Look, here's Socrates crying out from his prison cell (the cell he purified simply by entering and left behind more noble than any *curia*), "What madness has possessed you? What kind of nature, hateful in the eyes of gods and men, do you have that you would vilify the virtues and blasphemy against holy things with your malicious words? If you are able, praise good men—if not, go away. But if you all like to practice this filthy overreaching freedom of speech, take it out on one another. When you rage against heaven, I wouldn't say that you're committing sacrilege but that you're wasting your breath. **27.2.** I gave Aristophanes material for his jokes some time ago and all the comic playwrights, those thugs, poured out their poisonous wit all over me.[26] But my virtue was put in the right light through the very things they attacked me with. You see, it's good for virtue to be brought out and tested, and no one understands how strong virtue is better than the man who has felt its strength by attacking it. Those who strike granite know better than anyone how hard granite is. **27.3.** I present myself as a rock, alone in the rough sea, which the waves never stop crashing against, however the wind blows— but they don't move it from its place or wear it down over the ages with their unceasing attack. Jump at me! Make your attack! I will beat you by withstanding you. Whatever attacks something solid and invincible uses force to its own bad end. So, go look for something soft and squishy to stick your stones and arrows into. **27.4.** Do you have enough free time to find out other people's bad deeds and judge anyone you like? 'Why does this philosopher live without discipline? Why is he eating such an elegant dinner?' Are you watching other

---

25. This was a practice followed by worshippers of Cybele, another mystery religion from the East.

26. Aristophanes' farcical comedy *Clouds* was cited in Plato's version of Socrates' *Apology* as a factor in the charges brought against Socrates in 399 BCE, almost twenty years after the play was performed.

people's pimples when you're absolutely covered with raging acne? It's just like someone with a putrid rash laughing at the birthmarks and moles on very beautiful bodies. **27.5.** Take a swipe at Plato because he asked for money or a swipe at Aristotle because he took it. Take one at Democritus because he ignored it or Epicurus because he used his up.[27] Accuse me because of Alcibiades and Phaedrus[28]— how happy you will be when you reach the point of imitating my vices. **27.6.** Wouldn't it be better to look around at your own bad deeds,[29] which stab at you from all over, some attacking you from the outside, others burning you from the inside? The mortal world has not reached the point (even if you aren't aware enough of where you stand) of having so much free time that there's time to gripe about your betters.

28.1. "But you don't understand this, and you put on a face that doesn't match your real circumstance, like people sitting in the Circus or Theatre who haven't got the bad news that their houses have gone into mourning.[30] But I, looking down from above, see the storm clouds threatening you—soon they will break open or come nearer and sweep you and yours away. What more is there? A tornado is whipping your spirits around, isn't it, even if you can't feel much? It is spinning them as they run away from or run to the same desires, lifting them up high then smashing them down . . ."[31]

---

27. This is an anachronism, because these events and people post-date Socrates. But, as the next sentence shows, it is clear that Seneca is still speaking with Socrates' voice.
28. One of the charges against Socrates was for corrupting the youth of Athens, of whom Alcibiades and Phaedrus are prominent in Plato's *Dialogues*.
29. There is a famous fable by Phaedrus (4.10), who wrote in the early empire: Juppiter gave mortals two sacks, one in the front for others' sins, and one on the back for our own.
30. The Roman custom was for a house to go into mourning for nine days (women themselves had longer mourning periods), during which time all activity stopped and special precautions were taken to ensure the purity of the house and household.
31. The manuscripts do not preserve the end of the dialogue.

On Retirement

(*De Otio*)

1.1. . . . .[1] [T]hey commend faults to us through general consensus. Even if we try nothing else that might promote health, withdrawing into seclusion will be beneficial in and of itself: we will all become better people on our own. What about the option to withdraw to the company of the best men[2] and to choose some role model to whom we can align our life? This doesn't happen except in retirement, when it's possible to hold on to what one has decided to do, when no one can interrupt and distort our resolve when it is still weak, with the help of the crowd. Then life, which as it is we split between many different purposes, can progress on a single, level track. **1.2.** Among other bad things, the worst is that we switch from one vice to another. The result? We do not even keep doing the bad things we know well already! One thing after another pleases, and irritates us too, because our decisions are not only perverse but also lightly made. We waver and we grab at one thing after another: we let go of what we wanted before and we want to get back what we let go. We alternate between desire and regret. **1.3.** We, you see, depend entirely on the judgments of others. It's not what ought to be praised and desired that seems best to us, but whatever a large number of people desire and praise. And we don't look to see whether a path is good or bad in and of itself, but whether there are a lot of footprints on it—even when none of them come back.[3]

1.4. You're going to say to me, "What's going on, Seneca? Are you breaking ranks? Surely your Stoics say, 'We will work on the business of the state up to the minute we die. We will never stop working for the common good, helping each and every person, and giving assistance even to our enemies with our aging hands. We are the people who give no exemption from service at any time and, as that most eloquent of men said,[4] "We put helmets on heads white

---

1. The manuscripts do not preserve the beginning of the dialogue.
2. That is, philosophers from the past, whom we can know through their writings.
3. Seneca is referring to the famous fable in which an animal refused to enter a lion's cave because there were no footprints leading out, although many led in.
4. Vergil, *Aeneid* 9.610–12, where a warrior describes the hardiness of his native Italians.

with age." We are the people according to whom, to the same degree that there was no break from our work before death (and if our circumstances allow), the moment of our death itself should accomplish something.' So why are you quoting Epicurean orders in the Stoics' main camp?[5] Why don't you desert to the other side altogether if your own side is troubling you, instead betraying it?" **1.5.** For now I'll say this to you: what more could you want than for me to show that I am acting like my generals? What more can I say: I'll go where they've led me, not where they've sent me. **2.1.** What's more, this will prove to you that I am not parting company with the precepts of the Stoics (since they didn't part ways with their own precepts). And anyway I would be totally innocent of the charge you've laid even if I *weren't* following their precepts, and only following their example.[6]

I'll divide my topic into two parts. First, I argue that a man can, even from a very early age, turn himself over completely to the contemplation of truth, seek an examined way of living and practice it in retirement. **2.2.** Then I'll discuss how a man can be very well justified in doing this in the golden years when working life is over, and passing on what he's learned to others because of his great understanding—like Vestal Virgins do, who learn to conduct the sacred rites during their years spent in service, and, after they have learned, teach. **3.1.** I'll demonstrate that this was acceptable to the Stoics, too, not because I'd say it's my rule to do nothing against the dictates of Zeno or Chrysippus, but because the matter itself makes me willing to accept their position; someone who always conforms to one doctrine is not making his own decision but toeing the line.[7] If only we already knew everything, if only the truth were self-evident and incontrovertible and we were to change none of our principles! But in reality we are seeking the truth with the very same people who are teaching us the truth.

3.2. The two philosophical schools, Epicureans and Stoics, are especially at odds on this question, but each guides us, by different roads, toward retirement. Epicurus says, "The wise man does not

---

5. There is an extended military metaphor in this section.
6. That is, Seneca is doing what they did *and* what they said, and will refute the charge that has been leveled against him.
7. Literally, "not in the *curia* (the place of democratic debate for members of the Senate), but in a faction (when people vote as they're told)."

enter into service of the state unless something compels him." Zeno says, "The wise man enters into the service of the state unless something hinders him." **3.3.** The first seeks retirement on principle, the second with good reason: the reason, however, varies considerably. If the state is too ruined to be helped, if it is taken over by bad people, the wise man won't make a useless effort. He doesn't apply himself if he will be of no benefit. If he has too little power or authority to effect a result or too little strength and the state does not intend to consult him, or if ill health hinders him, he won't enter upon a course of action that he knows is untenable, just as he wouldn't launch a leaky ship on the sea or enlist for active duty if disabled.

3.4. It's possible, therefore, for a man who is entirely untouched, before he experiences any of the storms of life, to take a stand in safety, to continuously devote himself to the liberal arts, and to spend his entire life in retirement. He'll be a devotee of the virtues, which can be practiced also by those most removed from public life. **3.5.** Without a doubt, a man is required to be of benefit to others, to many if he can. If not many, then to a few. If not that, to those closest to him. And if not that, to himself. You see, by making himself useful to others, he is rendering a public service. A man who makes himself into a worse person harms not only himself but all whom he might have helped if he'd been a better person. In the same way, anyone who treats himself as he deserves is a benefit to others simply because he is making himself into the kind of person who will be of benefit to those around him in the future.[8]

4.1. Let's think about it this way, that there are two republics. One is extensive and truly "public" and it encompasses gods and humans. In this state we don't look to this spot or that to measure boundaries, but measure them by the sun. The other state is the one we are assigned by the circumstance of birth, for instance, Athens, or Carthage, or some other city that belongs not to everyone but to a specific group of people. Some people work for both republics at the same time, the greater and the lesser, some only for the lesser, some

---

8. That is, anyone who acts according to his nature (virtue), even if he lives in isolation, has the possibility of being useful to others in the future. Retirement properly used allows for the realization of one's full potential through study, etc. So, although one's usefulness seems to lie in a potential future, it has its source in what real actions one chooses to make in the present.

only for the greater. **4.2.** We are able to serve the greater republic in retirement also—actually, I'm not sure whether we cannot serve it better in retirement. In retirement we can ask what virtue is, whether it is one virtue or many, and whether nature or training makes men good. We can ask whether this world, which comprises the seas and the lands and the things in the sea and on the earth, is unique or whether god spaced out many such worlds. We can ask whether all matter from which everything arises is whole and without spaces or is separated, by which I mean void mixed with solids.[9] In retirement we can ask where god resides, whether he just watches creation or engages with it, whether he, separate from it, surrounds it or is infused in it entirely, whether the world will never end or should be counted among those things born for a time and destined to perish. What does a person who pays attention to these things give to god? He makes sure god's works, as great as they are, will not be without an eyewitness.

5.1. We usually say that the highest good is to live according to nature. Nature produced us for both purposes, contemplation and action. Let me prove the first statement now. But what is there to say? Isn't the statement proven true, if each person asks himself how much desire he has for knowing the unknown or how much enthusiasm he has for every story? **5.2.** Some people set sail and suffer through the exertions of a long journey for a single reward: knowing something hidden and isolated. This is what draws people to public spectacles and games, compels them to pry into what has been shut, to hunt out what is hidden, to unravel antiquity, to hear about the customs of foreigners. **5.3.** Nature has given us an innate curiosity and, because she is aware of her own skill and beauty, has produced us to be an audience for the great spectacles of the universe. She would derive no benefit from her work if she showed it—so huge, so brilliant, so artfully woven, so precisely planned, so bright and beautiful in many ways—to solitude. **5.4.** To fully understand that Nature wanted to be examined and not just seen, consider the place she provided for us: she set us in the middle of everything and gave us a clear view. Not only did she make the human being upright but set his head upright

---

9. Atomist philosophies, such as Epicureanism, hold that there must be space in which atoms can move, called the void. Stoicism asserts that god, divine reason, assembled and fashioned the universe out of amorphous, but continuous, matter.

on a flexible neck, to make him suited for contemplation, so that he could follow the stars slipping from rise to fall and keep his face turning to gaze on the whole. Then, bringing forth six constellations by day and six by night,[10] she displayed every part of herself, so that by what she showed our eyes, she might create a desire for the rest. **5.5.** We do not see everything, or even the extent of what exists. But our sight opens up paths of inquiry for itself and builds a foundation on truth for our search to move from what is seen to what lies hidden and to find something older than the universe itself. Where did the stars come from? What did the universe look like before things fell one by one into their divisions? What rational plan separated what was joined and jumbled? Who designated the places for the kinds of matter? Did the heavier elements sink and the lighter lift because of their nature, or did some higher power (other than the weight and pressure of physical bodies) lay out a natural principle of behavior for each? Is it true, as some argue, that human beings are divine spirits, parts—like sparks—of the stars, that fell to the earth and are stuck in a place not their own?

5.6. Our ability to think breaks through the walls of heaven and isn't satisfied to know only what we can see. It says, "I want answers! What is outside the universe? Is the universe immense and boundless, or is even something this big limited and confined? What does the stuff outside the universe look like? Does it have no form or order, taking up the same amount of space in every direction, or has it also been grouped and carefully arranged? Does it stay close to the universe, or is it far away, leaving the universe to revolve in emptiness? Are all things, all that was and will be, made up of indivisible particles, or is the raw material substantial and wholly changeable? Do the elements fight among themselves or are they uniting harmoniously, not fighting, because of their diversity?" **5.7.** Although born to seek answers for these questions, consider how little time a person gets to do so, even if he appropriates every last bit of time for himself. Even if no time is lost because he's good-natured, even if he doesn't let any slip away through negligence, even if he safeguards his hours like a miser and ages all the way to the very limit of the human lifespan, even if

---

10. The dominant theoretical understanding of the zodiac constellations in Seneca's time was that the sky, divided equally into twelve segments, held half of the constellations during the day and half at night.

Fortune doesn't attack what Nature gave him, a human being is far too mortal to acquire knowledge of immortal things. **5.8.** Therefore I am living according to my nature if I give myself entirely to Nature, if I am her admirer and worshipper. Nature, moreover, wanted me to do both things, to act and to make room for contemplation. And I am doing both, since not even contemplation is devoid of action.

6.1. "But it matters," you say, "whether you approach contemplation for pleasure, only seeking continual reflection without any outcome. After all, a contemplative life is pleasant and has enticements of its own." On this point I can tell you that it matters just the same in what spirit you conduct a life of civic service, whether you're always upset and never take time to turn from human affairs toward the divine. **6.2.** It is hardly an acceptable thing to enter politics without a love of virtue or concern for talent or to accomplish useless deeds, since virtue and talent and accomplishment ought to be mixed and entwined together. In the same way, virtue banished into retirement without action, never passing on what it has learned, is an incomplete and feeble good. **6.3.** Who can deny that virtue needs to test its own progress by taking action, or that virtue shouldn't only consider what must be done but also sometimes set to work and make what it has practiced internally become a reality. But if the wise man is not just hesitating to take action—I mean, if it is not the doer that is absent but something to be done—will you allow him to be alone then?

6.4. In what spirit does the wise man retreat into retirement? When he knows that he'll also be doing things then that are useful for those who come after him. We are, truly, the people who say that Zeno and Chrysippus did more important things than if they had led armies, held offices, or written laws. Well, they did write laws, just not for one city but for the whole human race. Why is it, then, that retirement isn't appropriate for a good man, if it's the kind of retirement that enables him to govern generations to come and to address not a few people but *all* people of *every* nation, now and in the future. **6.5.** To sum up, I ask you: did Cleanthes, Chrysippus, and Zeno live according to their own principles? No doubt you'll reply that, yes, they lived how they said one ought to live. But none of them ran a country. "They weren't," you'll say, "born into the status or the rank that are usual for those who manage countries." Even so, none of them led an inactive life: they found a way for their own quiet lives to be more useful for people than the back-and-forth debating and sweat others produced. As a result these men seem to have done a lot, even though they didn't go into politics.

7.1. Besides, there are three kinds of life. Which of these is best is a common question. One has time for pleasure, the second for contemplation, and the third for action. Setting aside the bickering and the implacable animosity we aim at people who follow paths different from our own, let's see how all of these lives, under one label or another, amount to the same thing: the man who endorses pleasure is not without contemplation; the one who engages in contemplation is not without pleasure; and the man whose life is headed for action is not without contemplation. **7.2.** You say, "There is a huge difference whether something is the main goal or the by-product of another goal!" Yes, of course there is a big difference, but the one cannot exist without the other. The one man doesn't contemplate without acting, the other doesn't act without contemplating, and the third—and we share a low opinion of him—doesn't endorse useless pleasure, but pleasure that he sanctions for himself through reason. So, even this hedonistic school of thought has action. **7.3.** But of course it's active, since Epicurus himself says that he will pull back from pleasure, and even seek pain, if the pleasure would have produced regret or if he could substitute a lesser pain for a greater one. **7.4.** Why am I saying these things? So that it'll be clear to you that contemplation is acceptable to every kind of life. Some people make contemplation the goal, but for us it's a stop on the journey and not the end.

8.1. Here's something else to add: it was a precept of Chrysippus that one could live in retirement. I don't mean tolerate retirement but choose it. Our school does not advocate that a wise man should enter into the service of just *any* state. And anyway, what difference does it make how a wise man ends up in retirement, whether a state finds him lacking or he finds a state lacking? Besides, when one exercises stringent judgment, every state comes up short. **8.2.** I ask you, what state would a wise man serve? Athens, where Socrates was sentenced to death? Which Aristotle fled so that he wouldn't be? Where dark envy crushes virtue? You will tell me that the wise person shouldn't serve that state. So, will the wise man serve Carthage, where treason happens daily, where freedom of speech is dangerous for a noble man, where there is the greatest contempt for what is just and good and inhuman cruelty against the enemy, even enemies from their own people? A wise man will avoid this state too. **8.3.** If I wanted to think carefully about each state in turn, I wouldn't find any that could tolerate a wise man, or that a wise man could tolerate. Now, if we can't find the state we imagine for ourselves, retirement begins to be a necessity for everyone, because the one thing that could have been preferable to retirement, a state we can serve, doesn't exist.

8.4. If someone says that sailing is the best thing to do, but then says that I shouldn't sail on a sea because it routinely causes ship-wrecks and there are very frequent storms that can come up suddenly and drive a helmsman into danger, then even though he may speak in favor of sailing, he is, I think, advising me not to launch my ship.

On Serenity of the Spirit

(*De Tranquillitate Animi*)

1.1. "As I spent time reflecting on myself, Seneca, some faults kept appearing to me as if laid out in front of me so that I could pick them up in my hand. Some were a little harder to see, back in the corner. Some weren't always there but kept coming back from time to time. I would say that these last are the most exasperating. They're like guerilla soldiers, attacking every once in a while. Because of them I can't stay prepared as if there were a war and I can't be worry-free as if there were peace. **1.2.** Nevertheless, the condition I find myself in most of the time (why shouldn't I tell the truth, as I would to a doctor?) is that I'm not truly free of the things I fear and hate, and on the other hand I'm not a slave to them either. It's not as if I'm in the worst condition, but I am extremely dissatisfied and sad: I'm not sick and I'm not healthy.

1.3. "There's no need for you to say that the first steps for all virtues are wobbly, but in time we acquire stability and strength. I'm not unaware that even things that are based on mere appearances grow stronger over time—I mean things such as respect, a reputation for public speaking, and whatever else comes from other people's opinions. Things that provide real strength and things that provide us with a kind of coat of paint to be pretty both require years for the long period of exposure to make appearance reality, bit by bit. But I'm afraid that habit, which makes things consistent, may fix this particular fault deep inside me: prolonged association imbues one with a love for bad things as much as for good things.

1.4. "I can't show you all at once what kind of a spiritual weakness this is to waver between two things (I can show you better by presenting it bit by bit): my spirit doesn't turn itself resolutely to what is right or to what is wrong. I'll tell you what happens to me and you can find a name for the illness. **1.5.** I admit that I have a deep appreciation of thriftiness. I don't like it when an audience chamber is set up to enhance a person's reputation. I don't like clothes that come in special chests and are smoothed with weights and given a million violent brushings to make them shine. I like everyday, common clothes that don't need much care or need to be put on carefully. **1.6.** I don't like the kind of food that a crowd of servants prepare and inspect that was ordered up many days before and dished up by many hands. I like easily prepared and simple food that isn't unnatural or expensive or hard on the wallet and the body and that won't come out the way it went in.[1] **1.7.** I like an unsophisticated attendant, a bit rough and homebred,[2] and I like my father's heavy silver (it didn't have a maker's mark)—he was a simple farmer.[3] I like tables that aren't remarkable for the different colors of stain or that become known in the city for holding many dinners in succession with sophisticated guests. I like it when a table is placed for practical use, so that it doesn't catch the eyes of dinner guests with its beauty or make them really jealous.

1.8. "But although those things are pleasing to me, my spirit and resolve are weakened when I see slaves who escort their master's sons to school in fancy outfits, and other servants dressed more carefully than if they were in a formal procession, decked out with gold. I love seeing a crowd of gleaming slaves, or even a house with floors of precious material, and shining ceilings too, with expensive things scattered about in every corner and a whole 'population' of slaves to keep the master company while the family's wealth is destroyed. Should I mention water, crystal clear to the bottom, flowing around the dinner guests, or meals that match the ambience? **1.9.** Conspicuous consumption flows all around me. I can see it clearly, because I have a long habit of being frugal, and it echoes loudly all around. The sight of it has me teetering on the brink, but I can make my spirit resist indulging in luxury more easily than I can make my eyes resist looking. And so, I go away not a worse man, but a sadder one, and I don't walk quite as tall among my insignificant possessions. A hidden pain catches hold of me, and I become uncertain whether the luxurious things might be better. None of these experiences changes me, but even so they all hit me hard.

---

1. That is, Serenus is not interested in purging his stomach by vomiting to make room for more food, as one might at certain kinds of dinner parties involving many dishes.

2. Most Romans thought that a *verna* (a slave born in the household) would be more loyal to the household and easier to manage, in part because slavery was all they had ever known. In addition, *vernae* could be trained from a young age for specific high-skill jobs (e.g., secretary, accountant) within a household, or trained and then sold.

3. Not enough is known about Serenus' family to be able to complete this picture, but a landowning farmer whose son rose to hold the important office of *praefectus vigilum* may have enjoyed the simple life but this does not mean he was poor.

1.10. "I am happy to follow the commands of the teachers and to enter into politics.[4] And I'm happy to have obtained public offices and the *fasces*, not motivated by the purple robes and the rods,[5] but so that I might be more helpful and useful for my friends, my relatives, all citizens, and finally all human beings. Under orders and ready, I follow Zeno, Cleanthes, and Chrysippus. Although none of them went into politics, all of them lead us to serve in this way. **1.11.** But when something happens to shock my spirit (which is unused to being battered), I reverse-march back to retirement. It's the same when some degrading thing happens (there are so many events like this in life), or when something doesn't come very easily to me, or when things that really shouldn't be thought very important demand a lot of my time. I'm just like cattle when they're weary: the path back home is quicker. **1.12.** At that point, I'm happy to keep my life within my own four walls again. At home, let no one take up any of my day as if he could pay me back with anything worth such an expense on my part.[6] Let my spirit stick to itself, nurture itself, and not work on another's business or anything that depends on another's judgment. Let me appreciate a tranquility that is free from care, public and private. **1.13.** But then when a very good reading lifts up my spirit and some noble examples of living have spurred me on, I leap willingly back in the fray of the forum, lending my public-speaking skills to one man and my support to another. Even if nothing will come of it, nevertheless it's worth it to try. And it's worth it to try to bring down the arrogance of a man totally carried away by his successes in the forum.

1.14. "In my studies I think that it's better, by Hercules, to pay attention to the subject matter itself, and to speak to the point. The words should follow the subject in such a way that wherever the subject leads an uncomplicated style of language follows. Why should I write something that will endure for generations? I talk to myself: 'Don't you want future generations to speak about you? But you were born for death: a silent funeral is less annoying for everyone. And so, write something with an unpretentious pen, because you want to use your own time to

---

4. Zeno and Chrysippus advocated activity in public life under certain conditions; see *On Retirement* for this question.

5. The *fasces* were an axe bundled with rods. These together symbolized the power of an elected Roman magistrate with *imperium* (the legal right to command in a specific area of responsibility) to execute and punish.

6. See *On the Shortness of Life* for a full discussion of this thought.

do something for yourself. Those who study daily don't need to work so hard.' **1.15.** On the other hand, when my spirit is uplifted by the weighty significance of its thoughts, it seeks unusual expressions and words. Just as it longs to be inspired, it longs for inspired speech. Then a style of language suited to the dignity of the subject matter emerges. Forgetting my rule and my more controlled judgment, I am carried aloft and speak with a voice no longer my own.

1.16. "I don't want to go through examples one by one, so I'll just say that this problem of willpower (when my mind is otherwise strong) follows me in every case. I'm afraid that I'm slipping into weakness bit by bit or, what is more troubling, that I am hanging like a man always about to fall and that there's perhaps more to all this than I can clearly see. We look at our private affairs with friendly eyes, and our bias always gets in the way of our judgment. **1.17.** I think that many people could have become wise if they hadn't already thought they were wise: they fooled themselves about some things and leapt over other things with their eyes shut tight. So there's no reason for you to think that we are destroyed more by the adoration of others than by self-adoration. Who dares to be truthful with himself? Who, even though he's among a crowd of admirers and flatterers, has not been his own greatest supporter? **1.18.** So, if you have a remedy that can center this vacillating spirit of mine, I ask you to consider me worthy of receiving it: I would owe my tranquility to you. I know that these waverings of my spirit are not terribly dangerous and aren't a sign of any serious disorder. Maybe I can explain how what I'm complaining about really feels with an analogy: I'm not drowning in a storm, just a little seasick. So take whatever this bad thing is away, and help me—I'm still afloat and within sight of land."

2.1. My goodness, Serenus! I have been quietly asking myself for a while now to what I can compare the state of spirit you are describing. This is as close as I could get: you're describing the behavior of those who, although they've healed from a long and serious illness, are still affected by slight fevers and mild aches. Even though they have escaped from the previous illness, they are nevertheless troubled by worries. They're quite healthy, but they hold out their hand to the doctors and interpret every flush in their bodies the wrong way. It's not that their bodies, Serenus, are not in good health, but that they are not really used to good health. In a similar way, there is still a kind of tremor and movement when a body of water is recovering after a storm, even though it is calm. **2.2.** So, you don't need the harsher treatments, which we have already talked about (i.e., that you stop yourself, or be angry with yourself, or be stern with yourself), but the last stage of treatment: that you trust yourself and be confident that you are heading along the right path, rather than be diverted by the crosswise tracks of many people rushing here and there, some of whom get quite close to the real path.

2.3. What you want is an important goal, the highest, and one near to god: to be undisturbed. This unwavering position of the spirit the Greeks call *euthymia*. (Democritus' book on this is the best.) I call it "serenity." There's no need to copy the Greeks' word and to use the transliteration. The topic itself, the one we're working out, needs to be represented with a Latin word that ought to have the inner meaning of the Greek, not the outward appearance. **2.4.** Therefore, what we are seeking to know is how the spirit may travel a smooth and pleasant track, be kind to itself, view its current circumstances happily, and not disrupt inward joy but maintain it with a peaceful attitude, never overjoyed nor depressed. This will be serenity (*tranquillitas*). Let's try to see how one might reach this point in general, and you can take away what you like in particular from this universal treatment.

2.5. Meanwhile, we need to drag this human flaw wholly into the light, so that we each can understand our share in it. At the same time, you will recognize how much less difficulty you have with your dislike for your situation than those who are trapped in their own charade more through their sense of shame than by their choice, bound as they are to their splendid public statements and struggling under weighty titles. **2.6.** Everyone is in the same state, both those who are disturbed by lack of seriousness, by weariness, and by constant changes of purpose (they're always happier with what they gave up), as well as those who flop about and yawn. Add to the mix those who flip back and forth like people having trouble getting to sleep, who settle themselves first one way, then another, until they finally get some rest because they're exhausted. In restructuring their approach to life frequently, they finally stop changing when old age overtakes them (old age hates change), rather than any aversion to change. Add further those who aren't very flexible, not because they are dedicated to a particular point of view but because they are lazy. These people don't live how they want to live; they just keep living the same way they've happened to be living.

2.7. There are countless characteristics of the fault you describe—
I could list one after the other—but just one result: being dissatisfied with yourself. The condition arises from an imbalance of the
spirit, more precisely from desires that are cowardly or unacceptable,
when people either don't dare to try for what they desire or don't
follow through and rely on hope entirely. They're always wavering
and indecisive because that's what happens to people who live in
suspense. They head down every path that leads to what they pray
for, and teach themselves—even compel themselves—to do dishon-
est and difficult things. And when there's lots of work but no success,
they torture themselves pointlessly: they aren't sad to have wanted
shameful things but to have wanted them and not gotten them.
2.8. At that point, remorse for what they've done takes hold of them
as well as a fear of getting started on something else. Then the spiritual
anguish of a life that is not finding its way out of trouble sneaks up
on them, since they aren't able to take control of their desires or obey
them. And with this comes indecisiveness. They can't get their lives
in order; their spirits lie numb among abandoned vows.

2.9. All of these things are more serious when people flee into
retired life and isolated study because they have come to hate the failed
prosperity they worked so hard for. A spirit raised for civic duties, eager
for action, and restless by nature cannot endure studies since it can't
really offer itself any relief. When all the delights that an active life
offers busy men have been taken away, the spirit cannot endure the
house, the seclusion, or the walls. It sees, unwillingly, that it only has
itself left. **2.10.** Weariness comes after this, then dissatisfaction with
one's surroundings and the disquiet of a spirit that never finds retirement, as well as an aggravating and unhealthy lack of concern shown
even for how one might spend the time one has. This situation is particularly acute when it becomes embarrassing to talk about the causes
of these feelings I've described: a sense of shame drives the anguish
deeper inside. Desires that are backed into a corner, without any way
out, suffocate themselves. After that, grief and melancholy, and a thousand different ways an uncertain mind wavers when it is propped up by
imperfect hopes and sad about hopes given up for dead. Then people
start to curse the fact that they have free time in retirement, complaining that they have nothing to do. They develop a jealous hatred of
others' achievements. You see, their unproductive inactivity feeds their
spite, and they want everyone to be brought down, since they can't

go forward. **2.11.** Finally, because of this loathing of others' progress and this hopelessness about its own, the spirit rails against Fortune and complains about how tough things are at that moment and draws itself into the corner, fixating on its own suffering until it is weary and hates itself. This is because the human spirit is by nature inclined toward motion. Every opportunity for rousing itself and pulling itself away is welcome, and more so to all of the worst types of people who happily use themselves up in keeping busy. Hands seem compelled to pick at some scabs and abscesses, and it feels good to do it. A disgusting bodily itch is happy with whatever scratches it. I would say that it's the same for minds in which desires have burst just like bad abscesses—they're happy for the work and aggravation. **2.12.** There are, after all, certain things that our bodies enjoy that come with some pain, such as turning over and changing to a side that isn't uncomfortable, and getting cool by alternating positions. The Homeric Achilles was like that, first lying on his front, then his back, arranging himself in a variety of positions and—this is quite normal for a sick man—tolerating nothing for very long. He used a change of position as a kind of therapy.

2.13. And that's why people begin traveling and wandering up and down the coasts. They practice their impulsiveness, the eternal enemy of the present, first on land and then at sea. "Let's go to Campania now." But luxury is already boring so, "Let's head for valleys of Bruttium and Lucania—things are so uncivilized there." Nevertheless, they start looking for some pretty spot in the empty wilderness where they can refresh their eyes after the tedious filthiness of the rough countryside. "We should go to Tarentum—it's famous for its harbors, has milder weather in the winter, and the region was well-off enough to support many people even in antiquity . . . actually, no, let's go to Rome. I really miss all the applause and the noise, and it would be lovely to see some human blood spilled." **2.14.** So, one route shifts to another, and one show is exchanged for another. It's as Lucretius says, "Thus each man [always] only flees himself."[7] But what for, if he can't get away? He follows along after himself, and is his own very worst travel companion.

2.15. So, we need to see that we aren't troubled because of the shortcomings of the places we go, but because of our own. We're in

---

7. Quoted from Lucretius, *De Rerum Natura* bk. 3, with the addition of the word "always."

no shape to endure everything, and we can't handle work or pleasure or ourselves, or anything actually, for long. This has led some men to kill themselves, because by always changing their plans they kept coming back to the same things and there was no place for novelty. Life begins to be a bore, even the world itself, and this question arises from our pleasures as they fester: "Will it always be the same?"

3.1. You ask what help I think could be used to treat being weary of life. It is best, as Athenodorus[8] said, to occupy oneself with official duties, the administration of the state and public office. Some people, for example, spend the day in the sun, in exercise and the care of their bodies. And it is by far the most useful thing for athletes to cultivate their bodily strength, something they have entirely dedicated themselves to. Most of the time, it is by far the noblest thing for people like us to use our spirits, preparing for the contest of civic life. This is because whenever a person has the intention to make himself useful to citizens—by that I mean mortals—he both practices and develops the good at the same time: he has placed himself in the middle of his duties, serving public and personal needs through his skills.

3.2. "But," he continues, "in this world gone crazy with human ambition, among so many con men twisting what's right for the worse, being open and honest is not very safe and there will always be more working against honesty than resulting from honesty. So, one should withdraw from the forum and public life. A great spirit also has ways to set itself in order more fully in private life. It's not the same for humans as it is for lions and other predators: their attack is impeded by their dens, but the natural actions of humans happen in retirement. **3.3.** And so, I say, a person should hide away so that, wherever he tucks himself away in retirement, he can be of benefit to each and every person with his talent, voice, and advice. You see, it isn't only the man who disqualifies candidates for office, or protects defendants, or advises on peace and war who is of benefit to the state. But if a person can encourage the young, can embed virtue into their spirits (when there is such a shortage of good teachers), can stop them and drag them back as they rush like maniacs for money and lives of extravagance or, if nothing else, can delay them, that person is doing important work for the whole community, even though he is a private citizen.

---

8. Almost certainly Athenodorus Cananites (74 BCE–7 CE), who advised Octavian (later Augustus) and seems to have influenced Cicero's *On Duties* (*De Officiis*).

3.4. "Is he who, as *praetor peregrinus* or *praetor urbanus*,[9] speaks aloud the words of his assistant[10] a more admirable man than he who proclaims what justice is, what piety is, what tolerance is, courage, contempt for death, the mind of the gods, or how a good sense of right and wrong is a gift all can possess? **3.5.** You haven't, therefore, abandoned or rejected your obligations if you transfer the time you subtract from your duties over to your studies. A man isn't only a soldier when he's standing in the battle formation and keeping the right and left flanks secure. He's also a soldier guarding the gates, assigned a post (less dangerous, maybe, but not leisurely), keeping the night watch or in command of the armory. These jobs, although they aren't bloody ones, still count as military service. **3.6.** If you had called yourself back to your studies, you'd have escaped the boredom of life, and you won't wish for the night to come because you're tired of the sun and you won't be a pain to yourself or useless to others. You'll attract many people into friendships and all the best people will flock to you. Although it may be concealed, virtue can never be hidden: it sends out signs of its presence. Whoever is worthy will make the connection between virtue and its tracks. **3.7.** If we take away all interaction, and we renounce the human race, living turned inward only on ourselves, a need for things to do will be the consequence of this kind of isolation: it lacks all focus. We'll begin to build buildings, to demolish others, to push back the sea, and to get water to places that don't have any—that is, to use badly the time Nature gave us to use. **3.8.** Some of us use time sparingly, some extravagantly. Others of us spend it in such a way that we account for where we spent it. Others spend so there is nothing left at all—which is worst of all. Often, a very old man has no other proof to show he lived for a long time besides his age."

4.1. To my way of thinking, dearest Serenus, Athenodorus seems to have given in to the times too much and to have run away too quickly. I wouldn't deny that one must sometimes retreat, but slowly,

---

9. The former judged legal cases in which at least one of the parties to the suit was a non-citizen, the latter suits between those with citizen rights.

10. The office of praetor was held only for one year, but in a system not based on a body of legal precedent, there was need for groups of pseudo-professionals who acted as consultants on points of law or as bureaucrats of the court. Roman law is not formally codified until the sixth century CE under Justinian.

backwards, step-by-step, and keeping the standards safe,[11] along with one's honor as a soldier. Those who come to make a treaty with weapons in their hands are less vulnerable to their enemies and safer. **4.2.** I think this is what virtue must do, and what a student of virtue must too: if Fortune has the upper hand and cuts away the ability to act, he shouldn't flee immediately in the other direction, unarmed, looking for the shadows, as if there is a place Fortune can't follow. Instead, he should apply himself more sparingly to virtue's duties, finding and deciding on a way in which he can be useful to the state. **4.3.** If he can't be a soldier, he should seek public office. If he must live as a private citizen, he should be an orator. Is he required to keep silent? He should help his fellow citizens with silent legal advice. Is it even dangerous for him to go to the forum? He should be a good acquaintance, a faithful friend, and a self-controlled dinner guest in homes, at the games, and at parties. If he has lost the duties of a citizen, he should practice the duties of a human being.

4.4. Here's why we don't just shut ourselves up courageously behind the walls of one city, but set out to have contact with the whole world and proclaim that it belongs to us: it's so that we can give a wider playing field to virtue. If you're excluded from the judge's tribunal and forbidden from speaking from the rostra or in the assembly, look behind you and see how many of the largest countries and peoples lie open to you. You are never so shut out of the greater part of life that the better part of it is not left to you. **4.5.** But make sure that the whole situation is not your fault. So you don't want to govern the state unless you're consul, or *prytanis*, or *ceryx*, or *sufes*.[12] What if you wouldn't be a soldier unless you were the general or a staff officer? Even if others will hold the front line, and the luck of the draw placed you in the third wave,[13] be a soldier from there with your voice, your encouragement, your example, your spirit. Even with his hands cut off, in a battle a man can find some way to help his squad, even if he just stands there and helps by shouting. **4.6.** You should act in a similar way. If Fortune removes you from the first

---

11. Legionary standards represented the legion itself and were sacred. Their loss was a terrible indignity.

12. These are the highest or most prestigious offices of their respective cultures, Roman, Greek, and Carthaginian.

13. That is, not in the front rank with the youngest soldiers, but farther back from the action with the older veterans.

rank of the state, nevertheless you should stand and help by shouting. And if someone stifles your voice, stand there anyway and help silently. The effort of a good citizen is never useless: he is heard and seen. With a look, with a nod, with tenacious silence, even with his appearance alone, he is beneficial.

4.7. Just as certain medicines are effective with their aroma, setting aside oral and topical uses, virtue dispenses its benefit even from a long way away and even if it is hidden. Whether virtue is out in the open and under its own power or its departure is under the control of another and it is forced to shorten sail, whether it is idle and silent, locked away tightly or free . . . whatever its circumstance, virtue is beneficial. What, do you think the role model of a man who is nobly peaceful isn't extremely useful? **4.8.** And so, it is best by far to mix retirement with work, whenever a politically active life is constrained by the obstacles of fate or the state of the state. You see, no situation is ever restricted to the point that there is no place for honorable activity.

5.1. Could you ever find a city in a worse state than Athens was when the Thirty Tyrants were ripping her apart?[14] Thirteen hundred citizens, the very best, were killed, and that didn't even put an end to it: savagery provoked more savagery. In a city that had the Areopagus, the most holy and respected group of judges for murder cases, which had a Senate and a citizen population that acted like a Senate,[15] a grim committee of killers came together daily and the unlucky assembly was packed with tyrants of its own. Could this state become peaceful, when there were as many tyrants as there would have been bodyguards? There was not even any hope of freedom to offer the Athenians' spirits, and there was no room for a remedy against the brutal power of bad men. For such a wretched state, where could they find enough Harmodiuses?[16] **5.2.** Nevertheless, there was Socrates, in the middle of things, offering consolation to grieving fathers, encouraging those despairing about the state, and

---

14. Athens surrendered to Sparta in 404 BCE to end the Peloponnesian War. The Spartans instituted a very limited oligarchy, which was overthrown the following year.
15. This probably refers to the *Boule* (a group of elected officials) and the *Ekklesia* (the assembly of citizens who voted on legislation chosen by the *Boule*). The *Boule* was not strictly equivalent to the Roman Senate.
16. Harmodius was the older of two famous tyrant killers (Aristogeiton was the other) of the sixth century, whose assassination of Hipparchus, son of Peisistratus, in 514 BCE ushered in the Athenian democratic experiment.

criticizing rich men, who feared their own wealth, for their regrets (a bit late!) about their perilous greed. He went about, a noble role model for those who wished to imitate him, since he was a free man walking among thirty masters. **5.3.** And Athens itself killed him in jail; "freedom" could not endure the freedom even of a man who had safely insulted an army of tyrants. As a result, you know that in a troubled state there is an opportunity for a wise man to reveal himself, and that in a state that is prospering and blessed, money, spite, and a million other useless vices reign supreme. **5.4.** Therefore, as the state gives us opportunities and as Fortune allows—we shall not stop and be inactive, bound by our fear!—we shall either bring ourselves forward or pull back. No! Better to say that the real man is one who, while dangers threatened on all sides and weapons and shackles clattered all around, did not endanger his virtue or conceal it. Burying virtue does not keep it safe.

5.5. Curius Dentatus[17] used to say that he preferred to be dead than to live as a dead man, and I agree: it's the worst of all bad things to have left the living before you've actually died. But, if you happen to be in a state where things are less civilized, this is what you must do: free yourself for retirement and study, seek that safe harbor again and again, no differently than if you were on a dangerous voyage. Don't wait until public affairs forsake you, but instead separate yourself from them by yourself.

6.1. But we need to examine ourselves first of all, then the things that we are ready to undertake, and then those for whose sake or with whom we will act. [You should reflect whether your nature is better suited to a public career or to study and meditation in retirement, and you should be inclined to go where the strength of your abilities might take you. Isocrates dragged Ephorus bodily from the forum, judging that he was more suited to writing historical works.[18] Natural

---

17. Manius Curius Dentatus was an important figure of the beginning of the third century BCE, the victorious general of the Samnite War, who held the consulship three times. He used personal funds to finance the building of an aqueduct for Rome and was known for being incorruptible and untouched by wealth.

18. Ephorus was one of the most important historians of the fourth century BCE; although we have relatively little of his writing left, he was used as a source by many later historians. Isocrates was a teacher of rhetoric and philosopher at Athens. The suggestion here is that Isocrates stopped Ephorus from having a political career to pursue a life more appropriate to his abilities and nature.

ability responds badly to coercion—the effort is useless when your nature resists it.][19]

6.2. It's necessary above all to know your own worth because we usually seem to ourselves to be able to do more than we can. One person fails because he trusts in his powers of speech, another asks for more from his finances than they can endure, another burdens his body, although it's already weak, with a demanding duty. Some are far too self-conscious for public life, for which you need to control your expressions. The arrogance of some isn't successful in the royal court. Some don't have control of their temper and any insult prompts them to speak recklessly. Some people don't know how to control their wit, and they don't leave off making dangerous jokes. For all of these people, a quiet life is more constructive than a life in public business. A wild and intolerant nature should avoid what triggers a tendency to speak frankly because it will cause harm.

6.3. Next, we should evaluate what we're undertaking, and our strengths should be measured against the projects we're about to attempt. There should be more strength in the doer than is required for the job. It's inevitable that a load greater than the person bearing it will crush him. **6.4.** Besides, some things aren't so much very important things to do as they are self-generating, and some work brings with it even more work. You should flee from this kind of work, because many more new things to do are born from the old. And you shouldn't walk into anything you can't back out of freely. You should only set your hand to the sorts of projects whose completion you can accomplish, or at least hope for, and pass over those that get bigger while you work and don't stop where you had thought they would.

7.1. The choice of people must be considered the same way: we must ask whether those we're spending part of our life on are worthy of it and whether the loss of our time will help them too. Some people count the things we did for them as favors they did for us. **7.2.** Athenodorus said that he couldn't even go to dinner at a person's house if the person would not as a result be in his debt. You should take him to mean, I think, that he would rather not go to the houses of those who provide dinner equal to the importance

---

19. This passage occurs in the manuscripts at 7.2, but modern editors feel that it was accidentally moved by an ancient scribe from this section of the text, or inserted at 7.2 from a marginal notation.

of the positions the guests hold, who count dinner dishes as gifts-to-go, as if they were being extravagant to honor another. If you take away from them the witnesses and lookers-on, they won't enjoy a food-stall none can see.[20] **7.3.** Even so, nothing makes the spirit happy quite like a faithful and delightful friendship. What a good thing it is when there are hearts standing ready to hold all your secrets safely, whose moral sense you fear less than your own, whose conversation lessens your anxiety, whose advice resolves your plans, whose sense of humor dispels your gloominess, and the mere sight of whom gives you pleasure! We should choose those who are, as much as possible of course, free from passions. Faults creep along, and leap over to anyone nearby—exposure to them harms us. **7.4.** So, just as in flu season we must take care not to approach people already infected and feverish with the illness, since we put ourselves at risk and will even get sick from their breath, so too in choosing our friends we should have a concern for their natures: make friends with as few corrupt people as possible. The mixing of healthy things with sick is the beginning of illness. Now, I wouldn't advise you to follow after or invite no one but a wise man—where will you find a wise man, when we've been looking for one for years? The best friend is one who is least bad.

7.5. Your ability to choose would get better, if you were looking for good friends among the Platos and the Xenophons and the other offspring of the Socratic school,[21] or if you were to have the power to choose from Cato's age—there were many born in that time who were worthy. (Likewise, there were then many worse people than in other times, architects of terrible crimes. It was necessary, you see, to have a group of each kind, so that Cato could stand out: he needed to have good men, to whom he could compare himself favorably, and bad men, against whom he could test his strength.) But now, when there is such a shortage of good men, we have to be a little less fussy about our choices. **7.6.** But avoid above all gloomy people who whine about everything and happily make anything a reason to complain. Even if his trustworthiness and goodwill are unwavering, a man who is distraught and groans about everything is still an enemy of serenity.

---

20. The bracketed text at 6.1 is found here in the manuscripts. See n. 19.
21. The notion that one can build a beneficial relationship with a (dead) author through his works was not uncommon.

8.1. Let's talk now about personal wealth, the source of human suffering. If you compare all the other things that cause us pain—death, illness, fear, desire, enduring sorrows and struggles—with what bad things our wealth brings us, the latter will tip the scales. **8.2.** So, we should think about how much more bearable our sorrow would be to not have wealth than to lose it, and we will understand that in poverty there is a potential for less sorrow that correlates directly to the potential for less loss. You're wrong to think that rich people endure loss with more courage: to the smallest and the largest the pain of a wound is the same.

8.3. Bion[22] says, cleverly, that it is as painful for bald men to have their hairs plucked as it is for men with hair.[23] You should know then that it is the same for poor and rich men—their suffering is equal. You see, each group is stuck to their wealth, and it cannot be yanked off without them feeling it. But it is more manageable, as I said, and easier to not acquire wealth than it is to lose wealth you've got. For that reason you will see that people Fortune never glances at are happier than people she has abandoned. **8.4.** Diogenes the Cynic—what an amazing spirit!—saw this and made sure that nothing could be taken from him. You can call this poverty, indigence, need—put whatever disgraceful name you want on this safety of his. I'll believe that Diogenes didn't live in happy prosperity if you can find for me another person who can lose nothing. Either I'm fooling myself, or it is supreme power to be the only one who can't be harmed—even though surrounded by greedy men, cheats, thieves, and bandits.

8.5. If anyone has any doubts about Diogenes' happiness and prosperity, he can also have doubts about the situation of the immortal gods. Perhaps they aren't very happy because they don't have farms, or gardens, no productive estates to have tenant farmers on, or large loans to collect interest on? Doesn't it embarrass you that you are stunned by and enamored with money? Come on, look around at the universe! You'll see that the gods are naked, giving everything, keeping nothing. Do you think that Diogenes was a poor man or like the immortal gods when he stripped himself of everything that is brought

---

22. Likely Bion of Borysthenes (325–250 BCE), a Cynic-influenced Greek philosopher.

23. This seems illogical, except that the kind of depilation Seneca is talking about was commonly done on other parts of the body, such as armpits, forearms, and even more sensitive areas.

by chance? **8.6.** Maybe you think Demetrius Pompeianus[24] was more prosperous, because he wasn't ashamed to be richer than Pompey the Great. The number of his slaves was reported to him everyday, just like troop strength to a general. But for a long time the only wealth he was owed was two slave's slaves[25] and a roomier cell. **8.7.** But Diogenes' only slave ran away, and when he was pointed out, Diogenes did not think it worth taking him back. "It's shameful," he said, "that Manes is able to live without Diogenes, but not Diogenes without Manes." It seems to me that what he meant was, "Mind your own business, Fortune. There is nothing that you own in my house. A slave ran away me, but I walked away from you a free man."

8.8. A household requires clothing and food. The many stomachs of those voracious animals[26] must be cared for, their clothing must be mended, their greedy hands must be guarded against, and we must make use of the services of those who hate us through their tears. How much more prosperous would a man be if he owed nothing to anyone but himself—and could easily deny his own needs. **8.9.** But, since we're not so tough, we ought certainly to reduce our personal wealth, so that we are less exposed to the injuries Fortune can do. Bodies that can fit inside their armor are better suited to war than those that bulge out of it—their own enormity makes them vulnerable. The best quantity of money is what doesn't leave us in poverty,[27] and doesn't fall too far from it either. **9.1.** We'll be happy with this amount of money if we are happy being thrifty first. Without that, either the amount of resources will never be enough or it will always be too much, especially when the cure is at hand. That is, small means can be turned into riches if one makes use of thriftiness.

9.2. Let's make it a habit to remove public display, and to measure things by their utility, not their appearance. Food should overcome hunger, drink thirst, and desire should arise for what is essential. We should learn to stand on our own two feet, to clothe ourselves after

---

24. A freedman of Pompey the Great, who was himself extraordinarily rich.

25. Some masters allowed some slaves to acquire money and certain kinds of property (collectively called a *peculium*), of which one kind of property could be the *vicarius*, or a slave's slave.

26. It is quite rare for Seneca to describe slaves in this way, because he normally treats them as equal to all other human beings except in circumstance.

27. "in poverty": Latin *paupertas*. This is not abject poverty (*egestas*), but having barely sufficient resources.

the custom of our ancestors and not in trendy fashions. We should learn to increase our self-control, to suppress extravagant living, to regulate desire for glory, to soften our anger, to have a balanced view of moderate wealth, to cultivate thriftiness. Even if many are ashamed of it, we should apply simple treatments to natural needs, keep unbridled expectations and a spirit that looks to the future under control, as if in chains, and work at seeking riches from ourselves rather than from Fortune.

9.3. It's not possible to drive away the great variety and excess of calamities so that fierce winds mostly won't blast those who put up a lot of sail. We need to trim the sails so that Fortune's blasts fall without effect. This is why exile and calamity have sometimes been healthy and why more serious problems have been fixed by small inconveniences. When the spirit won't listen to good advice and can't be cured in a milder way, why shouldn't we be pleased if diminished wealth, a bad reputation, and the world set upside down get the job done? Bad is matched against bad. We should get in the habit of being able to eat dinner without a crowd, to be served by fewer slaves, to provide clothes that do only what clothes should, and to live in a more modest house. The inside lane is the one to take, not only on the track and at the horse races, but also in the walk of life.

9.4. For studies too, which is the most worthwhile expense for a free person, there is as much of a justification as there is a proper limit to the expense one can incur studying. That is, why have innumerable books and shelves when their owner can barely even read all the title pages in one lifetime? A mass of books does not educate the learner, but burdens him, and it is more than good enough to dive into a few authors than to drift along through many. **9.5.** Forty thousand books burned at Alexandria.[28] Some would have praised it as the most beautiful monument to a king's power, as Livy did, when he said that it had been the most preeminent product of the civilized care of kings. This wasn't culture or care, but an extravagance of the educated class—or rather, not truly educated, since they didn't collect them for learning, but for display. In the same way, for most people who don't even know what a child should know, books are not

---

28. The library suffered a major fire in 48 BCE when Julius Caesar accidentally set it ablaze when he set fire to the Egyptian navy during his attempt to reinstall Cleopatra to the throne.

devices for study but decoration for the dining room. So, you should have as many books as are enough, and none for appearance's sake.

9.6. It's more noble, you say, to pour your money into books than into Corinthian bronze[29] and paintings. But there is moral error wherever there is excess. Do you have a reason to excuse a man who hunts down book chests made out of Sandarac wood[30] and ivory, who acquires the works of unknown authors of little worth and, yawning in the middle of his thousands of volumes, enjoys the title labels and the book roll covers most of all?[31] **9.7.** In the homes of very lazy men you'll see all the speeches and histories there are, scroll boxes stacked as far as the ceiling. Personal libraries (a necessary frill these days along with pools and saunas) lend a sheen of sophistication to a house. I would completely understand if they went wrong out of a desire for literature and learning. But in reality these acquisitions—works of divine talent—are shelved under the bust of their authors, bought for display and to decorate the walls.

10.1. Maybe you've fallen into some kind of difficulty in your life: some public or private circumstance has caught you, unaware of the trap, and you can't undo it or break out. Think about how men in chains at first suffer under the weight and the restricted movement. But then, when they have resolved not to be angry but to endure, necessity teaches them to suffer bravely and habit teaches them to suffer easily. You'll discover delights, entertainment, and pleasures in every kind of life, if you're willing to think that bad things are trivial rather than to make them into something to hate. **10.2.** Nature deserves better from us for no other reason than because, when she saw what hardships we were born for, she invented routine and habit as medicines for difficult times, lending the harshest situations a kind of friendly intimacy.

None of us would survive if we constantly experienced our difficulties with the same force as we experienced the first blow. **10.3.** We

---

29. So-called Corinthian bronze, because the process was thought (probably incorrectly) to have been discovered at Corinth. An alloy of copper and gold or silver (or both), Corinthian bronze was resistant to tarnish, and because of its value became a cliché of wealth and culture.

30. *Tetraclinis articulata*, otherwise known as citron wood, is a variety of cypress, common in the Mediterranean (especially North Africa) and prized from antiquity for furniture.

31. Book scrolls often had an outer sheet for protection, and a tag attached to one of the ends with a description of the author(s) and work(s) contained within.

all are bound to Fortune. For some the chains are golden and loose, for others tight and crude—but so what? The same restraint was set over the whole universe, and even those who did the binding are bound, unless perhaps you think a chain is lighter when you wear it only on the left hand. Public office shackles one man, wealth another. A noble family keeps some men down, an insignificant family name keeps down others, another's authority threatens some men, and others are threatened by their own. Exile holds some in one place and priesthoods hold others.[32] Every life is an enslavement.

10.4. And so each must habituate himself to his situation in life and complain about it as little as possible, seeing whatever good is around him. There is nothing so unpleasant that a balanced spirit cannot find comfort against it. Small spaces have been opened up for many uses through skillful partition, and even though the area is tight, organization makes it habitable. Apply reason to your problems: hard things can be made soft, narrow wide—and problems weigh less heavily on those who bear them skillfully. **10.5.** More than that, our desires should not be given too long a leash: we should let them roam, but close by, since they don't like to be fenced in entirely. After leaving behind the things that are impossible or possible but difficult, we should pursue what is at hand and what we can legitimately hope for, as long as we understand that all things are equally inconsequential. Things have different appearances on the outside, but inside they are equally empty. And we should not envy those above us: what seems high up from below is usually a steep and difficult climb.

10.6. People unfairly placed by destiny in a hazardously high position will be safer if they remove a sense of superiority from their superior circumstances and if they bring their own good fortune, as much as possible, down to a normal level. There are many who must hang on at the pinnacle of success out of necessity, because they can't come down unless they fall down. But these same people swear that being forced to be trouble for others is their greatest burden, and that they were not so much lifted up to their position, as nailed upon it. They should prepare assistance ahead of time—through just behavior, kindness, compassion, and abundant generosity—to make their fall favorable. They might hang more safely from such a hope. **10.7.** Still,

---

32. Priesthoods were by and large exercised in connection with a specific temple or cult center.

nothing frees us from these fluctuations of the spirit better than always setting some limit on growth and success, not giving Fortune the decision about where growth stops but stopping ourselves short of Fortune's limit instead. In this way some desires will both keep an edge on our spirit's hunger, and—because they are controlled—not lead us into anything huge and uncertain.

11.1. This discussion of mine is aimed at incomplete, ordinary, unhealthy people, not the wise man. He must not walk fearfully or cautiously. You see, the wise man is so confident of himself that he doesn't hesitate to stand in Fortune's path and will never yield his place to her. He has no reason to fear Fortune either, since he not only counts his property, estates, and personal honor as temporary things, but also his body, eyes, hands, whatever makes life better and even his life itself. The wise man lives as if he had all these things on loan . . . and he'd return them without sadness to whoever wanted them returned. **11.2.** But just because he knows he doesn't belong to himself, he isn't as a consequence worthless in his own eyes. Rather, he will do everything as diligently and with as much careful thought as a very dutiful and scrupulous man looks after things entrusted to him. **11.3.** And when he's ordered to hand anything back, he won't quarrel with Fortune, but will say, "Thank you for what I had in my possession. I tended your property with great profit, but since you demand, I give it, I yield it to you willing, with thanks. If you still want me to have anything else that's yours, I'm at your service. If not, I return my silver (coins and otherwise), my house, and my household. I restore them to their owner." If Nature remembers what she entrusted to us earlier, we'll say to her also, "Receive again a spirit in better condition than when you gave it. I won't turn away and run. You possess a thing given back to you willingly, that you entrusted to me before I was aware—carry me away."

11.4. Why is it difficult to go back to where you came from? He who does not know how to die well will live badly. So, in this matter we should first drop the price we set on life, putting our life's breath in with other possessions of little value. "Gladiators," as Cicero said, "we hate them if they want to stay alive in any way they can, and we love them if they excel at disregarding life." You know, it's the same thing for us. Fear of death is often the cause of death. **11.5.** And Fortune, who puts on shows for herself, says, "Why should I save you, you bad, fearful beast? You should be sliced up and stabbed more because you don't know to offer your neck. But you who bravely accept the sword will live more fully and die more quickly, and not with your neck covered and your hands pushing death away." **11.6.** He who fears death will never do anything like a man who is truly alive. But he who perceives that his death was decreed as soon as his life began will live according to that contract. At the same time, because of his strength of spirit, he will guarantee for himself that nothing that happens will happen without him seeing it coming. You see, by expecting that whatever could happen will happen, the wise man softens the blows of all bad events, which bring nothing surprising to those who are prepared and waiting. Those who live a carefree life and who look only for the happy things find such events difficult to endure when they occur.

11.7. Illness, captivity, destruction, or fire: none of these is unpredictable. I have known for a while now how disturbed and distraught the travel companions Nature has imprisoned me with are. Many times now mourners have wailed in my neighborhood. Many times the torches and candles have made their way solemnly past my door, lighting funeral processions for those who died too young. I have often heard the crashing sound of a building falling down. One night has taken away many of those whom the forum, the *curia*, or conversation had brought into my life—and one night has come between the joined hands of friends. Should I be surprised that dangerous things sometimes happen to me when they've always been happening around me?

11.8. The majority of people don't think about the storm as they're setting sail. I'm not ashamed of a good saying from a bad author— Publilius, a more forceful talent than tragic or comic writers (whenever he left off writing his useless mime plays and sayings that please the audience[33]). Among many other things he said too bold even for a tragic actor, much less a comic one, is the following:

"What can happen to someone can happen to anyone."

A person who has taken this to heart and seen all the misfortunes of others (and there are a great many of these every day), watching them as

---

33. In fact, only those clever sayings survive to the present day; a collection of them seems to have been made very early (many sayings of Seneca snuck into that collection). Publilius Syrus lived during the first century BCE, and wrote and acted in his mime plays. Mimes were a popular theater entertainment based on stock plots and characters, sexual innuendo (and later sexual acts on stage), violence, and fantastic effects (such as a real fire on stage). The popularity of mimes increased greatly under the empire and were often sponsored by the emperor.

if they had a clear path to him too, this person will prepare himself for battle long before troubles come to find him. It's too late for the spirit to learn how to withstand dangers after they have come. **11.9.** "I didn't think this would happen!" "Did you ever believe this would happen to me?" But why not? Has there never been wealth that hasn't been followed closely by need and hunger and abject poverty? Or personal honor that hasn't had its purple toga, its augur's staff, its patrician reins followed by filthy clothes, condemnation, a million public insults, and utter contempt? Is there a kingdom that has not had destruction, subjugation, a master, and an executioner prepared for it? These extremes needn't be separated by a large amount of time—an hour can be all there is between sitting on a throne and kneeling before it.

11.10. You should understand, therefore, that every circumstance is changeable and whatever happens to anyone is able to happen to you too. Are you rich? Who was ever richer than Pompey?[34] But he didn't have bread or water when Gaius Caligula, an old friend, now a host, opened Caesar's house to him so that his own might be closed down. Although he had in his possession so many rivers that had their source on his land, and so many that had their mouth on his land, he begged for a drop of water. While his heir[35] was preparing a public funeral for the starving man, he died of hunger and thirst in the palace of a relative. **11.11.** So, are you holding public office? Did anyone hold offices as great and unhoped for and all-powerful as Sejanus?[36]

---

34. There is a problem here. All the manuscripts refer to Pompey, but it's hard to think which Pompey this could be because of the mention of Gaius Caligula (r. 37–41 CE). Some have suggested the nephew of Pompey the Great. A better possibility is Ptolemy, the king of Mauretania, who was killed in 39 or 40 CE by Caligula either for aspiring to rulership (Suetonius, *Caligula* 26) or for being very wealthy (Cassius Dio, *Roman History* 59.25.1). Mauretania then became a province under the control of the emperor; such provinces acted as a sort of "estate" for the emperors, and all profits went to the imperial treasury.

35. That is, Gaius Caligula—it was common practice for noble Romans and also client kings to leave a large portion of their inheritance (for kings even their whole kingdom) to the emperor.

36. Sejanus was a low-ranking equestrian soldier who rose to great power and influence under the reign of Tiberius (14–37 CE). As Tiberius withdrew from public life in stages, Sejanus, in his capacity as prefect of the Praetorian Guard (the emperor's honor guard, and the only troop force permitted inside Rome's boundaries at that time), consolidated power in his absence. Sejanus' plans became known to the emperor, who quickly ordered his execution.

On the day the Senate executed him, the people of Rome ripped him to bits. Gods and men had granted him whatever power a man could achieve, but the executioner couldn't find anything to drag away on his hook.[37] **11.12.** So, you're a king. I won't send you to Croesus for advice—he both climbed onto his own funeral pyre when commanded and watched it be extinguished, made to outlive not only his kingdom but even his execution![38] Nor will I send you to Jugurtha: the Roman people watched him paraded by after fearing him for less than a year.[39] We have seen Ptolemy, the king of Africa, and Mithridates, the king of Armenia, in Gaius Caligula's custody. The one was sent into exile, the other chose it so he could be sent away a little more safe from harm. With such mixed-up reversals of things, if you don't think that anything that can happen might happen in the future, you give unpleasant things strength to use against you. And these unpleasant things have broken every man who experienced them before.

12.1. After this it will be important to not work hard on unnecessary projects or work unnecessarily—that is, to not desire what we can't have or understand too late, when we get it after much sweat, that our desire was an empty one. To put it another way, our hard work should not be ineffectual and without result, or the result unworthy of the hard work. Sorrow almost always follows a lack of success or a success that is something to be embarrassed about. **12.2.** We should cut down our rushing about, which is what the majority of people do, drifting from houses to theaters to forum. They involve themselves in others' business, looking like people who have something to do. If you catch one of them coming out of their house and ask, "Where are you going? What are your plans?" he will answer, "Goodness! I don't know. I'll see someone—I'll have something to

---

37. Romans are known for a variety of gruesome executions. Those charged with *maiestas*, or damaging the authority and dignity of the state (and so by extension the emperor), were pierced through the neck with a hook and dragged down to the Tiber River.

38. Most famously told in Herodotus, *Histories* bk. 1, Croesus was a king of Lydia who, after losing his kingdom, was saved from being burned to death by a rainstorm.

39. Rome was victorious over Jugurtha, king of Numidia, in the Jugurthine War (112–105 BCE), but only after a difficult campaign. Jugurtha was part of the triumphal procession of Gaius Marius (these processions included displays of prisoners and wealth from the conquered area), and finally thrown in the Tullianum, a pit in the Mamertine prison where political prisoners were executed.

do." **12.3.** They wander without purpose, looking for responsibili-ties, and they don't do what they decide to do, but what they stumble upon. Their path[40] is accidental and useless, like ants that go up to the very top of a tree and all the way down for no purpose. Most live their lives like this. I guess you could say that they are frantically idle.

12.4. You'll feel pity for some of them, rushing as if to a house on fire. They even push aside people who are in the way and hustle them-selves and their companions along. Meanwhile, what they're hurrying to do is to greet a man who won't return the greeting, or to follow the funeral procession of someone they didn't know, or to hear a verdict for a man who's often in court, or to go to the engagement party of someone who keeps getting married over and over again. Sometimes they even carry the litter that they were following![41] Then, returning home weary but without accomplishing anything, they swear they don't know why they went out or where they've been. But on the next day they will retrace their own steps as they drift along. **12.5.** And so, let all your hard work be for something or play a role in something. People are not restless because of their activities—false impressions of things make them ill. You see, not even restless people act without some kind of expectation. The outward appearance of something tempts them, and their mind, a prisoner to passion, does not expose its worthlessness. **12.6.** In the same way each of those who leave the house without good cause, to join in with the crowds and to be led around the city for trivial reasons, are driven out by the dawn light although none have anything to work toward. And when, after knocking on many doors in vain and having many doors shut in his face, a man has given the morning greeting to nomenclatores,[42] none of these is more difficult to endure than spending time at home with himself. **12.7.** The result of this badness is a very offensive vice, eavesdropping and prying into people's public and private affairs, and one comes to know many things that aren't safe to speak of or to hear.

---

40. The Latin suggests that this could refer to a career path as well.

41. Attending to an important person in public (i.e., following a litter) was a normal function of the *cliens*. A litter bearer, however, was a slave.

42. A *nomenclator* was a slave whose primary responsibility was to remember names and relationships for his master. The implication is that the man tries to attend the morning *salutatio,* but does not ever get to greet the important man in person or is not personally known to the important man.

13.1. I think that Democritus, because he held this view, began his work in the way he did: "Whoever wishes to live with serenity should not work at many things either in private life or in public life," referring of course to unnecessary projects. You see, if there are enough necessary things to do, we should get to work in private life and public not only if they are many in number, but even if they are innumerable.[43] On the other hand, when no established duty exists, actions should be restricted. **13.2.** When a man works at many things he gives Fortune power over what is his. It is safest to test Fortune rarely and instead to be aware of her all the time, promising oneself nothing in her name. "I shall travel by ship, if nothing happens to stop me." "I shall become praetor, unless something prohibits me." "My business venture will bring me a good return, unless something interferes with it." **13.3.** This is why we say that nothing happens contrary to the expectation of a wise man. We don't set him apart from the misfortunes of humankind, but from its errors. And things don't always go the way he wanted, but as he thought they might. Indeed, he thought first of all that something might stand in the way of his plans. At any rate, when you haven't predicted a good result, it's inevitable that the pain of a frustrated desire rest more lightly on your spirit.

14.1. We should also make ourselves flexible in nature, so that we don't get too attached to what we've planned but transfer our attention to where chance has led us. We shouldn't fear a change in plan or in circumstance, provided that consistently changing our mind—a vice that is very damaging to a quiet life—does not take over. You see, sheer stubbornness is necessarily anxiety-ridden and pitiful, and Fortune can often squeeze something out of it. But a fickle mind is a much more serious problem, since it is never in control of itself. To be able to change nothing and to be able to endure nothing: both are the enemy of serenity. **14.2.** At any rate, the spirit should be called back into itself, away from all external matters. Let it confide in itself, enjoy itself. Let it be suspicious of its own thoughts, pull back as far as possible from others' thoughts, and devote itself to itself. Let it not feel hurts, and explain its hardships in a positive way. **14.3.** After news came of a shipwreck, when he heard that all his possessions had gone down, our Zeno said, "Fortune is ordering me to be a philosopher who can

---

43. That is, no effort should be spared to accomplish a necessary action.

be light on his feet." A tyrant threatened Theodorus the philosopher[44] with death, and no burial afterwards, and he said, "You can do as you please, half my blood is in your hands.[45] As far as a burial goes, you are an idiot if you think my body parts care whether they decompose above or below ground." **14.4.** Canus Julius, an especially magnificent man (not even the fact that he was born in our lifetime prevents admiration for him), had been at odds with Gaius Caligula for some time and after that Phalaris[46] said to him as he was leaving, "Just so you don't flatter yourself with a foolish hope, I have ordered that you be led away . . . to your death." "Thank you," said Canus Julius, "o most noble prince." **14.5.** I'm not sure what he meant by this—many things come to mind. Did he wish to be very insulting and to point out how great Gaius' cruelty was, when death was a good thing? Or was he rebuking him for his daily delusions? You see, people also used to thank Gaius when their children were executed and when their property was confiscated. Or did he accept death willingly as if it were freedom? Whatever the case, he answered with a courageous spirit. **14.6.** Someone will say, "After this Gaius could have ordered him to live." Canus didn't fear this outcome: Gaius' dependability about such orders was well known. Can you believe that he even spent the ten days between that moment and his execution completely free of anxiety? It's unreal what the man said and did, and how serene he was. **14.7.** He was playing latrunculi[47] when the centurion who was gathering a group of the condemned ordered him to come along also. Although he'd been summoned, he counted up his pieces and said to his opponent, "This is so you can't pretend you beat me after I'm dead." Then, winking at the centurion, he said, "You'll be a witness that I won by a head." Do you think Canus was having a

---

44. Theodorus of Cyrene lived from about the middle of the fourth century BCE to the middle of the third century BCE.

45. This seems to be proverbial in both Greek and Roman sources for "my life," but it is also literally the amount of blood that can be lost before death is inevitable. Current medical wisdom suggests that blood loss over 40% (class IV hemorrhage) leads to hemorrhagic shock and death without aggressive treatment.

46. Phalaris, to whom Seneca is comparing Gaius Caligula, was a despot at Agrigentum on Sicily in the sixth century BCE, renowned for his cruelty and violent behavior. He was said to have invented the "bronze bull," a torture device into which a victim was sealed and then slowly cooked over flames.

47. A two-player game, somewhat like checkers or chess, played with different colored pieces on a grid.

bit of fun with the board game? He poked fun with it. **14.8.** His friends were sad, since they were going to lose such a good man. "Why are you grieving?" he said. "You're still wondering whether the spirit is immortal or not—but I will soon know."[48] He didn't stop searching for the truth at the very end and he held an inquiry about his own death. **14.9.** His own philosopher followed him, and the hill where the daily sacrifice to our god Caesar was made was not far off when the philosopher said, "What are you thinking about, Canus? What do you have in mind?" Canus said, "I plan to observe whether in that swiftest of moments the spirit can perceive when it leaves the body." He also promised that if he found anything out, he would visit his friends and let them know what it was like for the soul after death. **14.10.** This is serenity in the middle of the storm, this is a spirit worthy of eternity. It called upon its own death as evidence for the truth, it investigated its life-breath at the very last moment, and kept learning not only up to the point of death but even learned something from death itself. No one has been a philosopher longer than that. This great man will not be quickly forgotten and we should make sure we talk about him. I shall put you in every memory, most noble Canus, one of the great men whom Gaius slaughtered.

15.1. Still, it's not beneficial to get rid of the causes of personal sadness, because without it hatred for humankind can sometimes take its place. When we think how rare straightforward honesty is and how unfamiliar innocence is, how hardly anyone keeps his word unless it is useful to do so, we come face to face with a multiplicity of financial misdoings, equally detestable gains and losses from lusts, and ambition so unable to set boundaries for itself that it polishes itself to a shine with filth. The human spirit is driven into the night and, as if virtue was destroyed and we couldn't hope for it or have it, the shadows rise up before us. **15.2.** So, we ought to change our thinking so that the vices of the crowd aren't despicable but laughable and follow Democritus' example more than Heraclitus'. The latter used to weep whenever he had gone out into public, the former used to laugh. You see, for Heraclitus everything we do is pitiful, but for Democritus everything seems meaningless. Therefore, we should relax about everything and endure everything with a good-natured spirit: it's more human to laugh at life than to weep over it. **15.3.** What's more, he who laughs at humankind deserves better from it than he who

---

48. Echoing Socrates as he faced execution at Athens.

expresses grief for it, since the first leaves it some good to hope for. But the second weeps foolishly over what he despairs of ever being able to correct. He who, in contemplating the universe, cannot keep from laughing has a greater spirit than the one who cannot keep from weeping, since only the lightest of emotions has touched him and since he thinks that there is nothing great or serious, not even sad, in so big a structure as the universe.

15.4. Each should imagine for himself, one by one, the things that can make us happy or sad, and realize that what Bion said is true: "All human endeavors are extremely similar to our human beginnings and our lives aren't more holy or more serious than they were at conception." **15.5.** Even so, it's better to accept social norms and human vices calmly, not descending to laughter or tears, because it is eternal misery to be tormented by the bad things others do and an unnatural pleasure to enjoy them. **15.6.** In the same way, it is an empty compassion to weep because someone is burying a son, or to fake emotion on your face. During your own misfortunes, too, it is appropriate to act so that you give in to your pain as much as nature, not social custom, requires. Most pour out their tears to make a show, and have dry eyes whenever there's no one to see, while they think that it's shameful not to cry when everyone is crying. This badness—to set a value on something based on another's opinion—is so deeply entrenched that people fake even the most honest and straightforward thing, grief.

16.1. Now comes the part when we usually get very sad—not without reason—and fall into worrying. When the deaths of good men are bad, when Socrates was forced to die in prison, Rutilius to live in exile, Pompey and Cicero to offer their necks to their own clients,[49] and Cato, a living image of the virtues, to slice open his own body by falling on his sword, and the state with the same blow,[50] it's inevitable that we should be distressed that Fortune gave out gifts so unfairly. What can any person hope for, when we see the best men suffer the worst things? **16.2.** What can we do? We can look to how each of these men endured and, if they were brave, you should desire to have their courage in your spirit. If they died weak and fearful, nothing was lost. Either they're worthy because their virtue satisfies you, or unworthy because

---

49. That is, Caesar and Octavian, who became Augustus, respectively.
50. It is a commonplace in Seneca and other Roman writers influenced by Stoic thinking that Cato represents or embodies the state and liberty.

their cowardice does not. What is more disgraceful than for the best of men to be afraid to die like a man? **16.3.** So, let's give a man praise every time he's worthy of praise and say, "How bravely done! What a happy outcome! You have escaped every accident, jealousy, and sickness. You have broken free of the prison. You aren't thought worthy of a bad fortune by the gods, but you are unworthy of one in which Fortune can affect you." But we must fortify those who back away and look back to life at the moment of their death.

16.4. I won't weep for a happy man or for a man who weeps. The former wipes away my tears himself, the latter, with his own tears, makes himself unworthy of any tears. Shall I cry for Hercules because he burned alive, or for Regulus because he was pierced by so many spikes, or for Cato because he ripped open the wound he gave himself? All of these men discovered that to live for eternity cost only a little of their time, and all became immortal by dying.

17.1. There is also plenty of scope for anxieties if you anxiously hide your feelings and don't put an honest face on for anyone. The lives of many are like that, made up, made for display, because consistent self-examination is agony and they fear to be seen other than what they normally are. We are never free from worry when we think we are being judged every time we're looked at, because many things happen against our will that leave us naked. And, even if so much trouble over one's outward appearance turns out well, life can't properly be happy or carefree for those who always live under a mask. **17.2.** On the other hand, straightforward honesty when it is sincere and uncomplicated, and when it hides none of its character, is such a pleasure! Yet a life lived in the open runs the risk of contempt, since there are those who loathe whatever they get close to. But for virtue there is no risk of being despised when people can see it, and it is better to be despised for honesty than to be damaged by constant pretending. Nevertheless, we should be balanced: there's a big difference between living honestly and living carelessly.

17.3. The spirit should also retreat far into itself. Even when it's properly done, close interaction with someone dissimilar can cause upset, bring back emotions and open up again whatever weakness of the spirit has not been completely healed. Time alone and time with people should be interspersed and alternated. The former will make us desire human company, the latter our own; each is a therapy for the other. Solitude will heal an aversion to crowds, crowds the weary boredom of solitude. **17.4.** The mind shouldn't be kept invariably at the same level of exertion either, but should be distracted for fun. Socrates was not embarrassed to play with little children, and Cato used to relax with wine when tired out by political concerns. Scipio too, a triumphator[51] and a soldier, used to dance to the beat—not strutting effeminately, as is the style now for those who sway with every step even more like a woman than a woman, but like our forefathers did. They used to leap and strike the ground to a manly beat during festival times and didn't think it was embarrassing to be seen dancing by their enemies. **17.5.** And our spirits should have time for relaxation: they return from rest better and keener than before. Just as we shouldn't ask too much from fertile fields (sowing without a break will swiftly drain them), so too constant hard work breaks the power of spirits. They gain back their strength after taking a break and resting for a while. A kind of dimness and sluggishness of the spirit comes from constant hard work. **17.6.** Humans wouldn't possess such a desire for recreation unless games and jokes had a kind of natural delight in them. But all the substance and all the energy is taken away from our spirits by enjoying games too frequently. Sleep, for instance, is necessary for revitalizing ourselves, but if we sleep day and night all the time, we are dead. There's a big difference between relaxing something and breaking it up.

17.7. Those who established our laws instituted holidays so that men could come together in public for fun. It's as if they were setting a required moderation on our hard work. Some sensible men give themselves holidays every month on set days, others divide up every day into work and retirement. I remember what kind of man Asinius Pollio, the great orator, was.[52] He never worked past the tenth hour.[53] He wouldn't even read letters after that, so that no new worry would come up. He shrugged off all the weariness of the day with

---

51. That is, a field general who had been hailed as *imperator* by his troops after a significant victory. This decision was ratified by the Senate, and the individual was given a public procession and lifelong glory. Under the Republic this was one of the most significant public achievements.

52. Gaius Asinius Pollio, a significant military figure during the civil war between Caesar and Pompey, was also a distinguished politician and author. He was an early patron of Vergil.

53. A Roman day was split into twelve equal parts of night and twelve of day, so the hours were longer or shorter depending on the time of year. The tenth hour generally falls somewhere between 3:00 and 4:00 p.m.

those two hours. Others rest in the middle of the day, and set aside the hours after noon for some less demanding work. Our ancestors also disallowed the introduction of new business in the Senate after the tenth hour. Soldiers, too, divide up the watches, but those returning from an expedition are exempt from watch duty. **17.8.** The spirit should indulge in and be given rest and retirement, which is a food for the spirit and a place to get strong.

We should stroll about in open spaces so that the spirit can lift itself and grow with the boundless sky and lots of fresh air; frequent changes of speed, direction, or locale will promote strength, and so will social occasions and generous amounts of drink. We should sometimes even come close to being drunk, not to the point that it overcomes us—just so that it loosens us up. Wine, you see, washes away our worries and rouses the spirit from deep within. Just as wine is a tonic for some illnesses, it's also a tonic for sadness. The god Liber[54] is not said to be the inventor of wine by some linguistic accident, but because wine liberates the spirit from slavery to our worries, claims it for his own, invigorates it, and makes it more daring in every endeavor. **17.9.** But, just as for Freedom,[55] the healthiness of wine can be found in moderation. People believe that Solon[56] and Arcesilaus[57] indulged in wine; Cato was often accused of drunkenness. But they will find it easier to prove a crime is an honest act than to show that Cato is a disgrace. Still, we shouldn't drink often, in case the spirit is led to adopt a bad habit. Nevertheless, sometimes the spirit needs to be dragged into playful freedom, and gloomy sobriety needs to be set aside for a little while. **17.10.** And if we trust the Greek poet, "Sometimes it's fun to get crazy too."[58] Or Plato, "A man in control of himself knocks

---

54. This is the name (Liber = "Free") of an Italic god of fertility, who was associated with the Greek god Dionysus.

55. *Libertas*, by the period Seneca was writing, had become a heavily charged term, often used as a rallying cry for those opposed to the Principate, because *libertas* encompassed the idea of the right to free speech. See the depiction of Cato in *De Constantia* sec. 2 (and sec. 16 above).

56. A central figure and political reformer in sixth-century BCE Athens, considered one of the Seven Sages of antiquity.

57. A Greek philosopher of the third century BCE, credited with shifting the Academy toward Skepticism; the Skeptic school of thought was very important for the development of Stoicism; see Introduction.

58. It's not clear whom Seneca is quoting here.

in vain at the doors of poetry's house."[59] Or Aristotle, "Great talent is not without its share of insanity."[60]

17.11. A mind can't formulate a magnificent thought, I mean one that goes beyond other thoughts, unless it is inspired. When it has disdained what is common and habitual and has risen up above all, driven up by a divine impulse, then at last it can sing something too sublime for mortal lips. As long as the mind is housed in the body, it can't touch lofty things, placed high out of reach. It must cut itself free from normal life, seize the bit in its mouth, take its rider, and run wild where it had been afraid to go by itself.[61] **17.12.** My dearest Serenus, you possess what is needed to safeguard serenity, to restore it, and to resist faults as they creep in. But know this: when you are seeking to preserve a fragile thing, none of these is strong enough without intense and constant care encircling the spirit as it wavers.

---

59. This is a close translation of Plato's *Phaedrus* 317.

60. This is a loose translation of Aristotle's *Problemata* 30.

61. An allusion to Plato's theories of the soul. This seems not to be the tripartite soul found in Plato's *Phaedrus* but the bipartite soul in *Republic*.

On the Shortness of Life

(*De Brevitate Vitae*)

1.1 Most of the human race, Paulinus, complains of Nature's maliciousness, because we are born for a short life and because the spans of time given to us are said to slip by so swiftly and hastily that, apart from a very few people, life deserts us at the very point when we are ready to live. And it has not only been the ignorant mob lamenting over this universal moment—a bad thing, as they call it. This bad attitude has brought out the complaints of honorable men too. This is the source of that famous quote from the greatest of healers, "Life is short, knowledge long,"[1] **1.2.** and the quarrel—not at all appropriate for a wise man—Aristotle had with the universe.[2] He complained that "Nature had given enough years to animals that they could live for five or ten generations but that for a human, although born for great things, a limit is set that much earlier."[3] **1.3.** It's not that we have too little time, it's that we waste too much of it. Life is long enough and is largely given over to the completion of very important deeds, if it should be well organized. But when time melts away because of excess and carelessness, when it is not spent toward a good result, we understand—as that last law of nature finally forces us—that what we didn't realize was going has gone. **1.4.** This is how it is: we aren't given a short life but we make life short, and we aren't deprived of it but throw it away. Just as the abundant resources of a king, when they fall to a bad master, are rapidly squandered, but others, though small, grow with discipline if they are passed on to a good overseer, in the same way our lifespan is wide open for one who arranges it well.

2.1. Why do we complain about the universe? It has been good to us: life, if you know how to use it, is long. But unquenchable greed holds one person back, eagerness to work hard at work that's unnecessary holds back another. One man is soaked with wine, another swollen with sloth. Desire for the kind of success that always depends on the

---

1. Hippocrates. This is the first Hippocratic aphorism translated into Latin from Greek.
2. Aristotle deals with such questions in his *Parva Naturalia*, but see note below.
3. This seems rather to be a saying of Theophrastus, who followed Aristotle as the head of the Peripatetic School.

approval of others wears one man down, and a reckless desire for trade leads another around every land and sea in the hope of profit. Some men are twisted by their craving for military service, always intent on taking others' lives or worried about saving their own. And there are some who have been ruined by adoring—but not being appreciated by—their superiors: they have become slaves by choice. **2.2.** The urge to live another's lot in life, or to complain about their own, takes hold of many others. And unsteady, uncertain, and dissatisfied inconsistency tosses most into new schemes, because they aren't following a set plan. Some aren't happy with any path they can take through life. Instead, their deaths overtake them while they're yawning languidly, so much so that I'm sure what the greatest of poets said, as if he was a prophet of the gods, is true: "The part of life we actually live is short."[4] Every other moment is not life, just time spent.

2.3. Faults push at and hem us in on all sides and don't allow us to raise or lift our eyes to an examination of truth. These faults hold down those who are sunk and stuck in their desires—men who can never return to themselves. If ever some peaceful moment comes upon them by chance, they rise on it and then fall. It's as if they are in deep water when there is still the swell of the waves even after a storm, but there is no retirement for them from their passions. **2.4.** Do you think I'm talking about those whose troubles are common knowledge? Look at those whose happiness and prosperity the mob rushes after: they are being smothered by their own wealth. My goodness! Wealth is such a heavy burden for many people! And see how skill at public speaking and daily worry over proving their talent bleeds many dry! Look how many get sick because they don't take a break from pleasures! Or how for many the surrounding mob of clients leaves no free time. Go through the whole list from the bottom all the way to the top: this man acts as legal counsel, this one lends his support, that one there is on trial, that one there defends, that one judges. No one works to free himself: each person gets used up working on someone else's behalf. Ask about those whose names everyone learns and you will see that they are distinguished by the following signs: that man serves the interests of the other, and this one the interests of yet another. But no one serves his own interests. **2.5.** Finally, the indignation some men feel

---

4. Many poets have been proposed, including Vergil, Homer, and Menander, but the lack of a clear source makes certainty impossible.

is the silliest of all: they complain about the scorn of their superiors, because their superiors didn't make time for them when they wanted. How can a man who doesn't even make time for himself dare to complain about a snobbish rejection from another? That important man looked at you, whoever you are, at some point, even if it was with an arrogant glance, he turned his ears to your words, he called you to his side. But you never think it's right to take a look at yourself, to hear yourself. So there's no reason for you to total up the favors you've done to anyone's bill—after all, when you did the favors you didn't want to be with that person and you weren't able to be with yourself.

3.1. Even if all the brilliant minds that ever burned bright were to consider this one problem together, they could not sufficiently express their astonishment at the blindness of the human mind. People don't allow anyone to occupy their farms, and if there is the slightest disagreement about boundaries, they scurry for rocks and weapons. But they do allow other people to march into their own lives—no, they even bring the people who will take over their lives themselves. No one can be found who wants to divide up his money and give it away, but each and every person hands out his life to as many people as possible! They all feel obliged to guard their wealth, but when they come to spending time they are most extravagant with the one thing it's noble to be stingy with.

3.2. So I'd like to pull someone out of a crowd of old people (and say), "We see that you've made it to the limits of a human lifespan— one hundred or more years are weighing on you. Come now, think back over your life so you can balance your 'accounts.' Total up how much time a creditor or a girl took, or how much a king took, or a client, or quarrels at home, or arguing with slaves, or business concerns up and down the city. Add to that the illnesses we bring upon ourselves and the time that was wasted for no good purpose too. You'll see that you have fewer years to your credit than you thought. **3.3.** Think back and remember: When were you faithful to a plan? How many days passed as you had intended? When was a day set aside just for your use? When did your expression show what you actually felt? When was your spirit unshaken? What have you done in such a long life? How many men stole your life away while you didn't notice what you were losing? How much did suffering without cause, foolish pleasures, greedy passions, and empty conversations take away? The years left to you are very few: if you think about it, you'll see that you're going to die an untimely death." **3.4.** Why does this happen, then? Because you all live as if you'll always be alive. It never occurs to you to think about life's fragility. You don't pay attention to how much time has passed already. You waste time as if it comes from a full, deep well when in the meantime it may be that today, which is being sacrificed for some person or for some business or other, is your very last. You fear everything as a mortal might—but you desire everything as if you are immortal. **3.5.** You'll hear many say, "I'm going to take it easy after I'm fifty, and I'm going to retire fully when I'm sixty." Tell me, what guarantee of a long life are you getting? Who's going to allow these plans of yours to go the way you're arranging them? Aren't you embarrassed to be leaving the leftovers of your life for yourself, for your good mind, and to buy on layaway only the time that can't be devoted to any other activity?

4.1. You'll see very powerful and prominent men drop the following kinds of comments: They desire some retirement, they praise it, and they value it more than all their possessions. Meanwhile they want to come down from the pinnacles of their success, if there were some way to do it safely. You see, even when nothing shakes or strikes it from the outside, Fortune falls in on itself. **4.2.** The Divine Emperor Augustus, to whom the gods offered more than to any other, did not cease to pray for quiet time and to seek freedom from his duty to the state. All of his conversations came back to this: that he hoped for time to rest. With this sweet, if false, comfort he used to lighten his hard work: that at some point he would live for himself. **4.3.** I found these words in a letter he sent to the Senate, when he had promised that he would not retire in a way that didn't recognize his position or that would be at odds with his earlier glorious public recognitions: "It is a more beautiful thing to do something than to promise it. But the desire for the retirement I most hope for pushes me to take some delight even in the pleasure of talking about it, since I must delay the pleasure of the actual experience." **4.4.** Time for retirement seemed such an important thing to him that he imagined it in his thoughts since he couldn't put it into practice. He who saw everything depending on him alone, he who affected the fates of men and countries, used to think very happily about the day when he would cast off his greatness. **4.5.** He knew by experience how much sweat those good deeds, famous throughout the lands, demanded from him, how much hidden anxiety they covered over. Forced to settle things by war, first with fellow citizens, then with fellow magistrates, and in the end with in-laws and family, he poured out blood on land and sea. Driven by war through Macedonia, Sicily, Egypt, Syria, and Asia, and almost every other land, he ordered his armies, worn out with killing their countrymen, to do an about-face to attack enemies outside our borders.[5] And while he brought peace to the Alps and crushed enemies mixed in and among the peaceful parts of the Empire, while he extended the borders beyond the Rhine, the Euphrates, and the Danube, back in Rome the swords of Murena, Caepio, Lepidus, Egnatius,[6] and others were being sharpened against him. **4.6.** He hadn't quite escaped their plotting even then: his daughter and many young noblemen bound to her in service by adultery as if by a soldier's oath[7] alarmed him, when he was already worried about old age. There was Jullus too, and a woman with an Antonius again, a thing Augustus could really worry about.[8] He amputated these open sores with the limbs they were on too, but others grew up underneath. Just like a body swollen with too much blood, the Empire was always coming apart somewhere. And so he kept wishing for retirement, and his good works rested in his hopes and imaginings. This was the wish of a man who was able to make any wish come true.

5.1. Cicero, while he was tossed about among Catilines and Clodiuses, Pompeys, and Crassuses (some open enemies, others fair-weather friends), while he was driven back and forth with the state, keeping it from getting worse—and he was banished in the end, neither peaceful in happy circumstances nor patient in adversity—how many times he must have cursed his own consulship, which he

---

5. During Augustus' life, all of these places had been under Roman rule and some had been bases for his political enemies.

6. Marcus Aemilius Lepidus, son of the *triumvir*, was implicated in a conspiracy to kill Augustus in 30 BCE after the Battle of Actium. Aulus Terentius Varro Murena was executed in 22 BCE along with Gaius Fannius Caepio. Marcus Egnatius Rufus was executed in 19 BCE for his part in a conspiracy surrounding elections.

7. Julia is presented in our sources as a notorious adulteress, and she was eventually relegated (a form of exile) by Augustus never to return to Rome. She was given in marriage at the age of 14, widowed at 16, then given in marriage to Augustus' chief advisor Marcus Agrippa again at 18 and then again at 28 to Tiberius, Augustus' successor. Julia's marriages (like those of many women of noble families) were a means to secure political relationships.

8. Julia's affairs seem to have become public after Tiberius fled Rome for Capri in 6 BCE. Jullus Antonius was a son of Marcus Antonius, Augustus' chief opponent for power until the Battle of Actium in 31 BCE.

praised justifiably but unceasingly.[9] **5.2.** The words he utters in that
letter to Atticus (after the elder Pompey was defeated and the younger
was reviving his broken army in Spain) are so terribly sad: "What am
I doing at this point, you ask? I am lingering, half-free, in my villa
at Tusculum."[10] He adds other comments later, in which he weeps
over his former life, complains about the present, and despairs of the
future. **5.3.** Cicero called himself "half-free" but, by Hercules, a wise
man will never present himself under so dishonorable a name, will
never be half-free, but always has his liberty intact and true. He is set
apart, under his own power, and more noble than the rest. What can
conquer a man who conquers Fortune?

6.1. Livius Drusus,[11] a passionate and strong man, brought forward
unusual legislation—I mean proposed bad solutions, like the Gracchi
did[12]—supported by a huge gathering of all Italy. Although he did not
see the outcome of his efforts, it is reported that Livius, after cursing
a life troubled from birth, said he was the only person who had never
had a holiday, even as a boy. He wasn't permitted to direct his legisla-
tive campaign and wasn't free to let it go once it had begun. You see,
he dared, although a little orphan boy and wearing the *toga praetexta*,[13]
to speak on behalf of defendants in court. And he threw about his

---

9. Cicero did in fact write both prose and verse accounts of the events of his consulship
in 63 BCE, which included the suppression of a revolt led by Sergius Catilina, and
encouraged others to write also. Legal questions around the death of Catilina were
the basis of his exile in 58 BCE.

10. Although we have many of Cicero's letters from this period of his life, Seneca
does not seem to be quoting exactly from one we know about. Cicero's letters were
compiled for publication by his freedman Tiro.

11. Marcus Livius Drusus was a tribune of the plebs in 91 BCE who, although he
proposed many pro-senatorial reforms, was assassinated after proposing full citizenship
for Rome's Italian allies; his death led to the Social War (91–88 BCE).

12. Tiberius Gracchus (ca. 168–133 BCE) and then Gaius Gracchus (ca. 159–121 BCE),
almost a decade after his brother's assassination, proposed and enacted a series of legislation aimed at reforms, especially land reform. Gaius was also murdered. The period of
the Gracchi brothers is generally considered a turning point in Roman Republican
politics, leading to the extensive and bitter conflicts of the first century BCE.

13. Seneca is having a bit of fun here to draw a contrast between Drusus' age and his
activity. The *toga praetexta* (which had a broad purple stripe on the hem) was worn by
current or former magistrates with *imperium* (i.e., the highest-ranking officials, who
would naturally use their considerable influence in court on behalf of their friends
and supporters), and also by boys under 16. Drusus' father, of the same name, was
also politically active. He died in 108 BCE.

political influence so effectively that it's well known he forced some rulings to go his way. **6.2.** At what point could such a malformed ambition not rip itself apart? You can be certain that his recklessness, ripe before its time, would have turned into monstrously bad fortune both for his public as well as for his private life. He, a troublemaker from childhood and difficult in the forum, complained too late that he had never had a holiday. There isn't agreement about whether he killed himself: he collapsed all of a sudden with a wound to the gut. Some wondered if his death had been a suicide, but no one wondered if it was appropriate.

6.3. It isn't necessary to mention more examples of people who, although they seem to others very fortunate, give true testimony against themselves that they weren't, because they hated every deed they did over their lifetime. But by complaining like this they didn't change others or themselves. You see, when they finished their grand speeches, their attitudes settle back to that habitual place. **6.4.** My goodness, your life, even if it should last a thousand years or more, will become a short, very brief thing. Your bad habits would eat up a lifetime of any length. But it's inevitable that this lifespan should swiftly slip away from us; rational thought lengthens it, although nature rushes it past. But you don't grab at it, catch it, and hold it back, or even slow down this most swiftly moving thing of all. Instead, you let a lifetime slip away as if it were at the moment unneeded property that you could put your hands on later. **7.1.** I put those who make time for nothing but wine and lust at the top of the list: no one spends time more disgracefully. Others, even if they are controlled by the empty idea of public acclaim, are nevertheless splendid as they go astray. You might include on my list greedy men, men full of rage, or those who act on their hatreds and wage war unjustly, but at least they all fail in a rather manly way. The diseased rot of those who have fallen prey to their appetites and lusts is disgusting. **7.2.** Scrutinize all their time; examine how long they calculate, plot, fear, flatter; how much time they spend securing bail bonds[14] for themselves or others; and how much time they spend at parties, which have become a job for them. Then you'll see how their actions, good or bad, are suffocating them.

---

14. A *vadimonium* (like a bail bond) was usually deposited at the beginning of a civil suit to ensure the appearance of both parties at the time of trial.

7.3. Finally, it's generally agreed that nothing important—not the art of speaking, not the liberal arts—can be done by a busy person, since a divided spirit takes nothing in deeply but spits everything back out as it had been stuffed in. Nothing is less important for a busy man than living, and nothing is more difficult than knowing how to live. There are lots of common teachers of the other arts out there, arts that even boys seem to have learned well enough to be able to teach. But living well must be the study of a lifetime and—what might perhaps surprise you more—so must dying well. **7.4.** So many of the greatest men, after all their burdens had been left behind, when they had renounced their riches, duties, and desires, worked on only one thing to the end of their life: to learn how to live. Even so, most of them die having admitted that they have not yet learned. The others I mentioned above know even less than these greatest men.

7.5. Believe me, it is a quality of a great man, and I mean one who has passed beyond human error, to allow none of his time to be plucked away from him. His life was a long one since he made available to himself every bit of time given to him. Nothing lay untended or idle, nothing was under another's power. Because he was a very frugal steward of his time, he found nothing that was worth exchanging it for. And so, his time was enough for him. But for those from whose lives the mob takes so much, there must always be too little time. **7.6.** And there's no reason to think that the latter do not sometimes see their loss. You will certainly hear most of those weighed down by great prosperity exclaim from the middle of their herds of clients, their law cases, and their other noble misfortunes, "I am not being allowed to live!" **7.7.** But why aren't they being allowed? Everyone who asks you to take a case for them takes you from yourself. How many days has a defendant taken away? A candidate for public office? An old lady tired of burying her heirs? A man pretending to be sick so he can get legacy-hunters all worked up? Or a powerful friend, who keeps you, not in his heart, but as a tool to use? I say balance the books and take stock of the days of your life. You'll see that only a few are left in your account, and even those are spent on nothing.

7.8. The successful candidate wants to set aside the symbols of office he wished for, and says again and again, "When will this term end?" That fellow over there is sponsoring the games, and he considered being in charge of them very beneficial for himself. But he says, "When will I be done with this?" That patron over there rushes around the whole forum and amasses a crowd so big the outer edge can't even hear him plead his case. But then he says, "When will court adjourn?" Each person rushes headlong through his life and struggles under desires for the future and aversions for the present. **7.9.** But the one who gathers up all his time for his own use, who plans every day as if it's his last, doesn't wish for tomorrow or fear it. You see, what could an hour of some unusual pleasure bring him? He knows everything, understands everything, to the fullest. As for the rest, well, Fortune plans that as she wants—but his life is already safe. Fortune is able to give or subtract nothing from his life, and Fortune gives him what he doesn't desire but takes anyway, like food given to a man full to bursting already. **7.10.** So there's no reason for you to think that you have lived because you have gray hair and wrinkles. A man like that has not lived for a long time, but has existed for a long time. What! Do you think that someone is well traveled if a violent storm took him here and there, after being snatched out of a harbor, and with winds from all sides drove him around in a circle? He's not well traveled—he's just been for a bumpy ride.

8.1. I am often amazed when I see people asking others for their time and those who were asked being entirely willing to give it. Both see the thing on which time will be spent, but neither see the time itself. It's as if nothing was asked for, and nothing given. But they're playing a game with the most precious commodity of all. They are deceived because it's intangible. And because they can't see it, they don't value it much—no, they don't value it at all. **8.2.** Men receive big annual salaries and valuable gifts, selling their work, service, and industriousness for them. But none of them values time. They use it as carelessly as if it were free. But look at them when they're sick, or if the danger of dying has moved closer, when they're pleading with doctors, or when they're afraid they're going to get the death penalty. At that point they're prepared to pay out everything they have to live. There are such mixed feelings in them! **8.3.** Now, if the number of years that had gone by and the number yet to come could somehow be published for every person . . . oh, how scared they would get when they saw that few years remained! Oh, how carefully they would use them! It's an easy thing to manage a defined quantity of something, even if it's a small quantity. But when you don't know when something will run out, it ought to be conserved even more carefully. **8.4.** Now, there's no reason to think that they don't know how precious a thing time is. These people often say to those they love very much that they are ready to give up part of their own years for the other person. They do in fact give years, but don't understand in what way. Moreover, they give them in such a way that they take away from their own years without adding on to the other person's. Because they don't realize what account they're taking this amount from, they tolerate the expense of a hidden loss. **8.5.** No one can restore your years to you and no one can give you back to yourself. Your life is going to return to where it began and won't reverse course or stop. It won't raise a fuss and it won't warn you about its speed: it will slip away silently. It won't stretch out longer at a king's command or because of the people's goodwill. It will run on as it has since the first day, and won't ever be diverted or pause. What will happen, then? You're busy and life rushes by . . . but death comes closer, and you'll have to make time for it, whether you like it or not.

9.1. Can anything be more foolish than what some people think? I'm talking about those who brag about their good sense. They expend great effort to spend their time; in order to live better they buy life by paying with their life. They set up plans for the future, but delay is far and away the greatest waste of life. Delay strips away each day, taking away the present while making promises about things that are far in the future. Anticipation, which sets a value on tomorrow but devalues today, is a very powerful obstacle to living. You're trying to manage what's under Fate's control and abandoning what's under your own. In what direction are you looking? In what direction are you exerting yourself? All of the future is uncertain: live every instant. **9.2.** Hear how the greatest of poets cries out and sings a song for your benefit, as if possessed by the divine:

"Every best day of a life for miserable mortals flees first."[15]

"Why are you hesitating," he's saying, "Why are you hanging back? Unless you seize the day, it will flee!" And when you have seized the day, it'll flee anyway. So, we must counter the speed of time with the swiftness of our use of it. We must drink it in quickly, as if from a rapid stream that won't always be there. **9.3.** And he's saying it very elegantly in order to throw our limitless planning back in our faces: he says "every day" and not "every stage." Why do you carelessly and slowly, when times flies so fast, count out your months and years in a long sequence, as your greediness thinks best? He's talking to you

---

15. Vergil, *Georgics* 3.66–67.

about a day, and I mean this one, the one that's already slipping away from you. **9.4.** Is there any doubt therefore that every best day for miserable, I mean busy, mortals flees first? Old age crushes the still childish spirits of these men when they reach it unprepared and defenseless. You see, they didn't really think ahead: they fell into old age suddenly, totally unaware—they didn't realize that it was approaching them every day. **9.5.** Just as conversation or reading or deep thought give travelers a false impression and they realize they've arrived before they think they've gotten close, so the road of life, which we walk down at the same pace awake or asleep, is constant and very short and is not apparent to those who are busy, except at the end.

10.1. Now, if I wanted to divide up what I intended to talk about and to separate out the arguments, I can see there would be many ways I could show that the life of busy men is the shortest. Fabianus[16]—not one of those armchair philosophers, but one of the real, old-fashioned kind—used to say, "One must fight passions head on, not with cunning, and counter their attack not with many little strikes but with an all-out offensive." He did not approve of empty words. "You see," he said, "passions ought to be ripped to pieces, not picked at." To show people the error of their ways, they must be taught as well as criticized.

10.2. Life can be split into three periods: what was, what is, and what will be. Of these, what we're doing is brief, what we're about to do is in doubt, what we did is certain. You see, Fate has lost its power over the past, which can't be brought back under another's authority. Busy men lose this time, because they don't make room for being mindful of the past. And even if they do make room, the recollection of something they regret is unpleasant. **10.3.** So, these men don't willingly focus on time spent badly. And they don't dare to try to do again those actions whose faults, even though they were masked by the lure of an imminent pleasure, become obvious after a reassessment. No one willingly makes himself look at the past, except someone who has done everything with a capacity for judgment that can't be deceived. **10.4.** The man who has desired in excess, shown scorn out of arrogance, conquered without mastery, ensnared through trickery, taken greedily, spent out of overindulgence . . . this man will necessarily fear

---

16. Papirius Fabianus, who lived in the first part of the first century CE, was apparently known to Seneca, and certainly to Seneca's father. Fabianus' early career was spent as a rhetorician, but he later turned to philosophy; he is admired by Seneca for both.

his own memory.[17] And this period of our time, the past, is set apart and dedicated, passing beyond all human failures and removed from the tyranny of Fortune. Neither poverty, nor fear, nor illness can get to it. The past can't be ruined or taken away: it's a permanent and unshakeable possession. Days are present to us only one at a time, and these only minute by minute. But all the days of time past, whenever you command, will be there for you, will allow themselves to be examined with a critical eye and be remembered. This is something there's no time for busy men to do. **10.5.** It is characteristic of a secure and peaceful mind to examine all the parts of its life. The spirits of busy men, however, like oxen under the yoke, aren't able to turn and look at themselves. Their life, then, slips away into the abyss. It doesn't matter how much is given to them if there is no place for it to be stored, just as it's no use to dump as much of something as you like into a container if there's nothing on the bottom to receive and retain it. Time passes through their spirits as if they were battered and full of holes.

10.6. The present is the briefest kind of time, so brief that it doesn't seem like anything at all to some people. It's always in motion—it flows and tumbles along. It ceases to be before it arrives, no more allowing itself to be delayed than the universe or the stars do, whose never-resting motion never remains in the same moment. So, the present moment, which is so brief that it can't be caught, is all that matters to busy men, and even this much is taken away from them because they are pulled in many directions.

11.1. In short, do you want to understand how short a time they live? Then look at how much they want to live for a long time. Old men, shadows of what they were, pray like beggars for a few additional years. They pretend that they're younger than they are, flatter themselves with lies, and happily deceive themselves—as if they could trick death at the same time. But at the moment some frailty reminds them of their mortality, how fearfully they begin to die, not so much departing life as being hauled away from it. They wail that they have been so stupid not to live and, if only they could get well again, they would live in retirement from public life. Then they think about how they prepared in vain for things that did not come to pass, how every effort was sacrificed to no purpose. **11.2.** But for those who live life far from

---

17. There is a play on words in the Latin here. *Memoria* for the Romans was not just your own memory, but also what people remember you for after your death.

all kinds of business, how could life not be long? None of it is handed over to another, none strewn about here and there, none given up to Fortune, none wasted through neglect, none drained away through excess, none redundant. All of it, one might say, pays out dividends. So, even a very small amount is more than enough. That's why, when the last day comes, a wise man does not hesitate to walk steadily into death.

12.1. You may be asking yourself whom I mean when I say "busy men." You shouldn't think that I'm talking only about those whom the night-patrol dogs chase out of the courthouse, or those whom you see either jostled in their own crowd of supporters to put on a good show or jostled with contempt in someone else's crowd. I don't only mean those whom duty calls from their own houses so they can knock on other peoples' doors, or those whom the praetor's spear keeps busy for their disreputable profit,[18] a profit that will fester like pus one day. **12.2.** Even retirement keeps some men "busy": in their own villa or in their own bed, surrounded by solitude, withdrawn from everything, they are a danger to themselves. We shouldn't say they're living in retirement but that they're busy at being lazy. Do you say a man is living in retirement when he arranges his Corinthian bronze-ware—which has become valuable because of the crazy obsession of a small number of people—in a meticulously fussy way and spends the greater part of each day consumed with his tarnished plates? What about the man who eagerly watches boys roll about in the ring? (My god! We are suffering from vices that aren't even *Roman!*[19]) What about the one who separates his flocks of slaves into pairs by age and color or trains athletes according to the newest fad? **12.3.** What, do you think men are "retired" when they waste many hours at the barber while anything that grew the night before is plucked out and there's a big discussion over each and every hair while it's all neatly arranged and the stray ones pulled back to the front? Oh, they get angry, don't they, if the barber isn't careful enough. As if he were shaving a real man! They explode with rage if any of their mane is cut off, if any of it's messy, if it's not all

---

18. That is, busy at auctions carried out under the authority of a praetor. A spear was thrust into the ground to symbolically represent the praetor's (and his agent's) ownership and authority to sell the goods and/or property.

19. Wrestling was considered a Greek sport, but there are also intimations here of the kind of voyeurism and boy-love often associated with the Greek *palaestra*.

in tiny ringlets! Is there a single one of them who wouldn't prefer that the state got messed up instead of his hair, or who wouldn't be more concerned for the state of his hair than the state of his health? Wouldn't each prefer to look a better man than to be a better man? Are we saying they're retired when they're busy moving between comb and mirror? **12.4.** And what about those who are occupied with writing, hearing, and learning poems? They strain their voices, which nature gave the best and plainest range, into useless variations of melody. Their fingers are always keeping the beat to some song they're practicing in their head. And their silent melody can be heard plainly when they're guests at some important event, or even at sad events. They're not retired—they're ungainfully employed. **12.5.** Good grief, I can't even count their dinner parties as relaxation time, since I see how anxiously they set out the silver, how carefully they belt up the tunics of their perfumed and oiled slaves. They hang by a thread worrying about how the cook will prepare the boar, how quickly the smooth-cheeked slave boys will hurry to their duties when the signal is given, how artfully they'll carve up the birds into bite-sized chunks, and how carefully the poor little fellows will wipe away drunk guests' vomit. On such things, after all, a reputation for elegance and sophistication is built! And their badness follows them so far into every private place of their life that they don't drink or eat without looking for popularity. **12.6.** I don't think the men who take themselves here and there on litters or sedan chairs and rush to spend hours being carried around (as if they couldn't go without) are retired either. Someone else tells them when to wash, when to swim, when to eat: their precious little spirits are so soft with too much inactivity that they don't even know on their own whether or not they're hungry!

12.7. I hear that one of these precious darlings (if indeed you can call unlearning life and human behavior "precious"[20]), when he was carried out by hand from his bath and set on his litter, said in a questioning tone, "Am I sitting yet?" Do you think this man, who didn't know whether he was sitting or not, knows whether he is alive, can see, or is relaxing in retirement? I can't easily say whether I would pity him more if he really didn't know, or if he just pretended he didn't know. **12.8.** Men like this have forgotten many things but they also pretend to have forgotten many more. Some vices please

---

20. That is, unlearning the patterns of living that a human being has by nature instead of, as a Stoic wise man, living according to nature.

them as if they were visible proof of their prosperity. As far as they're concerned, it seems to be characteristic of a common and contemptible person to know what one is doing. Go ahead, think that the mime writers have to make stuff up to criticize luxury. My goodness, they pass over more real stuff than they make up. In fact, in an age so creative in this area, such a wealth of unbelievable vices has been generated that we can actually accuse the mime writers of not keeping up! Is it so strange in this age that there can be a man so deadened by his little pleasures that he has to depend on another person to tell him whether he is sitting down or not? **12.9.** This man, therefore, is not retired from public life—you must put some other label on it. He's sick—no, he's dead. A man can only be in retirement if there is also some awareness of his retirement. But a man is only half-alive if he needs someone else to help him understand the state of his own body. How can such a person be the master of his time? **13.1.** It would take a long time to go one by one through those whose lives are wasted in gambling, or ball games, or an interest in roasting their bodies in the sun. They're not retired if pleasure is their business.

No one will have any doubt about the following men either: those who are occupied with the study of useless literature are spending a lot of effort doing nothing. And there are now a great number of them who are Roman too.[21] **13.2.** It was a sickness for the Greeks to ask how many rowers Odysseus had or which was written first, the *Iliad* or the *Odyssey*, and whether or not they were both by the same author. There were other things like this that don't help you understand yourself at all if you keep it quiet. And if you tell others you don't seem more educated, just more irritating. **13.3.** This empty eagerness for learning empty facts has infected the Romans too. Lately, I heard someone reporting each of the first Roman generals to do certain things. Duilius[22] was first to win a naval battle, Curius Dentatus was first to have elephants in a triumphal procession. Now, even if these facts do not contribute to true renown, they do get passed around as examples of civic greatness. There is no benefit to such knowledge, but it is knowledge that entices and entraps us with its splendid nothingness.

---

21. In Seneca's time, many people, called *grammatici*, wrote and argued about the interpretation of literature and about proper grammar and usage.
22. Gaius Duilius was the first Roman to command a decisive naval victory, during the First Punic War (264–241 BCE).

13.4. We should also forgive those investigating who was the first to persuade Romans to embark upon a ship (it was Claudius and because of this he was called Caudex,[23] since a joining together of many planks of wood was called a *caudex* by the ancients, which is why public records are called *codices*[24] and ships that go up and down the Tiber, now as well as in olden days, are called *codicariae*). **13.5.** Perhaps this matters too, that Valerius Corvinus was the one who first conquered Messana and the first of the Valerii, after he added the name of the conquered city to his own,[25] to be called Messana. Bit by bit, as common use changed the sound, he was called Mesala. **13.6.** Perhaps you'd also not mind if someone cared that Lucius Sulla[26] was first to offer lions loose in the circus? They'd been offered before that, but chained, with javelin throwers sent by King Bocchus[27] to kill them. This could be allowed too, surely. Does it matter in the least that Pompey was the first to have offered eighteen elephants in the circus for a fight with criminals sent in to battle them? A man, *princeps* of the state and famous among ancient *principes* for his extremely kind-hearted nature,[28] thought that it would be a kind of show to kill men innovatively. A fight to the death? Not enough. Ripped to shreds? Not enough. Let's have them crushed under the weight of enormous

---

23. Roman naming practices sometimes included a *cognomen* after the *praenomen* and *nomen*. The *cognomen* almost always made some reference to an identifying characteristic, often physical, that was associated with the individual or his ancestors.

24. Originally the *codex* was a set of pieces of wood or wood tablets with wax bound on one or both sides. The knots could be sealed with wax and a stamp, thus making a secure document.

25. Another naming practice: victorious generals were allowed to assume the name of the conquered region as a fourth name, the *agnomen*. Marcus Valerius Corvinus led successful attacks on several Sicilian towns during the First Punic War.

26. Lucius Cornelius Sulla (138–78 BCE) began his career under Gaius Marius in the African campaigns of the Numidian and Jugurthine wars. After rising in power to compete with Marius and marching on Rome with his armies twice to secure concessions and power from the Senate, Sulla was made dictator. Author of a number of important pieces of legislation and constitutional reforms during this time, Sulla also instituted the notorious proscriptions, as a result of which many Romans were executed summarily and their property confiscated. Relinquishing power in 79 BCE, Sulla died in 78 BCE.

27. Bocchus was king of Mauretania in North Africa during Rome's war with King Jugurtha of Numidia (who was his son-in-law). Bocchus eventually betrayed Jugurtha, handing him over to Lucius Sulla and ending the war.

28. This is ironic, because Pompey was known to have a mean streak.

beasts! **13.7.** It would have been better for such things to be forgotten, so that some powerful person couldn't learn about it afterwards and emulate so inhumane an action. Goodness! Great prosperity throws a great blindness over our spirits. When he was throwing so many troops of wretched men to beasts born under a foreign sky, when he was making war between such different creatures, when he shed so much blood in full view of the Roman people—and was soon going to shed more Roman blood[29]—Pompey believed he was greater than the world. But, the same man was later deceived by scheming in Alexandria.[30] He finally understood that his cognomen, The Great, was an empty boast[31] when he let himself be stabbed by the least of his slaves.

13.8. But, to get back to my point and show the carefully useless work of some men on this very topic. The same writer was saying that Metellus,[32] after the Carthaginians on Sicily were defeated, was the only Roman to have led in procession before his chariot one 120 captured elephants. Sulla was the last Roman to have extended the pomerium[33]: it was the custom before that to extend it only because of the acquisition of Italian territory, not provincial territory.[34] Is it more beneficial to know this than to know that the Aventine Hill is beyond the *pomerium*, as this writer argues, because of one or the other reason, either because the plebs seceeded[35] there, or because when Remus took the auspices on that place the bird-omens had not been favorable? Anyway, there are uncountable stories like this, either full

---

29. In the Civil War with Caesar from 49–45 BCE.

30. In the Civil War between Caesar and Pompey, Caesar won a final crushing victory at Pharsalus in 49 BCE. Pompey then fled to Egypt, where he was killed by his own men as he landed.

31. Gnaeus Pompeius Magnus was his full name. His *cognomen* Magnus means "The Great."

32. Lucius Caecilius Metellus (born ca. 290–221 BCE) defeated Hasdrubal, father of Hannibal, at the Battle of Panormus. The Carthaginians were known for their use of elephants in battle.

33. The *pomerium* was the sacred boundary marking the limits of the city of Rome.

34. Provincial territory refers to any land outside of the Italian peninsula, which would then be governed by an elected or appointed Roman magistrate. Sicily was the first Roman province.

35. At critical moments in the history of the early Republic, the *plebs* (the large underclass of the Roman people, although there were many very wealthy and politically active plebeians) withdrew from the city of Rome as a symbol of their withdrawal of support or to leverage a concession from the ruling class (or both).

of lies or just like lies. **13.9.** Although you may admit that these men tell us things in good faith, that they pledge to write the truth, whom do they help avoid mistakes? Whose lusts do they control? Whom do they make stronger, more just, more generous? Our friend Fabianus used to say that he wondered whether it was better to be motivated by no learning at all than to be tangled up in learning of this kind.

14.1. The only ones who are retired, the only ones who are alive, are those who make time for wisdom. They don't just watch over their own life well, they add every past generation to their own. They have gained all the years that passed before they were born. Unless we're extremely ungrateful, these founders of holy beliefs, these very noble men, were born for our benefit and have prepared a life for us. We are being led by another's labor to the most beautiful things, things that have been rescued from the darkness and brought into the light. No century is denied to us—we are allowed into all of them. And if we can manage to pass beyond the limitations of human weakness because of our strength of spirit, there's plenty of time through which we can travel. **14.2.** We can debate with Socrates, be skeptical with Carneades, have a good time with Epicurus, conquer human nature with the Stoics, depart from it with the Cynics.[36] Since nature allows us to participate in every generation, why shouldn't we pass over with our whole spirit from this time, brief and fading, to those times, immeasurable, eternal, and shared with better men? **14.3.** People who rush about with their obligations, who make themselves and others unsettled—after they've become truly insane, after they've called on everybody every day and not passed by any open door, after they've disseminated their "Good Morning, sirs!" for money at all sorts of different houses[37]—how many of them will be able to see each person in a city so huge and confused by many different desires? **14.4.** How many will send them away because of sleep, extravagance, or impoliteness? How many, after making them wait for a long time, will run past pretending to be in a hurry? How many will avoid going out

36. Socrates' philosophical method was founded on debate around an ethical question (dialectic). Carneades was an important proponent of Skepticism during the second century BCE, who also visited Rome; Skeptics held that true knowledge was impossible. The Cynics (whose name means "doglike") believed like the Stoics that happiness could be attained through virtue and living according to human nature, but took a much more ascetic view, embracing extreme poverty.
37. That is, not passed up any opportunity to give the morning *salutatio* or to receive the *sportula.*

through an atrium filled with clients and will slip out their houses' hidden doors? As if it's not more impolite to trick someone than to deny them entry! How many important men, half-asleep and sick with yesterday's hard partying, and through a very rude yawn, will barely say the name (it's been whispered to him very softly a million times) of the poor fellow who's cut short his own sleep to wait for him to wake up.

14.5. Those who, as they might say, wish to consider Zeno and Pythagoras and Democritus and the other chief priests of the noble arts, and Aristotle and Theophrastus, as their closest friends[38]—I think these are spending their time on real obligations. All of them will make time for another person. All of them will send a visitor away happier and liking his own life better. None of them will allow anyone to go away empty handed. They can meet with all mortals, day and night. **15.1.** None of these will tell you to die, but they'll all teach you how to die. None of these will take away your years, but will pass down their own to you. It's not dangerous to have a conversation with any of them, or a capital crime to be their friend, or too expensive. You'll take from them whatever you want, and it won't be their fault that you didn't drink in as much as you could have. **15.2.** An amazing happiness and a beautiful old age await a man who makes himself a client to these philosophers! He'll have people with whom he can consider matters big and small, whom he can consult every day about how he's doing, from whom he can hear the truth without being insulted, by whom he can be praised without flattery, and in whose image he can make himself. **15.3.** There is a saying: it was not in our power to choose the parents we ended up with—they were given to us by chance. But it is possible to be the child of these good men by choice. Among them are families of the noblest blood: choose which you wish to be adopted into. You will not only be adopted in name, but with an inheritance. This inherited property must not be managed selfishly and with a miser's heart: it will get bigger the more you divide it up among many others. **15.4.** These men will give you a path toward eternity and will raise you up to that place from which no one can cast you down. This is the only conceivable plan for extending your mortal life or, rather, for making your life immortal. Public office, monuments, anything ambition orders by its decrees or builds with its deeds are quickly corrupted—there's nothing the long years don't shake and demolish. But it isn't possible to harm

---

38. Seneca means philosophy here, given the examples he names.

things wisdom has raised to immortality. Time will not erase them or diminish them. The next age and the one after that will always add a degree of sincere respect because spiteful jealousy is only turned against people close by and because we admire things that are farther away more honestly. **15.5.** Therefore, the life of a wise man is extended greatly. The limit set for other men is not the same for him: he alone is released from the laws of humankind and every age treats him as if he were a god. He catches hold with his memory of time that has passed, he uses the present time, and is ready for the future. He makes his life long by collecting all times into one.

16.1. For those who forget the past, don't care about the present, and are afraid for the future, life is very brief and mostly full of worry. When they arrive at their last breath, they understand too late, poor things, that they had been busy for so long accomplishing nothing. **16.2.** And there's no reason to think they led a long life because they sometimes cry out for death—that's not proof. Their ignorance plagues them with passions that are unsteady and that rush toward the very things they fear. Here's the reason they desire death: because they are afraid. **16.3.** And don't think that people live a long time because the day often seems long to them, or because they complain that the hours go by slowly until it's time for the dinner party. You see, whenever the things that keep them busy go away, they are indecisive. Left behind with retirement they don't know how to arrange things in order to prolong it. And so they keep themselves busy somehow, and all the time that lies in between events is hard for them. My goodness! It's just like when the day for the gladiatorial games is announced, or when they're waiting for the time fixed for some spectacle or show or whatever—they want to skip over the days in between. **16.4.** For these people every delay for something they hoped for is a long one, but the time they enjoy it is short and quick, and briefer by far than their own mistake. You see, they run from one thing to another and can't even stand their ground for one lust. They don't have long days—they hate them. On the other hand, the nights seem so short, and they spend them wrapped around whores or a wine bottle. **16.5.** This is where the folly of the poets comes from, when they feed the faults of humankind with their fictions. That Jupiter should double the length of night enticed by the pleasures of sex seemed right to the poets. What other way is there to ignite our ignorance than to give us immoral behavior that is excused by some sick archetype of the divine, to justify them with the gods? The nights that people pay for at such cost—how can they not seem very brief? They waste the day waiting for the night and the night fearing the light of day.

17.1. Their pleasures are hurried and unsettled because of their various fears. At the moment of greatest delight an anxious thought creeps in, "How long will this last?" This attitude makes kings mourn the power they still have, and the magnitude of their good fortune does not entice them from worry. Instead they're terrified of the end that will, eventually, be near. **17.2.** Although he stretched out his army over huge areas of land and didn't count it up in numbers of people but in numbers of units, the king of the Persians,[39] an immoderately extravagant man, wept profusely because within a hundred years none of these fighting men would be alive. But he—the same one who wept—was going to cause their deaths, and would lose some at sea, others on land, some while fighting, others while fleeing. Within a short period of time he wasted those men in combat—and he was fearful about what would happen a century later. **17.3.** Why be surprised that people's joys are also their anxieties? They don't build a foundation of firm motivations, but build on motivations that are toppled by the same futility that produced them. What should we think about times that even they call miserable, when the times they rise up and exalt themselves beyond mortal man are quite flawed? **17.4.** Each of their greatest goods is anxiety-ridden and there is no thought for any good fortune less than the very best—happiness has to be maintained with the next happiness and they have to make more prayers in place of the very same prayers that were answered. You see, everything that comes by chance is impermanent—the higher something rises, the more liable it is to collapse. On the other hand, things that are going to collapse don't delight anyone. Therefore, when people acquire through hard work what they can only keep hold of with even more work, it's inevitable that their lives be not just very short, but also very much to be pitied.

17.5. They pursue what they want with effort, and they hang on to what they pursued fearfully. Meanwhile, there's no consideration for time (it's not going to come back bigger and better than before!). New activities are substituted for the old ones—hope stimulates hope,

---

39. That is, Xerxes, who after the victory at Thermopylae in 480 BCE led the Persians to devastating losses at Salamis (a sea battle) and Plataea (a land battle) and was subsequently hunted back out of Greece.

ambition stimulates ambition. They don't seek an end for their miseries, they just change the raw material that makes misery. Do our own public offices torment us? Those of others take more of our time. Did we stop working after we were candidates for office? We began to get votes for others. Have we avoided the irritation of being in court? We were given the irritation of being a judge. Has a man stopped being a judge? Now he is a fact finder for the court. Did he grow old supervising other people's property for a fee? Now he is occupied with his own wealth. **17.6.** Was Marius discharged from the military? He went on to hold many consulships.[40] Did Quinctius rush to end his dictatorship?[41] He will be called from his plow again. Scipio would do battle with the Carthaginians, although too young for such a duty. As conqueror of Hannibal and conqueror of Antiochus,[42] renowned for his own consulship and the guarantee for his brother's, he would have been set on par with Juppiter if he had not put a stop to it. Political strife would later disturb the savior Scipio and, after he disdained honors equal to the gods in his youth, as an old man he would enjoy flattery from his stiff-necked exile.[43] Causes of anxiety, be they happy or sad, will never be lacking. Life is worn away in activity: retirement is never acted on, always prayed for.

18.1. So, separate yourself from the mob, my dearest Paulinus, and return at last to a calmer harbor, since you've been tossed about too much for someone your age. Consider how many waves you have survived, how many storms you have weathered in your private life, and set sail into in your public life. You have displayed your virtue well enough: the evidence is in your constant hard work. Experience what virtue can accomplish in retirement. The majority of your life, and certainly the better part, has been given to the state. Take some of your own time

---

40. The two consuls (the highest elected officials) were originally given command over armies in the field. Marius held a stunning six consulships; the standard was for a person to only hold the consulship once in a lifetime, rarely twice.

41. That is, L. Quinctius Cincinnatus, who as the story goes was elected dictator (and so had sole command of the Republic in a time of emergency) while he was plowing his field. He fulfilled his duty, then went back to his plow.

42. P. Cornelius Scipio Africanus, victor over Hannibal at Zama in 202 BCE at the age of twenty-six was given the command at an amazingly (for the time) young age. In 189 BCE he accepted the surrender of King Antiochus III.

43. This puts a good face on it: Scipio was charged with financial mismanagement and corruption, and withdrew from public life in 184 BCE to die the next year at his villa in Liternum.

for yourself too. **18.2.** I'm not inviting you to idle and useless rest, to plunge whatever natural energy you have into sleep or the pleasures the mob loves. Such behavior is not "finding rest." When you are at peace again and free from care, you will discover things to do that are more important than all the deeds you have accomplished to this point with so much hard work. **18.3.** You manage the grain supplies of the whole world[44] with as much self-control as if they belonged to another, with as much careful attention as if they belonged to you, and as devoutly as if they belonged to the state. You are well liked, holding an official position in which it's difficult not to be hated. But—believe me—it's better to have a balanced account for your own life than for the public grain supply. **18.4.** Withdraw your vitality of spirit—so capable of handling the greatest of matters—from a public service that is full of honor, of course, but too little suited to a happy life. Think about it! You didn't work from early childhood at every aspect of liberal education so that you could be (rightly) trusted with many thousands of measures of grain! You had promised yourself something better and nobler. There is no shortage of men who are virtuously thrifty and hardworking. Steady beasts of burden are so much more suited to carrying loads than noble racehorses. Who would ever weigh down the dignified speed of a racehorse with heavy sacks? **18.5.** Think too how much danger there is in throwing yourself at such a huge job. Your business involves the human stomach, which doesn't allow for logic and isn't mollified by fairness. And a hungry population is not turned aside by pleading. Just recently, during the days after Gaius Caesar died—if the dead can feel anything he must be upset that he died and the Roman people survived—there was only seven or eight days' worth of grain left! While Gaius had joined ships to make bridges[45] and played with the might of the nation, there was a grain shortage, the worst of all bad things (for the besieged too). The pretend-play of this totally crazy, strange, and calamitously arrogant ruler very nearly brought death, famine, and the

---

44. Paulinus was *praefectus annonnae* from 48 BCE to 55 BCE. This office, appointed by the emperor, had the vital task of ensuring grain supply to Rome (this supply was distributed to the urban populace). Seneca is exaggerating somewhat, but is accurate to the extent that Rome would draw its grain supplies from wherever it could.

45. In 39 CE Caligula built a pontoon bridge using merchant ships across the Bay of Naples (about three miles wide), covering the decks and spreading earth on top, then paraded back and forth for two days imitating Xerxes, according to Suetonius (*Life of Caligula* 19).

total devastation that follows famine. **18.6.** What must those to whom the care of the public grain supply had been entrusted have felt in their spirit at that moment, when they were about to endure stoning, stabbing, being set on fire—and Gaius Caligula. They covered up the great evil hidden[46] in the belly of the state with very skillful deception—and of course they did so with good reason. Certain illnesses must be cured without the patient knowing what's wrong: knowing the nature of an illness is the cause of death for many.

19.1. Retreat to these more peaceful, safer, and more important things! To be concerned with the transport of the grain over the ocean unspoiled by the scams and carelessness of the traders, or with protecting the grain from excessive humidity or heat or with matching the records by volume and weight—do you think all this is the same as it is to approach the sacred and the sublime, ready to learn what is the essence, pleasure, condition, and form of god, or what end awaits your spirit. Or to learn where nature brings us together when we've been released from our bodies, what it is that keeps each of the heaviest things of this world in the middle, raises up the lighter things, carries fire to the highest point, sets the stars into motion in their courses, and all the other things full of profound marvels? **19.2.** Do you wish to see these things with your mind, leaving the earth behind? Now, while your blood is warm and you have energy, it's time to set out for more important things! In such a life the noble arts await you in abundance, as do love of the virtues and of productivity, destruction of passions, knowledge of living, and dying and profound tranquility.

20.1. All who are busy are in a pitiful situation. And it's the most pitiful for those who don't even work on their own work, but sleep on another's schedule, walk on another's route, and are commanded to love and to hate, which should be the things least subject to another's will. If these men wish to know how short their own life is, let them think about how much of it is actually their own. **20.2.** So, when you see the robes of office worn often, when a name is heard in the forum often, don't be resentful. Such things are achieved at a great cost to life. People spend all their years so that just one year can be named after them.[47] The early years of the struggle leave some men behind before they have worked their way to the height of their ambition. The pitiful thought that they

---

46. That is, the short supply of grain.
47. Years were named after the two elected consuls.

had labored for a title to put on their tomb overcomes some people, after they escape through a million indignities to reach the height of dignity and respect. Some grow sick in the last years of life and fail in the middle of grand but inappropriate ventures while lining up new hopes, as young men do. **20.3.** It's a shameful thing when an old man's breath fails him in court, speaking on behalf of plaintiffs who aren't friends, trying to win the support of an ignorant crowd. It's disgusting when a man, tired out by living sooner than by working, collapses on the job. Disgusting, too, when an heir who's been denied his inheritance for a long time laughs as someone falls dead over the account books.

20.4. I can't resist relating an example that has occurred to me. Turannius was a very exact and careful old man, who at ninety years of age,[48] when he had finally been forced by Gaius Caesar to leave his post as procurator, commanded that he be laid out on his bed and—as if dead—to be mourned by his household standing around him. The house was in mourning for the old master's retirement and didn't conclude its grief until he got his job back. Is it really such a distinction to die on the job? **20.5.** Most people have a similar spirit: their passion for work lasts longer than their capacity for work. Because they fight the weakness of their body, they think that old age is a burden, for no other reason than that it makes them old. The law does not allow a soldier to be older than fifty, and does not require a senator to be present for deliberations after sixty. Men have a harder time asking for retirement from themselves than from the law. **20.6.** In the meantime, while they rob and are robbed, while one man disturbs another man's rest and while they make each other miserable, their life is without reward, without pleasure, and without any spiritual improvement. No one keeps their death in sight and no one reaches for hopes that are reachable. Instead, some even make arrangements for things that are outside their lifespan, such as the massive structures of their tombs, donations of public buildings, public spectacles at their funerals, and flattering funeral processions. My goodness, funerals for such men ought to be conducted with torches and candles, as if they had died as children.

---

48. Gaius Turannius preceded Paulinus as *praefectus annonae.* Although Seneca makes him about a decade older than seems likely, based on other offices and dates associated with him and Gaius Caesar's death in 41 CE, he would still have been very old indeed at that point, into his eighties. Turannius was still holding office and advising Emperor Claudius in 48 CE.

Consolation to Polybius

(*Ad Polybium De Consolatione*)

1.1. If you compare cities and monuments built of stone to our lives, they are solid. But if you stack them up against Nature, which breaks down everything and brings it all back to the place it came from, they are fragile. What immortal thing was ever made by mortal hands? The Seven Wonders of the World,[1] even if the aspirations of subsequent generations build something more wonderful, will be seen razed to the ground someday. That's the way it is. Nothing is permanent— few things are lasting. Some things are fragile in one way, others in other ways, and the manner of their death varies. But whatever has a beginning also has an end. **1.2.** There are some things that endanger the world. Even the universe, which embraces everything, human and divine, will someday be scattered—if you hold to this belief— and fall into its former chaos and darkness. Let someone go now and weep for any one single life, or for the ashes of Carthage, Numantia, and Corinth, or any more powerful cities that have fallen, if there were any. Even the universe, which has no place to fall, will perish. Let someone go and whine that Fate has shown him no mercy—Fate that will someday dare to do the unspeakable. **1.3.** Who is so full of arrogant self-importance that he would want only himself and his dear ones to be exempt from the inevitable aspect of Nature that calls all things back to the same end? Or want only *his* home to escape the destruction that hangs over the world itself? **1.4.** It's a very great comfort to consider that you have experienced something everyone who lived before you has experienced, and that everyone will experience in the future. This is why, it seems to me, Nature has made her most terrible creation a common experience: so that through our equality consolation can be offered for the cruelty of death.

---

1. Lists of the Seven Wonders of the Ancient World familiar to the modern world were being made by the second century BCE, usually including the Walls of Babylon, the statue of Zeus at Olympia, the Hanging Gardens of Babylon, the Colossus of Rhodes, the Pyramids, the Mausoleum of Halicarnassus, and the Temple of Artemis in Ephesus. Earlier lists comprised Greek buildings.

2.1. It will help you a great deal if you also consider that nothing useful will come from your grief, either for the one you're missing or for yourself. You won't want to spend a long time doing nothing useful. If we could accomplish anything with our sadness, I'd willingly pour out for you whatever tears are left after weeping for myself. I might even now find some to shed from these eyes of mine, even though they are drained from personal grief, if only it were good for you. **2.2.** Why stop now? Let's grieve together, and I'll add my own accusation, "Fortune, everyone thinks you're terribly unfair. In the past you seemed to protect this man, who was held in such high esteem through your favor that his prosperity and happiness didn't even provoke dangerous jealousy—and that's a rare thing for anyone! But now you're crushing him with pain and sorrow, the most he could have felt while Caesar lives.[2] And although you set a tight siege line all around him, you understood that he was vulnerable to your attacks only from this direction. What else could you have done to him? Taken away his wealth? He never depended on it. Even now, as much as possible, he keeps it at arm's length and, given his attitude about possessions, wants no greater return from his investments than to be able to ignore money. **2.3.** Take away his friends? You know he was such a friendly man that he could easily have found others to replace the ones he lost. I think that in him I know, out of all the powerful men in the Emperor's court, a man whose friendship has been much more than an advantage—it has been a pleasure, for everyone. Take away his good reputation? His good name is too well established even for you, Fortune, to destroy. Take away his good health? You know that his spirit has its foundation in the liberal arts (he was a natural, not just well brought up), so it can rise above physical pain. **2.4.** Take away his life's breath? That wouldn't have harmed him at all. Fame has promised him a long life through his talent. And he has made sure that the better part of himself will endure and rescue him from mortality through his exceptionally eloquent literary works. As long as literature is held in honor, as long as the power of Latin or the beauty of Greek still stands, he will stand strong among the greatest of men, whose talent he equaled—or, if his sense of modesty rejects the term 'equaled,' I'll say 'emulated.' **2.5.** So, you discovered the one way to harm him the most. You see, the

---

2. Caesar in this dialogue is Claudius (10 BCE–54 CE), the successor of Gaius (Caligula) after he was assassinated in 41 CE.

better someone is the more he gets used to enduring you, you who rage without reason and are most fearsome when giving gifts. It would have been very little effort for you to keep this man safe from this injury. It seemed like your affectionate support was being given to him on purpose before that—not falling out of the sky at random as usual."

3.1. Let's add to these complaints, if you like, that this young man's natural talent was cut down in the bloom of youth. He deserved to be your brother. And you certainly deserved most of all not to suffer undeserved pain because of your brother. Everyone swears that his contribution to your family's good name is missed and that he had a good name of his own too. There was no part of him that you were not happy to acknowledge. **3.2.** You would have been a good brother to a less good brother too but, because it was working with the good raw material in him already, your brotherly duty and love applied itself much more fully to supporting him. He didn't make his power and influence felt when anyone hurt him, and he never used the fact that you were his brother to threaten anyone. He molded his conduct to match yours and used to reflect on how great a jewel and a burden you were for your family. It was not too heavy a load for him. **3.3.** O, Fate, you are harsh! And you never come in proportion to a person's virtue! Your brother was taken before he came into a prosperity and happiness of his own. I understand that I'm not being indignant enough about it. Nothing's more difficult than finding words to equal a great sorrow. Even so, if it could somehow make a difference, let's cry out in grief together, "What do you want, Fortune? You are so unjust and so brutal! Do you regret so quickly that you showed him your favor? **3.4.** What a cruel thing, to attack these brothers and make them fewer in number—they were of one heart and mind—with such a brutal theft! What a cruel thing, to throw a family so blessed with the best of children into confusion. None of them were a disappointment and to subtract a little from it wasn't justified! Is there no benefit, then, in following every law without doing harm and in living with old-fashioned thriftiness? Is there no benefit in being moderate by controlling a strong potential to achieve great wealth? Is there no benefit in a heartfelt love for literature, or a mind without defect? **3.5.** Polybius is grieving and, because he has been forewarned through the one brother about what he should fear for the rest, even the solace for his sorrow, the brothers left to him, makes him afraid. What a crime! Polybius is grieving and feels pain while Caesar favors him! This was self-indulgent Fortune's purpose, without a doubt: to show that against her there is no defense—not even Caesar!—for anyone." **4.1.** But we can't accuse Fate any longer, and we can't change it. Fate stands inexorably firm. No one can change Fate with insults, tears, or arguments. Fate spares no one and gives no one a second chance. Therefore, let's stop tears that have no effect. This sorrow will take us to join the dead more readily than it will bring our dead back to us. And if sorrow isn't helping us but hurting us, we should set it aside as soon as possible and rescue the spirit from useless consolations and the bitter pleasure of grief.

4.2. Fortune will not bring an end to our tears if reason won't. Look around you—everyone's mortal—there are plenty of reasons to weep every day. Abject poverty makes one man work for a living every day. Ambition harasses another endlessly. Another fears the riches he once desired and struggles against the thing he prayed to get. One man is tortured by loneliness, another by hard work, and yet another by the crowd camped out on his doorstep. This man here is sad that he has children and that man that he lost some. Our tears run out before we run out of reasons to cry. **4.3.** Don't you see the kind of life we were promised by Nature? She wanted humans to cry as soon as they were born. This is our first act, and the entire succession of our years matches it: we live our lives this way. For that reason, whatever we must do often we ought to do with moderation. Looking behind at how much sadness is coming toward us,[3] surely we should save up our tears, if not stop them. Nothing should be more carefully rationed than something used frequently.

5.1. It will help you a lot if you think that your pain isn't pleasing anyone, much less the man it seems to be offered to. He either doesn't want you to suffer or he can't understand that you're suffering. There is no rational purpose for this duty of grief, which is useless for the one it's offered to, if he can't perceive it, or unpleasant if he can. If I can be so bold, there's no one in the world who would delight in your tears. **5.2.** What, then? Do you believe your brother would hold you to a standard no one else would, that this pain and suffering should harm you and distract you from your duties—that is, from your studies and from the Emperor? Not likely. He offered you the affection one gives to a brother, the respect one gives to a parent, and the attention one

---

3. The Romans, and Greeks, visualized humans as walking backwards into the future, able to see the past but not what is coming.

gives to a superior. He wants you to miss him, not to suffer. So how is it helping for you to be wasting away from a grief your brother—if the dead can feel anything—wants you to end? **5.3.** For any other brother whose wishes might be less clear I'd be more cautious and say, "If your brother wants you to suffer from tears that never end, he's unworthy of your affection and emotion. But if he doesn't want it, throw off the grief that's clinging to you both. A brother who didn't have brotherly duty and love for you shouldn't be missed so much, and a brother who did wouldn't want to be." But in this case, since his brotherly duty and love was so strong and obvious, it must be clear that nothing is crueler for *him* to endure than his death being too cruel for *you* to endure, or causing you any pain, or disturbing and wearing out your eyes with endless tears. Your eyes don't deserve this badness!

Even so, nothing will redirect your own brotherly duty and love from these empty tears than thinking that you ought to be an example for your other brothers of enduring bad fortune in a brave way. **5.4.** You need to do now what great generals do when things are tough: they fake a good mood intentionally and cover up serious situations with feigned cheerfulness, so their soldiers' spirits won't waver seeing their general's mind broken. Put a good face on it or, if you can, throw off this sadness entirely. If not, bury it deep inside, so it doesn't show, and help your brothers imitate you. They think whatever they see you doing is noble, and they will make their spirits match your attitude. You need to be their solace and their solace-giver. You won't be able to counter their grief if you indulge in your own.

6.1. It's possible that you can also stay away from excessive grief if you admit to yourself that nothing you do can be hidden. The people's vote has imposed a public role on you that you must protect. A crowd of people offering sympathy stands around you, asking how you're holding up and looking to see how much strength of spirit you have against sorrow: to see whether you know how to enjoy the good times only or if you can endure the hard times like a man too. They are watching your eyes. **6.2.** Everything is less restricted for those whose emotions can be hidden. But for you there's no such thing as a guarded secret because Fortune has set you in the limelight. Everyone will know how you behaved in this painful situation, whether you threw down your weapons at the first attack or held your ground. Some time ago Caesar's affection and your studies promoted you to a higher rank and status. Now nothing common or ignoble is appropriate for you.

6.3. What is more ignoble and weak than to resign yourself to be consumed by grief? While your grief is equivalent, what is permissible for your brothers isn't permissible for you. The public understanding about your studies doesn't give you much room and men require a lot, and expect a lot, from you. If you wanted freedom, you shouldn't have turned all eyes on you. As it is, what you promised must be provided. All those who praise your writings, who make copies of them, for whom your talent (if not your happiness) are necessary—all of them are jailers for your spirit. **6.4.** For this reason, you can't do anything that is unworthy of your public reputation as an excellent and cultured man or the mob will regret admiring you. You can't weep uncontrollably— and this goes for other things too. You can't sleep in or run away from the crush of work into retirement in a hideaway in the quiet of the countryside. You can't recuperate a body worn out from the continuous duty your position requires by taking a fun trip. You can't distract your spirit with a variety of games and spectacles or schedule your day as you wish. **6.5.** There are many things you can't do that the lowest of the low, even drunks lying in an alley, can. Great good fortune comes with a kind of slavery. You can't do what you like. You must listen to countless numbers of men; you have to take care of many reports and letters. There's such a pile of business coming in from all over the world that you have to make sure it gets prioritized for the Emperor. You don't have time to weep. You need to dry your eyes so that you can hear the tears of many others and so that you can dry the eyes of those in danger or seeking the benevolent mercy of Caesar.

7.1. These comments I've made will help you right now with gentler cures for your grief. But when you want to forget it all, think about Caesar. Can you see how much faith and hard work his affection for you deserves? If so, you'll understand that you can't bend under the pressure any more than Atlas, whose shoulders support the world—if, of course, one can believe the stories. **7.2.** Even for Caesar, who can do anything, many things aren't allowed because he, on guard through the night, is defending the sleep of all people. His hard work means retirement for everyone else, his persistence means pleasure for everyone else, and his constant effort means everyone else gets a break. Because Caesar has dedicated himself to the world, he is deprived of himself. Just like the stars, which always follow their path without rest, he is never allowed to sit back and do his own thing. So, you must be held to essentially the same standard: you are not allowed to act in your own interests or to turn your attention to your studies. **7.3.** Although Caesar rules over the whole world you can't share yourself with any desire or pain or anything else. You owe your whole self to Caesar. Add to that the fact that, since you always say Caesar is dearer to you than your breath, it isn't right for you to complain about your own fate while Caesar is safe: your loved ones are safe while he is safe. You've lost nothing—your eyes shouldn't only be empty of tears, they should be full of joy. Everything for you lies in Caesar and Caesar benefits all. Your exceptional respectability and your sense of duty is helping you avoid this mistake, but you're not showing enough gratitude for your happiness and prosperity if you allow yourself to weep at anything while Caesar lives.

8.1. Now I will show you a therapy that isn't better than Caesar, it's just better suited to your private life. Whenever you are at home, you should fear your sadness more, because as long as you can see the divine power, your sadness will have no way in. Caesar will have your full attention. But when you go away from him, as soon as the opportunity presents itself, your pain will lay a trap for you in your loneliness and will creep bit by bit into your spirit while it rests. **8.2.** So, there's no reason why you shouldn't spend every spare moment with your studies. This is when your writings—so long and faithfully cared for—should return the favor. This is when they should claim you as both their master and their servant, and have Homer and Vergil spend time with you. These writers merit the respect of the human race as much as you merit *their* respect (and the respect of everyone) for wanting them to be known to more people than they had written for.[4] Every moment you commit to their protection will be safe. And this is when you should compose a poem on the deeds of your Caesar, as best you can, so that they will be told throughout the ages by the voice of someone on Caesar's staff. Caesar himself will give you both the raw material and the example for shaping, and recording, history. **8.3.** I don't dare suggest that you, with your usual elegance, compose fables and stories like Aesop, something a Roman talent hasn't attempted.[5] It's difficult for a spirit, suffering such a forceful

---

4. Polybius was known to have translated Homer from Greek into Latin, and Vergil from Latin into Greek.

5. Much to the consternation of commentators, Phaedrus, a freedman of Augustus (d. 50 CE), had in fact written Aesopic fables in Latin. Seneca uses the phrase *Aesopeos logos*, which might suggest that he was thinking here of a Roman writer composing fables in Greek.

blow, to move so quickly to this cheerful kind of literature. But you should consider it proof that your heart is recovering and returning to stability, if it is able to shift from more serious writing to this less serious kind. **8.4.** You see, the gravity of the subject matter of the former kind will keep the mind's attention even when it's still sick and struggling in itself. But one can't manage pleasant fables, which should be attempted in a happier mood, except when the heart has reestablished itself in every way. So, you'll need to train up the heart again with the more severe material then soften it with stuff that's more fun.

9.1. It will provide great relief too, if you often ask yourself, "Am I grieving for my own sake or for the sake of the one who died? If I'm doing it for my own sake, this outward display of affection is wasted. From a pragmatic point of view my grief (I overlooked it before because the pain was noble) has begun to be a perversion of my brotherly love and duty. But nothing is less appropriate for a good man than to put grief for a brother on a balance sheet. **9.2.** If I am grieving for his sake, I need to decide between the following two propositions. If the dead can feel nothing, my brother has escaped all the difficult aspects of life and has been returned to that place where he was before he was born. Removed from every bad thing, he fears nothing, desires nothing and suffers nothing. How crazy would I have to be to grieve for him forever, if he's never going to feel grief? **9.3.** But if the dead do feel things, my brother's spirit, released from a sort of life sentence and finally free and independent, is going where it wants, enjoying Nature's spectacular show. His spirit is looking down on human affairs from a higher vantage point and at the gods from a place nearby—the gods whose plan he had questioned for so long without result. So why am I eaten up inside from missing him, if he's either blessed or nothing at all? To weep over a blessed man is envy. To weep over no one is madness."

9.4. Or maybe the fact that he seems to have lost the good things in life, just when they were raining down upon him in huge numbers, is upsetting you? But when you think he's lost many things, think also that there are more things he doesn't fear. He won't get twisted up with anger, illnesses won't make him suffer, suspicion won't shake his confidence, malicious envy (greedy and always hostile to another's achievements) won't persecute him, fear won't worry him. And fickle Fortune, who transfers her rewards so swiftly, won't make him anxious. If you tally it all up, he has been saved from more than he has lost.

9.5. He won't enjoy the fruits of his labor, or the favors you and he together are owed. He won't receive them or give them. Do you think he's pitiable, because he has lost these things, or blessed, because he doesn't miss them? Believe me, a man whom Fortune has left alone is more blessed than the one to whom Fortune has given much. All of these good things you mention, which delight us with an illusory and false pleasure—money, respect, power, and many other things that the human race drools after with blind lust—are only achieved through hard work, are only admired with envy, and in the end oppress only those they adorn. They threaten more than benefit, are slippery and fragile, and are never firmly held. You see, although there is nothing to fear from the future, protecting great prosperity and happiness produces anxiety.

9.6. If you want to believe those who examine the truth more closely, all of life is a death sentence. Cast away on a deep and restless sea that changes with the flow of the tides, we rise and fall with the waves. At one point the sea will lift us with sudden increases and distinctions. At another it will bring us down after significant losses, tossing us about constantly. We're never in a stable place. Smashed one into the other, we are often shipwrecked and always afraid. There's no port for sailors on this roiling, storm-filled sea except death.

9.7. So don't envy your brother: he's at rest. Finally, he's free, safe, and immortal. He has left Caesar behind and all of Caesar's family. He has left you behind with your brothers. Before Fortune could change anything and remove her favor, he left her standing next to him, still dealing out rewards with a generous hand. **9.8.** He's enjoying the open sky now, and has flashed from this common and sad place to the place, wherever it is, that welcomes souls released from earthly bonds like a mother. He's wandering there freely now, witnessing all the good things Nature gives with great delight. You're wrong: your brother didn't lose the light, he's been promoted to a greater light. Our path, all of us, is the same—why weep over our fate? He didn't leave us—he has scouted out the path. There is, take my word on it, a great happiness and prosperity in the inevitability of death. There's nothing certain in any day. Who can know for sure, when truth is so dark and hidden, whether death hated your brother or was looking out for him?

10.1. It should help too, since you have a sense of justice in all matters, to think that no injury was done because you have lost your brother. Rather, you have received a favor because you were allowed to benefit from and enjoy his brotherly love for so long. A man who doesn't allow a gift-giver full control over giving a gift is an unfair man. A man who counts what he gives back as a loss but not what he brings in as profit is a greedy man. A man who calls the end of pleasure "damages" is ungrateful. A man who thinks that there is no use for good things unless they are used immediately is stupid. He doesn't find peace in what he has used up. And he thinks that things that are gone are more reliable because he doesn't have to be afraid they'll stop. **10.2.** You're limiting your happiness when you think that you can only enjoy what you can hold or see and when you think that the things you had in the past aren't worth anything. Every desire, you see, leaves us behind quickly, flowing across us and being carried away almost even before it has arrived. As a result, we should cast our spirits back on what has happened before, and frequently play over again in our heads whatever we enjoyed. The memory of pleasures is longer and more trustworthy than their enjoyment in the moment. Therefore, you should consider it among the greatest of good things that you had such a great brother.

10.3. There's no reason for you to think about how much longer you might have been able to keep him. Instead, think about how long you did keep him. The universe didn't give him to you, or others to their brothers, as property—he was on loan. Then, when it seemed right, the universe called in the loan, and was guided by its own rules, not your level of satisfaction. If a man gets upset that he has to repay a loan, especially an interest-free loan, wouldn't he be considered unreasonable? **10.4.** The universe gave your brother his life, and you yours. And if, well within its rights, it called in the debt from whomever it preferred to take back, and sooner than it will call in the debt from another, it's not guilty of a crime. No, it's that the human spirit's hope is greedy: it forgets what the universe is like right away, and never remembers its own lot—unless it is warned. **10.5.** So, be happy that you had a good brother and the pleasure of his good advice, though for less time than you wanted. Think of it this way: having him as a brother was a very pleasant thing, losing him was a very human thing. Nothing is more contradictory than for someone to be sad because such a great brother was in his life for so short a time, but to not be glad because he was in his life at all. **11.1.** "But he was snatched away so unexpectedly!" In this, we're all deceived by our own naïveté. And, in the case of the things we love, we willingly forget about mortality. Nature has proven that she gives no one favors to escape that necessity. We watch the funeral processions of those we know pass by, and those we don't, and we still act otherwise and think that death was sudden. But our whole life has been announcing that death will come.

11.2. So, it's not that fate is unfair, but that the human mind is perverse, insatiable in every respect, insulted at being banished from the place it got into by begging. How much more reasonable is the man who, when he heard about the death of his son, said something worthy of a great man, "When I fathered you, I knew then that you would die."[6] Of course, you won't be surprised that a man born from this man could die bravely. The father didn't accept the news about his son's death as if it were news at all. Is it news that a man has died, when his whole life is nothing but a road to death? "When I fathered you, I knew then that you would die." **11.3.** Then he adds a thought both more prudent and more spirited, "I raised him for this." We are all raised for this: anyone brought into life is destined for death. Therefore, let us be glad for what will be given, and let us return it when required. Death catches one man at one time and another at another, but it doesn't pass by anyone. Let our spirits stand on guard, never fear what is necessary, and always watch for what is changeable.

11.4. Should I tell you that generals and their children, and those who stand out because they held many consulships or triumphs, are dead? Whole kingdoms and their kings, and their people with them, have died. All people, I mean all *things*, await a last day. The end isn't the same for absolutely everyone: life abandons one man in mid-course, ditches another right at the beginning, and casts off another wearied by extreme old age and wanting to die. At one time or another, certainly, we're all headed for the same place, and I don't know if it's stupider to ignore the law of life and death or to shamelessly fight to repeal it. **11.5.** Come, pick up the poems of either poet who has become very well-known because of your hard work and talent. You put these poems into prose so well that although the arrangement on the page is changed their grace endures. In fact, you translated them from Greek into Latin and Latin into Greek in such

---

6. Telamon says this of his son Ajax after his death/suicide at Troy. Seneca is quoting Ennius' play *Telamon*. Ennius (239–170 BCE) is among the earliest and most influential poets at Rome, although he obtained citizenship only later in life. Very little of Ennius remains except through quotations other ancient writers made.

a way that—and this is really hard to do—you transferred all the virtues of each language into a foreign one. So, pick them up and you'll find that every chapter supplies many examples of life's changes, of unforeseen disasters and of tears shed for one reason or another. Read with the same vigor you used to recite the lines in the past. You'll be ashamed to suddenly be found lacking and to not live up to the greatness of the words. May you not be found guilty of making people who admired your writings as an example of greatness wonder how such grand and steadfast phrases came from such a frail spirit.

12.1. It would be better for you to turn from the things that are torturing you to the many wonderful things that are comforting your grief. Look at your excellent brothers, your wife, your son: Fortune put an installment with you on your account (your brother's death) in exchange for their health. You have many people among whom you can find peace. Free yourself from this poor reputation, so that it doesn't seem to everyone that one sorrow affects you more than so many consolations. **12.2.** You can see that your whole family felt the blow of his death along with you and that they can't help you— more to the point you can understand that they even look to you to lift *them* up. So you must interpose yourself even more against this shared bad event to make up for the fact that they have less training and talent. This is a substitute for solace: to divide one's own pain among many people. Since the pain is spread among many, it ought to weigh less heavily on you. **12.3.** I won't stop bringing Caesar up often. While he governs the world, while he shows us how much better it is to guard the Empire through generosity than through generals, and while he supervises human affairs there is no risk of feeling that you have lost something. This one fact offers enough protection and solace. Lift yourself up, and whenever tears start to well up, turn your eyes toward Caesar. The sight of his great and glorious power will dry them. His brilliance will blind them so that they can see nothing else and will keep them fixed on him alone. **12.4.** He must remain in your thoughts—you gaze at him day and night and the attention of your spirit never wavers. And he must be asked to help you against Fortune. No doubt he has already spread many comforting things over this wound of yours and applied many things to blunt the pain, since his compassion and affection for all your family is so great. **12.5.** So what? If he had done none of those things, isn't seeing and thinking of Caesar all by itself the greatest comfort you could have?

May the gods and goddesses favor the earth with his presence for many years! May he equal the deeds of the Divine Augustus and may he live even longer! As long as he is among mortals, may he never sense that anyone in his household is mortal! May he establish his son[7] through long-lived faithfulness as a leader of the Roman Empire. And before seeing the boy become his successor, may he see him become co-leader with his father. May the day on which his ancestors welcome him to the heavens come late and only in the lives of our grandchildren! **13.1.** Keep your hands off this Emperor, Fortune, and do not demonstrate your power in his life, except in the ways you are beneficial to people. Allow him to restore the human race to health, long since sickened in body and mind. Allow him to restore and renew whatever was battered by the madness of the previous Emperor.[8] May this shining star always shine, casting its light down on a world pitched into the depths and drowned in shadows! May he bring peace to Germany, make Britain accessible,[9] and celebrate the triumphs of his ancestors and new ones too![10] His mercy—which is the best of his many virtues—makes it possible for me to be spectator of these events also.[11] **13.2.** He has not, you see, thrown me into exile in such a way that he can't recall me, but he supported me, struck hard by Fortune, and set me down gently with restraint although I was rushing head first into trouble. He begged the Senate on my behalf, not only giving me my life but also asking for it. Let him see to it that he judges my case as he wants. May his sense of justice see that my life is good, or may his sense of mercy make my life good. His goodwill produces the same result as far as I'm concerned, whether he knows that I am innocent or wants it to be true. **13.3.** Until this happens, it's a great comfort to me to see his mercy permeating the whole earth. Even in this little corner of the world I'm trapped in he has dug out not a few who

---

7. That is, Brittanicus who, at the age of fourteen, was killed by Nero after Nero came to power in 54 CE.

8. That is, Gaius Caesar (Caligula).

9. Claudius suppressed the German tribes of the Marsi and Chatti almost immediately into his reign, and had by the time this dialogue was written already begun to make substantial inroads into southern Britain.

10. Julius Caesar had invaded Britain in 55 and 54 BCE. Augustus and Tiberius both had waged campaigns against the Germans.

11. Seneca was eventually recalled from exile by Claudius in 48 CE. Sources suggest that Claudius arranged a lesser sentence of exile (instead of execution).

were lost under the ruin of many years and led them back into the light. I'm not afraid he will only pass over me. He knows the very best time to help each person. I'll do my very best to make sure he won't be ashamed to come help me. **13.4.** How bountiful is your mercy, O Caesar, which makes it possible for exiles to live a more peaceful life under your rule than princes did under Gaius Caesar! They aren't fearful, and they don't expect execution every hour of the day or panic every time a ship is sighted.[12] Through your authority there is a limit to cruel fortune for them, hope for better fortune, and contentment in their present circumstance. One can be sure that thunderbolts were well deserved if they are worshipped even by the people they struck.

14.1. So, this Emperor, who is a comfort shared by all humans, has—unless I'm utterly mistaken—renewed your spirit and provided a cure stronger than your serious wound. I'm sure he has already strengthened you in every way, recalling from his unfailing memory all of the great role models through whom one can attain peace of the spirit. He has already set forth the commands of all the wise men with his usual eloquence. **14.2.** No one takes on the role of consoler better. When he speaks, words have a certain weight, as if conveyed from the mouth of an oracle. His divine authority subdues the power of your pain. Imagine that he's speaking to you: "Fortune has not only picked on you to hurt with a serious loss. There isn't now (and hasn't ever been) a household in the whole world that doesn't have some reason for tears. I'll pass over all the examples of common people who, even if they are less important, are no less numerous and I'll lead you straight to lists of senior officials of the state.

14.3. "Do you see all these *imagines*[13] that fill the atrium of the Caesars? Every single one of them is prominent for some misfortune in their family. All of them—shining examples who adorn the ages—were racked by longing for their loved ones or were missed by a family with grief-stricken spirits tortured by sorrow. Do I need to remind you about Scipio Africanus, whose brother's death was

---

12. Punishments for lower- and upper-class citizens were different. Instead of execution, convicted upper class persons were often sent into exile, or relegated to an isolated island (where they might, however, starve or await a less public execution).

13. *Imagines* were wax impressions taken of significant family members at the time of death. These portraits would be hung in the atrium or other public area of the household to demonstrate the family's prominence. The masks would also be worn by actors representing the ancestors during funeral processions.

announced to him while he was in exile?[14] This brother Scipio, who saved his brother from prison,[15] could not save him from death. His brotherly love and duty—and that he expected special treatment—was not doubted by any. You see, on the same day that he snatched his brother from the executioner's hands, he also blocked even a tribune of the plebs from action, though he was himself not in elected office![16] He missed his brother with as great a spirit as he had defended him. **14.4.** Do I need to remind you of Scipio Aemilianus, who watched the triumphal procession of his father and the funeral processions of his two brothers on very nearly the same day?[17] Although a young man himself—almost even an adolescent—he endured the sudden devastation of his family perishing just after the triumph of Paullus with as much spirit as a real man should, especially one born to make sure that a Scipio would never fail and Carthage never prevail over Rome. **15.1.** Do I need to remind you of the harmonious unity of the two Luculli brothers that was destroyed only by death?[18] Or the Pompeys?[19] Savage Fortune did not even leave them to be reduced by the same defeat at the same time.[20] Sextus Pompey survived his sister, by whose death the bonds of a secure and stable Roman peace were

---

14. P. Cornelius Scipio Africanus (235–183 BCE), who conquered Hannibal, went into self-imposed exile at the end of his life to his small villa at Liternum.

15. L. Scipio was being taken to prison after being fined for misappropriation of state funds.

16. Tribunes of the plebs were sacrosanct, and could prohibit the action of any other magistrate by literally or figuratively interposing their bodies. Scipio, therefore, was acting like a tribune of the plebs to counter the action of a tribune of the plebs.

17. L. Aemilius Paullus Macedonicus (222–160 BCE) was granted a triumph in 167 BCE for his victories in Macedon in 171 BCE. The son mentioned here (Scipio Aemilianus, or properly Publius Cornelius Scipio Aemilianus Africanus Numantinus, also known as Scipio the Younger) was adopted by the son of P. Cornelius Scipio Africanus (see n. 14); he is famous (and earned his *agnomina*) for destroying Carthage in 146 BCE.

18. Lucius Licinius Lucullus Ponticus and Marcus Licinius Lucullus. Lucius earned his *agnomen* after defeating the army of Mithridates in 72 BCE.

19. Gnaeus Pompeius Magnus (Pompey the Great) died in 48 BCE after his defeat by Caesar at Pharsalus. His sons Sextus Pompey and Gnaeus Pompey continued to fight against Caesar and then against Octavian (Augustus) until their deaths (Gnaeus in 45 BCE and Sextus in 35 BCE).

20. After Pompey's death in in 48 BCE, Sextus and Gnaeus raised an army in Spain, but were defeated by Caesar in 45 BCE, shortly after which Gnaeus was executed and Sextus a decade later.

dissolved.[21] Likewise, he survived his most excellent brother, whom Fortune had brought to such prominence so she couldn't cast him down from a lower height than she had cast down his father. And after all this misfortune Sextus Pompey had sufficient courage not just for his grief but also for war.

15.2. "Innumerable examples from all over of brothers separated by death fill my mind, but we hardly ever see any equivalent examples of brothers growing old together. I'll be satisfied to take examples from my own household, since no one is so devoid of sense and sanity that, when he knows Fortune has even desired to see Caesars' tears, he can complain Fortune has caused anyone else grief. **15.3.** The Divine Augustus lost his beloved sister Octavia.[22] The universe did not take the inevitability of grief away even from him, though he was destined to become a god. Instead, distressed by every kind of loss, he likewise lost his sister's son who had been prepared to be his successor.[23] In the end—I don't want to list his griefs one by one—he lost his sons-in-law and his children and his grandchildren. While Augustus was on the earth, no mortal perceived his own mortality more clearly.

15.4. "Even so, that heart of his, big enough to hold everything, took up so many and such great sorrows. The Divine Augustus wasn't just a victor over foreign nations but even over his own pain. Gaius, grandson of Augustus my great-uncle, lost his dearest brother Lucius while still a very young man: a *princeps iuventutis* lost a *princeps iuventutis* while preparing for a war against the Parthians[24] and was struck more seriously by this blow to the spirit than he was later by a blow to his body. He bore both with the utmost devotion and bravery. **15.5.** Tiberius Caesar, brother of my father Drusus Germanicus, held him in his arms as he died, although he was younger, kissing his face. Drusus was making the interior of Germany accessible and subju-

---

21. Seneca is referring to Pompeia's second marriage, to Lucius Cornelius Cinna, the brother-in-law of Julius Caesar.

22. Circa 10 BCE. Octavia had played a crucial role through her marriages (especially her last, to Marcus Antonius) in the shifting alliances of the end of the Republic.

23. Marcellus (b. 42 BCE), the son of Octavia and her first husband Gaius Claudius Marcellus, was adopted by Augustus as heir but died in 23 BCE.

24. The title was used in the early empire to indicate eligible successors. Gaius (d. 4 CE) and Lucius (d. 2 CE), sons of Marcus Vipsanius Agrippa and Julia, were adopted by Augustus in 17 BCE.

gating savage tribes to Roman rule. Even so, Tiberius set a limit on his grieving, and on the grief of others—he restored the army to the Roman custom of grief[25] although it, devastated and astonished, was demanding the body of Drusus for itself.[26] Tiberius judged that soldiers and mourners both need to preserve discipline. He would not have been able to suppress other men's tears if he could not have suppressed his own. **16.1.** My grandfather Marcus Antonius, at the point when he was regulating the Republic and had no one above him because he had been granted triumviral power,[27] heard that his brother had been killed.[28] Antonius—only the man who defeated Antonius was greater[29]—considered all to be inferior except his two colleagues in the triumvirate. O Fortune! What a game you make for yourself out of the bad things that happen in this world! At the very same time Marcus Antonius sat in court as arbiter of life and death for his fellow citizens, his brother was ordered to be executed. **16.2.** Nevertheless, he bore this sad hurt with the same greatness of spirit through which he tolerated all other adversity—and his grief was such that he sacrificed the blood of twenty legions in his brother's honor.[30] But let's forget about all the other examples and keep quiet about all the other deaths in my own life, except to mention that Fortune has attacked me twice with grief for a sibling, and has twice found out that I could be wounded but not vanquished. I lost my brother Germanicus,[31] whom I loved as much as devoted brothers love brothers—anyone who thinks about it will see that. But I governed my emotions in such a way that I did everything that ought to be done by a good brother, but did nothing that an Emperor could be criticized for."

---

25. That is, a moderate and strict period of mourning.

26. Tiberius took the body back to Rome, according to Suetonius (*Life of Tiberius* 7), accompanying it on foot.

27. The triumvirate formed in 43 BCE granted the three men (Octavian [later Augustus], Marcus Antonius, and Marcus Lepidus) extraordinary powers to restore the Republic. Each man was assigned a different area to control and regulate.

28. Gaius Antonius, who was killed while governor of Macedonia by Brutus and other killers of Caesar after fleeing to Greece in 44 BCE.

29. That is, Octavian (later Augustus) at the Battle of Actium in 31 BCE.

30. These were the legions Marcus Antonius committed to the Battle of Actium.

31. Germanicus, the adopted son and nephew of Emperor Tiberius (d. 19 CE) and Livilla (d. 31 CE).

16.3. Imagine, then, that the nation's father refers you to these role models, and explains how nothing is sacred or untouchable for Fortune, who dares to lead funeral processions out of the same households where she will look for gods. So, none should be surprised that Fortune could make something cruel and unfair happen. In fact, can Fortune truly show fairness and self-control with private families if her unquenchable savagery has brought sorrow so many times to the thrones of the gods? **16.4.** Even if we complain about the life of the state and not just our private lives, she won't change her ways. Fortune holds herself apart from all prayers and protests. Fortune has always acted this way and always will. She has tried everything—there's nothing she has left untouched. She'll continue to barge recklessly through everything, as she always has, daring even to bring harm down on houses that must be entered through temples. She'll wrap those laurelled doors with black cloth. **16.5.** If Fortune has decided to not destroy the human race, if she looks kindly on the name "Roman," let's hope our prayers and offerings obtain just this one thing: that our Emperor, given to us to restore humankind, be as sacred to her as he is to all mortals. Let her learn about mercy from him, and let her show kindness to the kindest of Emperors.

17.1. You should look to all the people I just talked about, whether they've become gods already or will soon, and endure Fortune's touch with a calm spirit—she doesn't even keep her hands off those on whose names we swear oaths. You ought to emulate their steadfast courage in enduring and conquering sorrow, at least to the extent that it's not blasphemy for a man to follow in the footsteps of the divine. **17.2.** Although in other things respectability and nobility make a huge difference, virtue is within everyone's reach. Virtue scorns no one who thinks he is worthy of virtue. Of course, it would be best of all to emulate those who, although they could be indignant that they weren't immune to this bad thing, in this one case concluded that it wasn't an insult to be equal to other human beings but a law of human nature. They didn't endure what happened too bitterly and too spitefully, or weakly and unlike a man. It is not truly human to not feel bad things—and not a real man who does not endure them.

17.3. I can't, since I've gone over all the Caesars who have had brothers and sisters snatched away by Fortune, pass over the man who should be removed from every record of the Caesars. In him Nature created a destructive force and a source of shame for the human race. The mercy of our most kind Emperor is recreating the Empire that the previous Caesar overturned and ravaged utterly. Gaius Caesar (Caligula), who was as unable to feel sorrow in a manner appropriate to an Emperor as he was able to feel joy, ran from the sight and company of his people after losing his sister Drusilla. He wasn't at his sister's funeral and didn't pay proper respects to her. Instead, he alleviated the bad things of that terribly sad funeral at his Alban estate with dice and games and other vulgar distractions. **17.4.** What a shame for the Empire! Dice were a comfort to the Roman Emperor grieving for his sister. Gaius was wildly inconsistent, at one point letting his beard and hair grow, then cutting them off, wandering all over or striding the length of the shores of Italy and Sicily, never really sure whether he wanted his sister mourned as dead or worshipped as a goddess. At the same time he was constructing a temple and altars to her he was also inflicting a very cruel retribution on those who weren't mourning enough. You see, he was carrying the pain of very difficult circumstances with the same unbalanced spirit that carried him away and became inhumanly elated by happy events. May every Roman man avoid this example of behavior: deflecting grief with inappropriate amusements, stimulating it with the filth of neglect and an absence of concern, or satisfying it by bringing bad things to others, which is hardly a normal human way to find comfort.

18.1. But you don't have to change your behavior, since you have prepared yourself to love the studies that promote the greatest happiness and prosperity and that most easily weaken the impact of disaster. These studies are the greatest enhancement and comfort for life a person can have. So, now is the time to sink deeper into your studies. Now is the time to set them up like fortifications around your spirit, so that sorrow can't find a way in. **18.2.** Bring your brother's memory into the world with a literary monument of your own. For memory is the one creation of the human world that no storm can harm and no passage of time can destroy. Other monuments—which endure because they're built of stone or blocks of marble or huge dirt mounds piled up high—will of course perish themselves one day. But the memory of a man of great talent is immortal. Grant this memory to your brother, make him a tomb out of memory. It would be better for you to hallow him with your enduring talent than mourn him with your unholy sorrow.

18.3. As for Fortune, even if it's impossible right now for you to hear her side of things (everything she has given us is hateful to you because of what she took away) eventually her side will need to be heard—as soon as time has made you a more fair-minded judge. Eventually you'll be able to be her friend again. You see, Fortune provided many things to make amends for the injury she caused with your brother's death, and she'll give many more in compensation. After all, she gave you the very thing she took back. Therefore, don't use your talent against yourself: don't sustain your sorrow. **18.4.** Of course, it's possible, because of your facility with words, to make the case that relatively minor things are of great significance, and likewise to take important things and make them insignificant. May your skill save its power for another time, and turn its energy entirely to comforting you. Perhaps, too, you need to think about whether by now it's past time for seeking comfort. Nature demands one thing from us, but our vanity leads us to drag it out longer. I'll never demand that you not grieve at all. I know that men of inflexible, rather than courageous, self-control can be found who deny that the wise man feels sorrow. These men never seem to me to have ever experienced such a terrible loss, or Fortune would have knocked this prideful wisdom out of them and compelled them to profess the truth of the matter, however unwillingly. **18.5.** But reason will have fulfilled its purpose well enough if it only takes away from your sorrow what is unnecessary and excessive. No one should hope or desire that reason could make sorrow disappear entirely. Let reason instead preserve a limit for grief: to imitate neither irreverence nor insanity but to maintain the behavior appropriate to a reverent and steady mind. Weep, and also stop weeping; let sobs come from the deepest place in your heart, but likewise finally set them aside. Govern your spirit in such a way that you find favor both with wise men and with your brothers. **18.6.** Make sure that you remember your brother often, that you mention him often in conversation, that you keep a picture of him in your mind every day. You'll be able to do this if your memory of him is happy rather than sad. It's natural, you see, for the spirit to avoid what's sad to think about. **18.7.** Think instead about his unassuming nature, think about his shrewdness in conducting business, his diligence in following through, and how consistently he kept his promises. Tell others what he said and did—and tell yourself too. Think about what sort of man he was and what we all hoped he would be: what promise would such a brother *not* have met?

18.8. I've written these things down as well as I can—my spirit is decaying and dulled by long disuse. If my words seem to offer advice inadequate for your talented mind or not therapeutic enough for your sorrow, consider how a person caught up in his own bad fortune can't really make time to console someone else. Consider, too, how proper Latin doesn't easily come to a man bombarded by the babble of foreigners—babble that is even hard for the more civilized foreigners to endure.

Consolation to His Mother Helvia

(*Ad Helviam Matrem De Consolatione*)

1.1. I have often, dearest mother, felt the urge to console you, and often I have held back. Many things pushed me to try. First of all, it seemed that I would have laid down all my own troubles for a while when I wiped away your tears, even if I weren't able to put an end to them. Second, I didn't doubt at all that I had enough influence to lift you up, once I had already lifted myself up. And I was worried that Fortune, conquered by me, might turn to conquer someone in my family. So, one way or another, I kept crawling along, trying to bind your wounds while I used one hand to keep pressure on mine. **1.2.** There were also things that interfered with my intentions. I knew that I couldn't confront your sorrow while it was still so fresh and causing pain, just in case the consolation itself aggravated and inflamed the sorrow. Nothing is worse for an illness than a medicine applied at the wrong time. So I was waiting until your sorrow could run its course and break. Alleviated by the time that had passed and ready for a cure, the hurt might then allow itself to be touched and treated. And although I had looked through all the great works of the most famous writers written to suppress and diminish grief, I couldn't find an example of someone writing to console his own family when he himself was the source of the sorrow. So I was stuck in an unusual situation and afraid that my words wouldn't be a consolation, but would make your sorrow worse.

1.3. Anyway, is it really necessary for a man to use fresh ideas, not ones taken from the usual, common sources, to console his family when he's lifting his head from his own deathbed? The magnitude of an exceedingly profound sorrow inevitably snatches away the power to choose words carefully, since it often even cuts off the voice itself. **1.4.** I'll try as I can, then, not because I trust my talent with words, but because I can be a very effective consolation just by offering consoling words. I hope that you, who could deny me nothing, won't deny me this either: though all mourning can be obstinately persistent, I hope you are willing to have me set you a limit on missing me. **2.1.** See how much I'm trusting your fondness for me? I've no doubt at all that I have more power to affect you than your sorrow does, and for people who are suffering there's nothing more powerful than sorrow. I'll give support to your sorrow first (I'm not going to start off by fighting with it), and I'll mention things that will strengthen it. I'll mention everything and expose whatever has been covered over. **2.2.** Somebody will say, "Some kind of consolation this is, bringing up bad things that were forgotten and putting the spirit right in the middle of all its burdens, when it can barely carry one of them!" But think about it: whenever a condition becomes so critical that it resists medicines, it is often treated with the opposite of medicine. So, I'll apply all of this grief and all of this mournfulness to your sorrow, not to give a gentle treatment, but to amputate and cauterize. What for? To make your spirit feel ashamed that, after overcoming so many other sadnesses, it is troubled by this one hurt—one open wound on a body covered in scars. **2.3.** So, let people whose tender minds have been made weak by much happiness and prosperity weep and wail for a long time; let them tumble and fall at the slightest hint of the most insignificant insult. But let the minds of those whose entire life has passed through every kind of calamity, let those minds endure to the end with a deep strength and an unshakeable perseverance. Constant misfortune gives this single good thing: in the end it hardens those whom it distresses.

2.4. Fortune didn't give you a break from the deepest kinds of sorrows; Fortune didn't even allow the day you were born to be a happy one: you lost your mother as soon as you were born—or rather, while you were being born—and so you were abandoned just as your life was beginning. You grew up under a stepmother, whom you made into a mother with your utter obedience and loyalty, as much of each as can be hoped for from a daughter. But even a good stepmother comes at great cost to a child. You lost a very affectionate uncle,[1] an exceptional and very brave man, just when you were expecting him to arrive home. And (so that Fortune could spread out her savagery for maximum effect instead of lumping the losses together) thirty days later you laid your beloved husband to rest, with whom you had three children. **2.5.** This sad news was brought to you while you were still grieving your uncle and while all your children were away. It was as if it happened at that time on purpose, all these bad things together, so you would have nowhere to lay your sorrow down. I won't mention all the dangers and all the fear that you have endured without a break. Only

---

1. See below, sec. 19.4 and following.

recently you took the bones of three grandchildren into your arms, the very same arms that sent them away on their trip. Twenty days after you buried my son, dead in your arms with your kisses on his face, you heard that I had been taken away into exile. This was the only thing left for you to experience: mourning as if dead one who was still alive.

3.1. The recent wound, I confess, is the most serious of those that have been inflicted on you. It didn't just break the skin, it split you right through the gut. New recruits who are lightly wounded put up a great fuss and fear doctors' hands more than any sword. But a veteran, even if he's badly wounded, lets his body be treated as if it belonged to someone else: tolerantly and without a sound. You ought to offer yourself now in the same way, bravely, to the cure I'm offering. **3.2.** Put aside your lamenting and your wailing, and the other ways women express their grief out loud. You've wasted so many bad events if you've not yet learned from them how to endure misery. Am I being too rough with you? If so, it's because I haven't left out any of the bad things in your life—I've piled them all together right in front of you.

4.1. I did this with a generous spirit, because I've decided to conquer your sorrow after all, not merely set a limit on it. And I'll conquer it, I think, if first of all I demonstrate that you couldn't call *me* pitiable and sad because of anything I've endured—still less could you call any who know me pitiable and sad; and second, if I switch focus to you and prove that your fortune, which depends entirely on mine, is not unfavorable at all. **4.2.** I'll try first to prove something your love for me as my mother wants to hear, that I'm not in a bad way at all. If I can, I'm going to demonstrate clearly that the things you think have harmed me are quite bearable. But if you can't bring yourself to believe this, then I'll be even happier to prove that I am alive, content and happy in circumstances that usually make men miserable. **4.3.** There's no reason for you to believe otherwise. I can tell you myself, so you won't be troubled by false speculation: "I am not miserable." I'll emphasize the point, so you'll feel even better: "It's impossible for me to be miserable."

5.1. We're born into a good condition, although we soon abandon it. The universe has arranged it so that we don't need much to live a happy life. Each and every one of us can give ourselves a happy life. External things, which anyway don't have much power for good or bad, aren't all that important: favorable circumstances don't lift a wise man up and adversity doesn't get him down. He can always work hard to depend mostly on himself, and to find every joy within.

5.2. What? Am I calling myself a wise man? Not at all! You see, if I were able to claim to be wise, I wouldn't simply deny that I'm pitiable, but I'd state that I'm the most fortunate of all, and even that I have been brought near to god. The truth is—and this is enough to soothe any misery—I've dedicated myself to wise men. Not yet strong enough to defend myself, I've fled to other men's fortresses, men who can easily defend themselves and their friends and family. **5.3.** I'm under orders to stand tall every day, as if I'm on guard duty, to keep watch for all the troop movements and attacks of Fortune long before they are made. Fortune is terrible only when she is unexpected, but a man who always expects her attack can withstand her easily. People caught by surprise fall in the first onslaught of the enemy. But people who have prepared themselves for battle beforehand, and are armed and in ranks, easily absorb the first and most destructive wave of attack.

5.4. I've never trusted Fortune, even when she seemed at peace with me. I put all of the things she affectionately gave me—money, public office, good standing—where she could take them back without affecting me. I maintained a no-man's land between these things and me. So, Fortune took them away—but she didn't *tear* them away. Fortune only breaks men she has smiled upon first. **5.5.** People who have loved the things Fortune gave them as if they were permanent gifts, who have wanted to be honored because of them . . . they fall and moan when their childish spirits, entirely ignorant of every true pleasure, are abandoned by those fake and fleeting delights. But the man who isn't improved by prosperity isn't made less by things that go away. Against both conditions of life he maintains an unconquered spirit with proven resilience. He has learned while he was prosperous and happy what could fend off bad times.

5.6. So, I've always thought that there's nothing truly good in any of the things everyone wishes for. I've found them hollow and covered up with a pretty paint job, which is deceptive because there's nothing pretty on the inside. Now, as far as what people call "bad things" are concerned, I find that nothing is as terrible or as harsh as the opinion of the mob suggests. By common consensus and belief even the word "evils" itself sounds rather harsh to the ear and hits those who hear it like something sad and detestable. At least, this is what the mob has decided. But wise men, for the most part, don't consider the mob's decrees to be legitimate. **6.1.** Setting aside, then, the opinion of the many, who are taken in by first impressions, however believable, let's see what sort of thing exile is. Of course, it involves a change of location. I don't want to seem to lessen exile's intensity and eliminate the worst part of it—unpleasant things do come with a change of place, such as poverty, public disgrace, and disrespect. I'll take these on later. In the meantime I want to examine first what difficult things just a change of place brings.

6.2. "It's unbearable to be away from your homeland." Come on, look at the huge crowd who barely fit under the roofs of this enormous city, Rome: most of this mob are away from their homeland. They have gathered here from their townships and colonies, from the whole world over. Ambition led some, the demands of public office led others. Some have come as ambassadors, others seeking a chance at the high-life or fertile ground for their vices. Some came desiring higher education, others desiring games and spectacles. Friendship drew some here and work others, because they saw a chance to show their virtue. Some brought beautiful bodies to sell, others beautiful speeches. **6.3.** Every kind of person has rushed to this city of ours, a city that sets a high price on both virtue and vice. Tell them all to say their full names and ask them all where they're from. You'll see that the majority are here having left their own homes behind—it's a great and beautiful city, but it's not theirs. **6.4.** After that, leave the city, which could be called the capital of the world, and travel around to all the other cities. Every one of them has a large group of foreign residents. Go from those that please many because of their beautiful locations and the opportunities the regions offer to isolated places or rocky islands, to Sciathus and Seriphus, Gyara or here on Corsica—take a census. You'll find that in every place of exile there is someone who is actually staying by choice. **6.5.** Can you find a hunk of rock that is as barren and craggy everywhere as Corsica is? Or more deprived of basic resources and with less civilized people? Is there any landscape more wild or sky more gray and gloomy? Even so, there are more foreigners here than there are citizens. Therefore, a change of location in and of itself is so much *not* a serious thing that even this place has drawn people away from their homeland.

6.6. I find some people say that a certain level of restless desire in the spirit for changing locations and moving homes is natural. The human mind is distracted and restless, you see, never keeping still. It spreads out, and spends its thoughts on everything, known or unknown. It wanders, it doesn't tolerate quiet, and it is utterly delighted by the newest thing.

6.7. Actually, this won't be much of a surprise if you think about the mind's origin. It's not made from earthbound and solid material, but comes from heavenly breath. The nature of heavenly things is to always be in motion, to flee, and to be moved along very swiftly. Consider the stars that light the world: none of them stay still. The sun is constantly moving and the points of sunset and sunrise change. Even though the sun moves with the heavens, it is carried in the opposite direction to the world. It passes quickly through all the signs of the Zodiac, never stopping. It's in perpetual motion, constantly changing location from one place to another. **6.8.** Everything always spins and is always moving. As the law and forces of nature have ordained, things shift from one place to another, and when over a certain numbers of years the planets have completed their orderly progression, they will travel that path again. Go ahead, then, and suggest that the human spirit, formed from the same essential substance as the heavenly bodies, doesn't like movement and travel even though the nature of god delights itself, or preserves itself, with constant and very swift change.

7.1. Turn from the heavens to the earth, and you'll see that nations and people the world over have migrated. Why else would there be Greek cities in the middle of barbarian regions? Why else would Macedonian Greek be heard in the middle of India and Persia?[2] Scythia, and that whole stretch of savage and wild tribes, has Greek cities along the southern coast. The brutal, everlasting winter, the tribes whose nature is as fearsome as the skies above them—these did not stop people from migrating there. **7.2.** There are lots of Athenians in Asia Minor.[3] Miletus sent out seventy-five cities' worth of people in different directions[4] and the entire southern and western coasts of Italy became *Magna Graecia*.[5] Asia Minor claims that the Etruscans came

---

2. During Alexander the Great's campaigns in the East, Macedonian troops were often settled in conquered areas.

3. Seneca is referring to the Ionian colonies of the western shore of Asia Minor (modern Turkey). Between around 800 BCE and 500 BCE there was a very robust period of colonization led by a number of city-states in Greece. Greek colonies were established all around the Mediterranean Basin and the Black Sea.

4. The suggestion is that Miletus dispatched seventy-five groups of colonists, each of which founded its own city.

5. *Magna Graecia*, or "Big (or Greater) Greece," is the name often applied to the region of Greek coastal city-states that stretched down the western shore of Italy and around the toe, including Sicily.

from there originally, Tyrians (Phoenicians) moved into Africa, and Carthaginians into Spain. Greeks imported themselves to Gaul, and Gauls to Greece. The Pyrenees did not stop the migrations of the German tribes. Human whim has moved down trackless and unknown paths. **7.3.** They dragged along their children, their wives and parents weighed down by age. Some, thrown off the path for a long time, didn't choose their location through careful judgment, but in their weariness took over the nearest place. Others enforced their own laws on a foreign land by the sword. The sea took some people, in search of unknown lands, and others settled where they ran out of supplies.[6] **7.4.** The reasons for leaving and seeking a homeland weren't the same for everyone. The destruction of a city by the enemy forced some away and they stumbled into foreign lands after losing their own. Internal conflict pushed some out and others were sent away to ease the strain of overpopulation. Pestilence, frequent earthquakes, infertile and unproductive land—all of these forced people out. And rumors (usually exaggerated) of a fertile land have seduced others. **7.5.** People have been shifted from their homes for various reasons, but it's quite clear that none have remained in the place they were born. Humankind scurries around all the time. On this huge globe something changes every day. New foundations are constructed for cities, and new peoples appear while others fall or are absorbed by the rise of a stronger nation. What are all of these movements of groups of people if not a kind of shared exile?

7.6. Why did I drag you along on such a long journey? What difference does it make to add to my list Antenor, the founder of Patavium, or Evander, who relocated the Arcadian Greeks to the shores of the Tiber? What about Diomedes and all the others—the winners and the losers—who dispersed to foreign lands after the Trojan War? **7.7.** Of course, the Roman state has respect for its founder, although he was an exile—a captured homeland, necessity, and fear of the conqueror led him, dragging along a small band of survivors and seeking a distant land, to Italy. And this nation has sent many, many colonies into lands it controls! Every place a Roman conquers, he inhabits. Romans willingly sign up for these relocations and, leaving their home altars behind, the old follow young colonists across the sea.

---

6. There are undertones here of the "migration" of Aeneas and the refugee Trojans from Troy to Italy, famously told in Vergil's *Aeneid*, which become explicit in sec. 7.7.

7.8. The question doesn't really need a longer list of examples, but I'll add one that comes to mind as I look about. This island itself has often changed inhabitants. I'll pass over earlier times shrouded in antiquity, but it was the Greeks who, after leaving Phocis, came to live here before moving on to Massilia[7] where they live now. It's uncertain what made them leave—perhaps the gloomy sky, or the sight of Italy growing in power, or the fact that there are few good harbors. That it wasn't the savagery of the indigenous peoples is clear enough because the Greeks established a settlement at the time when the indigenous Gallic peoples were especially fierce and wild. **7.9.** After that, Ligurians came to the island, then the Spanish too—this much is clear from shared customs. They have the same kind of hats and footwear as the Cantabrians, and some common words too. In fact, the dialect as a whole has drifted from its original form through contact with Greeks and Ligurians. Then two colonies of Roman citizens were sent out, one by Marius and the other by Sulla. The entire population of this dry, craggy rock has changed! **7.10.** You could hardly find any land that's inhabited now by indigenous people. Everything's mixed up and interbred. One thing follows another and then this group wants what that group's sick of; one group of people—forced out of somewhere else—ends up forcing another out. Fate likes it when fortunes shift, not staying in the same position.

8.1. Varro,[8] a very learned man among the Romans, thought the fact that the natural world is the same wherever we go was a good enough antidote for moving (setting aside the other disadvantages that exile brings). Marcus Brutus[9] thought that it was enough that people going into exile took their virtues with them. **8.2.** Although someone might not think these two things individually are good enough to console an exiled person, he must admit that they're more than

---

7. Modern Marseilles, which may be the oldest city in France. A trading post was established there around 600 BCE, with a settlement shortly after, by Greeks from Phocaea (in turn an Ionian colony on the coast of modern Turkey).

8. Marcus Terentius Varro (116 BCE–27 CE), like many of the Roman elite, held significant public offices and participated (as a partisan of Pompey) in the civil wars of the period. But Varro is best known as an antiquarian and scholar who studied and wrote on a wide range of topics.

9. Brutus was among the killers of Julius Caesar, and later became a sort of hero to many who opposed the rule of the emperor. He was also a favorite role model for the Roman Stoics.

enough when taken together. What a small thing we lose. But two very beautiful things follow us wherever we move: nature (which we all share) and virtue (which is our own). **8.3.** This was done on purpose, trust me, by whoever the creator of the universe was, whether an omnipotent god or formless reason, the ingenious artist of monumental works. Or perhaps it was the divine breath equally and consistently disseminated through everything, great and small, or even fate and a determined, continuous chain of events. It was done by design, I say, so that nothing except what is least valuable can come under the authority and control of another. **8.4.** The best thing a man has lies beyond human influence and power, and can't be given or taken away. This world, the biggest and most beautiful thing Nature has created, and the spirit, which reflects on and wonders at the world and is the most magnificent thing in the world, belong to us. They are lasting and will remain with us as long as we ourselves remain.

8.5. So, let's hurry eagerly and without fear, heads held high, wherever life takes us, and let's stride across whatever land we're in. It's not possible to be exiled from the world—for humankind nothing in the world is foreign. We view heaven from the same distance away wherever we are. All that is divine stands an equal distance apart from all that is human. **8.6.** In the end, what does it matter where I stand, as long as my insatiable eyes can always devour the spectacle of the heavens? What does it matter where I stand, as long as I can gaze upon the sun, the moon, and the bright lights of heaven? What does it matter, as long as I can study their rise and fall and how far apart they are or why they travel swiftly or slowly? What does it matter, as long as I can view so many stars twinkling at night, some unmoving, others only moving a bit within a prescribed space, some shining brightly all of a sudden, and others blinding the eyes with a blaze of fire, as if they were falling or flying across the sky very brightly with a long tail? As long as I stand among the stars and mix with heavenly things, as much as a man can, as long as I keep my spirit lifted up and focused on things with which I share a bond, what does it matter where I stand?

9.1. "But this land doesn't have an abundance of fruit-bearing or beautiful trees. It isn't irrigated by big rivers you can sail on. People in other places don't want anything that comes from here and the land is barely fertile enough to provide for the inhabitants. Precious stones aren't found here, and there are no veins of gold or silver." **9.2.** A spirit delighted by earthly things is a shallow one. It must be led from earthly things to the things that can be seen shining from everywhere equally. Consider, too, that earthly things impede our perception of true goods because earthly things are false goods, in which people blindly trust. The higher people build their porches or raise towers, the wider they stretch neighborhoods, the deeper they dig cool basements, the farther they lift up the peaks of dining halls—this is how much more the sky is blocked from their view. **9.3.** Let's say chance has thrown you into a region where a shack is the most elegant housing available: aren't you showing a poverty of spirit and making yourself just feel good if you can put a brave face on it because you know Romulus lived in a shack? It's better to say, "Without a doubt, this humble little hut can house virtues. It'll be more beautiful than every temple the moment it is occupied by justice and moderation, good sense and duty, thoughtfulness in the management of responsibilities, and knowledge of human and divine affairs. No place is shallow if it contains such a crowd of high virtues—no exile is harsh if you leave with virtues like these for companions." **9.4.** Brutus, in his book *On Virtue*, said that he had seen Marcellus in exile at Mytilene[10] and that he was living (as much as human nature allowed) a very happy life—and never more attracted by the liberal arts than at that time. Brutus added that, rather than leaving Marcellus behind in exile, he seemed to be going into exile himself because he was returning to Rome without him. **9.5.** It's amazing that Marcellus was much more fortunate when admired as an exile by Brutus than when admired by the Roman Republic as consul.[11] What a man he was! He made another feel like he was becoming an exile when the man was actually leaving an exile behind! What a man he was! He won the admiration of Brutus, whom even Cato had to admire! **9.6.** Brutus also said that Caesar had sailed past Mytilene because he couldn't handle seeing the man in disgrace. The Senate asked for Marcellus' reinstatement with popular support, so solemnly and so sadly that all of them seemed to be echoing Brutus' spirit: not pleading for Marcellus' sake but for their own, so they wouldn't have to be exiles, deprived of Marcellus.

9.7. Don't you think Marcellus, being the man he was, often said to himself (so he could endure his exile with a calm spirit), "It's not a

---

10. Marcus Claudius Marcellus, consul of 51 BCE, went into exile after Caesar's victory over Pompey.

11. While consul (and afterwards) Marcellus was fiercely opposed to Caesar's plans.

sad thing that you are away from your fatherland. You have studied philosophy deeply enough to know that every place is a fatherland for the wise man. What else is there to say? The man who sent you into exile[12]—wasn't he himself away from the fatherland for ten years in a row? Without a doubt, it was so the *imperium* could grow. But still, he was away. **9.8.** And now look at him! Africa, full of the threat of war again, is drawing him away. So is Spain, which is reviving factions that were beaten and broken, and traitorous Egypt, and indeed the whole world, intent on taking advantage of a distracted and disturbed *imperium*. What should he deal with first? Which threat should he turn and face? His own victory forces him to travel the lands. Let nations look to him and worship him. You should live, happy to be admired by Brutus." **10.1.** Marcellus, therefore, endured his exile well. The change in location didn't change anything in his spirit even though poverty came with it. There's nothing bad in poverty for anyone, as long as he isn't too far gone with the diseases of greed and overconsumption, which corrupt. How little it takes to support a human life! Can anyone who has even a little bit of virtue lack that amount of sustenance?

10.2. As far as I'm concerned, I understand that I have lost responsibilities, but not riches. The needs of the body are few: it wants to keep the cold at bay and to satisfy hunger and thirst. Whatever else is desired feeds our vices, not our basic needs. It isn't necessary to search the oceans or to fill up our stomachs with butchered animals or to bring up shellfish from the unknown shores of the farthest sea. The gods destroy those whose desire for extravagant things exceeds the limits of our imperium, which is enviable even without its excesses. **10.3.** People want something hunted east of the Phasis River[13] for their pretentious kitchens to prepare. They're not ashamed to capture birds from the Parthians, though we've not yet taken vengeance for our legion standards.[14] They pull together a menu from everywhere that a discriminating palate would appreciate and bring food from the edge of the world that stomachs, ruined by delicacies, can barely keep down. They

---

12. That is, Julius Caesar.

13. The Rion River in Georgia, which ends at the Black Sea. From the earliest ancient Greek literature this was considered the northeastern edge of the known world.

14. These standards were lost to the Parthians by Marcus Licinius Crassus' ill-fated attack against the East in 53 BCE. They were recovered through diplomacy by Augustus (a major political success) in 20 BCE, but without any punishment or military action against the Parthians.

vomit so they can eat and eat so they can vomit. They don't even stoop to digest the dinners they've brought together from the world over! How can poverty harm someone who despises such things? And even if someone desires them, poverty is still beneficial to him, because he—though unwilling—becomes healthier. That is, as long as he can't get what he wants, the result is the same as if he didn't want it at all: he gets the treatment without agreeing to accept it. **10.4.** Gaius Caesar, who was born, it seems to me, to show how big vices can become among the super-wealthy, ate ten million sesterces' worth of food in one day: he couldn't quite figure out how to spend the equivalent of the tax revenue from three provinces, though he got imaginative help from everyone.[15] **10.5.** Wretched people! Their palates aren't stimulated unless they taste very expensive foods. It's not that it's exceptionally savory or sweet that makes the food expensive, but that it's rare and difficult to prepare. For those who are happy to return to a healthy mindset, what use is there for skills that serve the stomach? Commerce? Clear-cutting forests? Deep-sea fishing? Food is lying around all over in all of the places nature has put it. As if they're blind, people pass over food that is right next to them and wander the earth, crossing the seas and spending a great deal to whet their appetite when just a little food could satisfy it.

10.6. It would be nice to say, "Why are you launching ships? Why are you arming yourselves against men *and* wild beasts? Why are you running around in such a rush? Why are you adding wealth to wealth? Don't you want to think about how small your bodies are? Isn't it madness and the worst mental illness to want so much, when you can only take so little? Although you are increasing your wealth and expanding your boundaries, you'll never grow a bigger body. Although your business ventures may turn out well and war may bring you lots of profit, although food hunted from everywhere may be brought to your table, you still won't have anywhere you can store these provisions of yours. **10.7.** Why do you want so much? Our ancestors, whose virtue still supports our vices, were unfortunate wretches, of course, weren't they? They made their food by hand, the ground was their bed, their roofs didn't sparkle with gold, and their temples didn't glimmer with gems then. At that time oaths were

---

15. Exact equivalents in modern currencies aren't really possible, but Seneca is basically claiming here that Caligula's dinner cost about as much as a year's pay for 12,000 Roman legionnaires.

made with reverence for the gods not just with hand-crafted statues of the gods. And those who had invoked the gods went back to the enemy, knowing they'd die, so they wouldn't break those oaths.[16]

10.8. "Our *dictator* Manius Curius lived less happily, didn't he? He received the Samnite delegation although he was cooking his own very plain food on the hearth,[17] cooking with the same hands he'd used many times by then to strike the enemy and to place a victor's wreath on the lap of the Capitoline Juppiter.[18] Surely he lived less happily than Apicius, who lived not long ago.[19] Philosophers were expelled, charged with being 'corrupters of the youth,' from the same city in which he tainted his generation with his teaching, lecturing on science . . . kitchen science." Learning about his death is rewarding. **10.9.** After he had thrown a hundred million sesterces at his kitchen and had sucked back many imperial handouts, and the Emperor's earnings, with one wild party after another, he for the first time took a look at his accounts because he was heavily in debt. He calculated that he had ten million sesterces left, and fatally poisoned himself. It was as if he would have been living at the edge of starvation if he had lived on ten million. **10.10.** What luxury he was living in if ten million was abject poverty for him! Go ahead, then, and think that it's the measure of your bank account that matters, and not the measure of your spirit. One person was afraid of having ten million and fled with poison what others seek with prayers. But for Apicius, since he had such a depraved mind, that final drink was his healthiest. Whenever he was enjoying his incredible feasts and even boasting about them, whenever he was putting his vices on display, whenever he was talking his fellow citizens into excessive living, whenever he was

---

16. A reference to M. Atilius Regulus, consul in 267 BCE and 256 BCE, who, released from imprisonment during the First Punic War (264–241 BCE) to deliver a message to the Roman Senate, returned to face terrible torture by the Carthaginians rather than break his oath.

17. Turnips, according to ancient sources. Manius Curius was a very successful general in the early third century BCE known for incorruptibility and for using war profits for public works.

18. This was one of the culminating rituals of the "triumph," a ceremony honoring exceptional generals. The victorious general gave his wreath to Juppiter to symbolize his disavowal of personal power.

19. That is, during the reign of Tiberius; Apicius was known for disreputably luxurious living.

seducing young people to imitate him (and they learn these things quickly even without bad role models!)—whenever he was doing these things, he was eating and drinking poison. **10.11.** These are the kinds of things that happen to people who assess their wealth not according to reason, which sets clear limits, but according to corrupt habits, which have a limitless and inconceivable power over decisions. Nothing satisfies lust, but even a little satisfies natural needs. Therefore, poverty in exile is not at all troublesome, since no place of exile is so desolate that it cannot provide enough to nourish a man.

11.1. "But an exile will miss his clothes and his house." He'll miss only what he is used to. He'll have a roof and a cloak. It takes little to cover the body and little to nourish it. Nature didn't make anything necessary for humans that was hard to acquire. **11.2.** Now, he misses his cloth tinted with expensive purple dye, with gold woven in and decorated with many different colors and designs. It's not Fortune's fault he's poor, but his own. Even if you give him back what he lost, it won't do any good. You see, after being recalled, he'll want what he doesn't have more than he wanted, as an exile, what he once had. **11.3.** He's missing his dinner table gleaming with gold dishes, his silver made by famous ancient artisans, his bronze made more expensive by the insanity of a few collectors, his crowd of slaves who would crowd any house you can think of, his force-fed pack animals, and the marble brought from all over the world. Even if you gather all those things together in one place, they won't fill his empty spirit, any more than any amount of liquid will satisfy the thirst of a man driven not by lack of water but by a raging fever: it's not a thirst he has, it's a sickness. **11.4.** This doesn't only happen with money and food. Every desire that's born from vice and not a basic human need has the same nature. That is, if you give anything to it, you won't end the desire but will reach the next stage. Whoever keeps himself within a natural limit will not experience poverty. Whoever exceeds a natural limit will be followed by poverty even in extreme wealth. Even places of exile supply all that is necessary, but not even kingdoms supply all that is unnecessary.

11.5. It's the spirit that makes men rich. It follows us into exile and, in our deepest isolation, after it has found enough to sustain the body, the spirit overflows with its own goods and enjoys them. Money matters no more to the spirit than to the immortal gods. **11.6.** All of the things men admire because of their unwise inclinations—things that are tied too closely to the body, such as gemstones and gold and silver and large polished tables—are just earthly weight. A spirit that is free and true to its own nature can't love them, since it is light and swift, prepared to spring toward the heavens whenever it is released. Until then, as much as it can, weighed down as it is by these limbs and this heavy bag of bones, it examines heavenly things on the swift wings of the mind. **11.7.** This is why the spirit—free, kin to the gods, and equal to every world and every age—can never be exiled. In thought it can travel all around heaven, can be sent into every past and future time. This poor little body, the spirit's guardian and prison, is tossed about here and there—it is tested by punishment, incarceration, illness. But the spirit itself is set apart from mortal things and eternal—no hand can touch it.

12.1. Don't think that I'm just using the sayings of philosophers to reduce the discomforts of poverty, which no one experiences as a serious thing unless he thinks it's a serious thing. Consider first of all how the large majority of people are poor, but note that they are no more or less sad or anxious than rich people. Or should I say that I don't know whether they're happier, in relation to how few things disturb their spirits. **12.2.** Let's finish with the poor and focus on the super-rich. How often the rich are like the poor! Their bags must be made smaller when traveling, and whenever the itinerary requires speed, their crowd of companions is sent away. When they're on military service they have only a small part of their property with them, since camp discipline removes all such supports. **12.3.** And it's not only the circumstances of a time or the barrenness of a place that make rich men equal to poor men. On certain days, when boredom with riches takes hold of them, they have picnics and use clay pots, leaving behind their gold and silver plates. Crazy! They sometimes want to experience the thing they always fear will happen. Their minds are so blind and so ignorant of the truth that they imitate for the sake of pleasure what brings them anxiety.

12.4. Whenever I look back at the ancient role models, I am ashamed that my current poverty is a comfortable one, since at this point in time extravagant living has come to this: the traveling expenses of exiles now are greater than the inheritances of the noblest men were then. Homer had one slave, Plato three, and for Zeno, the founder of the Stoics' stern and manly wisdom, none was enough. Will anyone therefore say that these men lived unhappy lives without seeming himself to be the unhappiest man of all? **12.5.** Menenius Agrippa,[20] who was the mediator for the Republic between the patricians and the plebeians, was buried with money that was donated. Atilius Regulus,[21] when he was beating the Carthaginians in Africa, wrote to the Senate that the supervisor for his country property had run off and deserted the farm. He asked that it be managed at public expense while he was away. Was it worth it to have no slaves so that the Roman people could become his tenant farmer? **12.6.** Scipio's daughters were provided with a dowry through the public treasury because their father didn't leave an inheritance.[22] Goodness! It was fair for the Roman people to give Scipio a contribution that one time, since he always made Carthage pay their tribute. How lucky the grooms were to have the Roman people stand in place of a father-in-law! Do you think fathers these days, whose daughters are pantomime actresses[23] but marry with a dowry of a million sesterces, are happier than Scipio was, whose children were given solid cast bronze for a dowry by the Senate, acting as guardian?[24] **12.7.** Does a person look down on poverty when it has such noble ancestors? Is an exile indignant because he goes without, when Scipio went without a dowry, Regulus a steward, Menenius a funeral? For all of these people, being given what they needed was a nobler thing—and only possible because they had a need in the first place. With these kinds of character witnesses, poverty is not only safe, it is desirable.

13.1. You could answer, "Why are you so cleverly dividing up things that cannot be endured at the same time, but can be endured

---

20. Consul in 503 BCE, victorious against the Sabines, and known for the famous speech related in Livy that ended a civil uprising (the first Secession of the Plebs).

21. Marcus Atilius Regulus (d. 250 BCE) was one of the most famous role models for the Stoics. After being captured by the Carthaginians and sent back to Rome to arrange for a ransom (which he opposed), he returned voluntarily to Carthage to face execution.

22. We do know from Valerius Maximus that the Senate provided a dowry for Gnaeus Scipio's one daughter, but while he was still alive. Perhaps Seneca knows of another instance (there were many famous Scipiones).

23. Although it was socially and legally discouraged, members of the upper class sometimes performed in pantomimes (a kind of comic play that incorporated elements of farce, and also nudity and sexuality). Such actors were often portrayed as morally corrupt.

24. Lumps of bronze were the basis of the monetary system in the early Republic before coins were used (early third century BCE). Seneca is referring here to *aes grave*, cast bronze bars of standardized weight.

one at a time? Moving is tolerable, if you are only moving. Poverty is tolerable, if it doesn't come with public disgrace, which can crush the spirit by itself anyway." **13.2.** Here are the words I would use against the man trying to scare me with bad things gathered together: "If you have enough inner strength against any one element of Fortune, you have enough to stand against all. As soon as virtue strengthens the spirit, it becomes invulnerable on all sides. If greed, humanity's most intense illness, is gone, ambition won't delay you. If you consider the end of your life to be a kind of natural law and not a punishment, and you cast from your heart the fear of death, you won't be afraid of anything else. **13.3.** If you think that the libido was given to humans not for pleasure but for propagation, every other desire will harmlessly pass by the man who hasn't been violated by lust, that destruction buried deep in the core of man. Reason does not defeat all the vices one by one. It conquers them all, all at once."

13.4. Do you think that the wise man can be disturbed by public disgrace when he is entirely self-sufficient and keeps himself apart from the opinions of the crowd? A disgraceful death is even worse than a disgraceful life, but Socrates entered prison with the same attitude he showed to bring the Thirty Tyrants back into line.[25] In fact, he took the disgrace out of the place, since a place that held Socrates could never seem like a prison. **13.5.** Who is so utterly blind to the truth that he thinks it was a public disgrace for Marcus Cato to have been twice defeated in elections, once for the praetorship and once for the consulship? The public disgrace was that neither office was held by Cato. **13.6.** No one can be disrespected by someone else unless he has lost respect for himself. An insignificant and abject spirit is open to insult. But the man who stands tall against the most brutal events and resists bad things that crush others wears his sorrows as a badge of honor. It's how we feel: we admire nothing as much as we admire a man bravely facing misery.

13.7 Aristides[26] was led back to Athens to face execution. No one he met could look him in the eye, but they groaned as if they were not

---

25. This probably refers to 403 BCE, when Socrates refused to follow an order given by the Thirty Tyrants on moral grounds.

26. The event related here actually concerns Phocion (the Good), an Athenian politician active at the end of the fourth century BCE. Seneca has confused him with Aristides (the Just), son of Lysimachus, who was an Athenian politician and general in the first quarter of the fifth century BCE famous for his mediation of allied contributions to the newly formed Delian League.

just seeing a just man, but Justice itself. Even so, one man spat in his face. He could have been very insulted because he knew only a foul-mouthed man would dare to do this. But he wiped his face and said with a laugh to the arresting magistrate, "Tell this fellow not to open his mouth so rudely in the future." He did it to match insult with insult. **13.8.** I know that some will say there is nothing more serious than disrespect and that even death is better. I'll say to them in reply that exile, too, is devoid of any kind of contempt. If a great man falls, he is great even when fallen too: he can no more be disrespected than the ruins of a temple that religious people revere just as if it were standing.

14.1. Since, dearest mother, you have no reason to weep forever for my sake, it must be that you are weeping for your own reasons. There are, it seems, two: either the fact that you seem to have lost your protection[27] or that you aren't able to endure your longing for me on your own. **14.2.** I should touch on the first concern briefly, because I know that you love your children with all your spirit for nothing other than what they are. Some mothers, with a woman's lack of control, use their sons' power to control events. Others, because women can't hold public office, are ambitious through their sons. And some both use up and seek to possess their children's inheritance and wear out their skill with words by lending it to others. May all of them see what kind of mother you are. **14.3.** You take great joy in your children's goodness but little in their usefulness. You've always set a limit on our generosity, though never on your own. You, although legally under your father's control, gave gifts out of your own money to already rich sons. You managed our inheritance as if you were working to preserve your own or abstaining from using another's. You used our influence as sparingly as if you were using another's property, and all you received from our elected positions was pleasure, and the expense of the political campaign. Your affection was given without a view to advantage. So, when your son has been taken away, you can't miss what you never thought was yours when he was safe.

15.1. I need to focus all my efforts to console you where the true force of a mother's pain comes from: "I miss my dear son's hugs. I can't enjoy seeing his face or talking with him. Where is he? The sight of him relieved my sadness—he carried all my worries for me. I miss our

---

27. That is, her son, Seneca, after whose fall from grace she might have been legally or socially more vulnerable.

conversations—I could never get enough. Where are his writings, in which I shared more willingly than a woman usually does, and more as a friend than a mother? I can't meet him, or see his childlike happiness when he sees me." **15.2.** You add to these thoughts the places where we were happy and sat talking and all the reminders of recent conversations that are, of course, so good at making your spirit ache. Cruel Fortune planned this for you, too, that three days before I was taken you would leave, worry-free and without any fear that anything like this would happen. **15.3.** It was good that distance had separated us before, and good that an absence of a few years had prepared you for this bad thing. Rather than returning to have the pleasure of your son's company, you returned to the daily habit of missing him. If you had been away long before, you would have endured my absence bravely, because the intervening time would have softened the ache. If you hadn't gone away, you would have enjoyed seeing your son for two more days. As it is, fate cruelly arranged it that you wouldn't be there for my misfortune or get used to my being gone. **15.4.** However difficult these events are, you need to call that much more upon your courage, and fight like you're fighting an enemy you know and have beaten before. Your blood isn't flowing from a body that has not been injured before—these are old wounds that have opened again.

16.1. There's no reason you should excuse yourself because you're a woman and allowed to be a little uncontrolled with tears (though not a lot). It's why our ancestors gave women ten months[28] to mourn their husbands: they were limiting how stubborn a woman's sadness can be with a public regulation. They didn't prohibit grief. But they did set a boundary on it, because when you have lost someone you love very much, unlimited sorrow is a silly indulgence and no sorrow at all is inhumanly rigid. Best of all is to choose something in between loving duty and reason—that is, to feel loss then control it. **16.2.** And there's no reason to take a lesson from certain women who put on sadness only to end it with death (you know, the ones who never took off the mourning clothes they put on when their sons died[29]). Life has demanded more courage from you from the start. A woman who lacks a woman's faults can't use a woman's excuses. **16.3.** You're not like most

---

28. Men were traditionally allowed nine days of public mourning.
29. This could be a reference to Octavia, sister of Augustus. See *Consolation to Marcia* 2.3–2.5.

people drawn to shameless behavior, which is the greatest badness of our generation. No gems or pearls catch your eye. Wealth doesn't glitter for you, as if it were the greatest good a human being could have. Since you were raised in an old-fashioned and strict home, the desire to emulate the worst—dangerous even for the best—doesn't affect you. You have never felt ashamed of your fertility, as if it were a bad thing to have children when older. And you never hid your pregnancy like it was indecent, as some do—women whose beauty is the only thing to recommend them. You never got rid of the hopes conceived within you for children. **16.4.** You haven't polluted your face with pigments and makeup. You've never liked clothes that leave you naked wearing them. Modesty seems to be your only enhancement—the best kind of decoration, the most beautiful, and a loveliness that suits every age. **16.5.** So, you can't use the fact that you're a woman as an excuse for maintaining your sorrow, because your virtues have set you apart from women. You should be as free from womanly tears as you are from womanly vices. Not even women will allow you to fade away in mourning—that is, if you want to listen to women whose exceptional virtue puts them in the company of great men. Instead, these women will tell you to rise up after you've completed the required mourning period.

16.6. Fortune left Cornelia[30] two out of twelve children. If you wanted to count up funerals, she lost ten—but if you want to measure their worth, she lost two Gracchi.[31] Even so, she forbade the women weeping all around her and cursing her fate from blaming Fortune, because Fortune gave her sons like the Gracchi. A son born from this woman had to be one who could say during a debate, "Are you insulting the mother who gave birth to me?!" The mother's words seem to me much more courageous: the son valued the day of his

---

30. Cornelia (ca. 190–100 BCE), the daughter of the famous Publius Cornelius Scipio Africanus, was the mother of Tiberius Gracchus and Gaius Gracchus (and also a third surviving child, Sempronia). She is one of several Roman examples of virtuous women, and one of the few non-Imperial women to have been voted an honorific statue by the Senate. Cornelia seems to have been heavily involved in her two sons' radical political careers, and studied literature and philosophy. There are some excerpts and fragments surviving from her letters, putting her in the company of a very small group of women from antiquity whose writings survive.

31. That is, Tiberius and Gaius, populist and revolutionary leaders during the Republic who were both killed in public rioting. One of Cornelia's speeches in support of her sons is preserved.

birth, the mother also valued funerals. **16.7.** Rutilia followed her son
Cotta into exile.[32] Her affection tied her to him so closely that she
preferred to endure exile than to miss him, and she didn't return to
her fatherland until he did. Then, after his return and at the height
of his political influence,[33] she lost him to death as bravely as she had
followed him into exile—no one saw her cry after he was buried. She
showed her virtue during exile and her good sense at his death: nothing held her back from her duty as a mother, and nothing held her
back in unproductive and silly sadness. I want to say that you belong
in their company. You've always imitated their lives. Follow their
example in bringing your grief under control and suppressing it.

17.1. I know that this kind of thing is not in our control, and that
no emotion follows our orders, least of all one that comes out of sorrow and pain. This kind is fierce and resists every kind of medicine.
Sometimes we want to bury it and swallow our grieving, but tears
still fall from our faces even if they are falsely serene. Sometimes we
distract our spirits with the Games or gladiatorial spectacles, but then
our defenses are broken down by some reminder of our loss that happens during the very entertainments that are distracting us. **17.2.** This
is why it's better to conquer your heart than to trick it. You see, after
grief has been deluded by pleasures and distracted by business it comes
back, and after the rest renews its savage attack. But whatever yields
to reason is given up forever. I'm not going to show you all the meth-
ods I know many use, such as distracting yourself with a long trip or
pleasant scenery, or examining the household accounts carefully, or
spending lots of time managing the family's wealth, or always involving yourself in new and different business. All of these things are good
for a short while but they interfere with your sorrow rather than cure
it. I would prefer that you end your grief, not avoid it. **17.3.** So, I'll
direct you where all who flee from Fortune ought to flee, the liberal
arts. They will heal your wound and erase your every sadness. Even
if you've not usually done so in the past, you'll find them useful now.
As much as my father's old-fashioned strictness allowed, you have a
passing familiarity with them even if you didn't study them all.

---

32. Gaius Rutilius Cotta was exiled in 90 BCE, and returned shortly after.

33. Rutilius Cotta was consul in 75 BCE, and proconsul in 74 BCE, leading troops
to a significant victory in Cisalpine Gaul (for which he was voted a triumph). He died
before celebrating the triumph.

17.4. If only my father, a very great man, had been less devoted to tradition and had wanted you to be totally immersed in philosophy, rather than just dipped in it! If he had, you wouldn't have to prepare it as a defense against Fortune. You'd just pull it out and use it now. He was less willing to allow you to throw yourself into studies because of those women who used them to attain status instead of wisdom. But, for the time, you did imbibe some wisdom because you have a voracious intellect. The foundations for these areas of study have been laid—go back to them now and they will keep you safe. **17.5.** They will also give you comfort and pleasure, and if they enter your spirit in good faith, sorrow and pain will never enter again, or anxiety, or the useless annoyance of unhelpful worry. Your heart won't be vulnerable to any of these feelings—it has long been closed to other faults. Studies are the surest protection, and are the only thing that can snatch you from Fortune's grasp.

18.1. But since, while you are traveling to the port in the storm that studies promise you, you still need something to help you stay afloat, so I want to tell you about the comforts you already have. **18.2.** Look to my brothers[34]—given their health and safety it's not right for you to blame Fortune. In both brothers there's something to be pleased about, though their virtues are different. One has pursued public office through hard work and the other wisely despises public office. Find peace in the public image of the first, in the quiet life of the second, and the love and loyalty of both. I know what they most privately want: one cultivates his public image to make you look better, and the other has withdrawn in a peaceful and calm retirement to make time for you. **18.3.** Fortune has arranged nicely for your sons to be an aid and a delight. You can be defended by the public image of one and enjoy the retirement of the other. They will be rivals in helping you and the devotion of two will push out your longing for the third. I can promise this with a bold certainty: you won't notice any difference except the number of sons around. **18.4.** After them, look to your grandchildren. Marcus[35] is a handsome young lad—

---

34. Lucius Annaeus Gallio, known before his adoption by Lucius Junius Gallio as Lucius Annaeus Novatus, who was politically active and successful during the reign of Claudius, and Marcus Annaeus Mela, whose son was the eminent poet Lucan.
35. This is usually thought to be Seneca's own son, but could be Marcus Annaeus Lucanus (the poet Lucan).

no sadness can last when you look at him. There is no savage pain so great or so immediate that he can't soothe it with his presence. **18.5.** Whose tears could his cheerfulness *not* dry? Whose spirit could his witty jokes *not* lift up, even a person weighed down with worry? Who could resist enjoying a joke around his naughtiness? He'll get anyone's attention—his chattiness will pull anyone away from sad musing, but they won't get sick of it. I pray to the gods that he outlives us! **18.6.** May all of fate's cruelty wear itself out on me! Whatever pain and sorrow a mother must have, or that a grandmother must have, let it come to me! May the rest of the family thrive as they are—I won't complain about my loss of family or my circumstances. Let me be the sacrificial victim so my family won't suffer anymore. **18.7.** Hug Novatilla,[36] who is about to give you grandchildren. I brought her into my household, adopted her—perhaps it seems like she has been orphaned by losing me, although her real father is still alive. Love her in my place. Fortune recently took her mother, but your devotion can make it so it doesn't feel as if she's lost a mother, though she may be sad that she has. **18.8.** Establish her character now, and shape it. Advice given at an impressionable age is more deeply absorbed. Get her used to talking to you, to be shaped by your judgment. If you give her nothing more than a role model, you'll still be giving her a great deal. And this solemn duty can be like a cure for you, because a spirit grieving out of love can't be turned from its pain except by reason or a noble task. **18.9.** I would mention your father in this list of comforts too, if he weren't living away from you.[37] Think about the affection he has for you instead. You know that it's better for you to be kept safe for him than to expend yourself for my sake. Whenever an uncontrolled wave of grief hits you and drags you with it, think about your father. You, certainly, have been so good at giving him grandchildren and great grandchildren that you yourself aren't his only outlet for affection. Nevertheless, the achievement of a life lived in such happiness stems from you. It's not right while he is alive to complain about your life.

---

36. Novatilla was the daughter of Seneca's brother Gallio. Adoption from living parents was a widespread practice at Rome among the elite.
37. We know that Helvia followed Seneca the Elder to Rome sometime between 3 and 5 CE from Spain. Presumably her father remained there.

19.1. I have remained silent so far about your greatest comfort, your sister,[38] who loves you most of all. You can share every care with her without holding back, because she loves us all like a mother. You have mingled your tears with the woman who held you as you took your first breath. **19.2.** She is always in tune with your emotions, but she doesn't mourn for me only because you do. I was brought to Rome by her, and because of her devoted and motherly care I recovered after being sick for a long time. She offered me her support and influence when I was campaigning for my quaestorship and for my sake overcame her sense of modesty because of her affection for me—and she wasn't even bold enough for conversations or conspicuous greetings. Her sheltered way of living, her reserve (when women are mostly so careless and unrefined), her peaceful life in retirement, and her private and studious character did nothing to stop her from canvassing for my sake! **19.3.** This, dearest mother, is the comfort that will make you whole again. Be with her as much as you can, cling to her hugs as tightly as you can. The grieving usually flee the things they love best and look for freedom from their sorrow. You should go to her no matter what you are feeling since, whether you want to keep being sad or stop, in her you will find either an end for your sorrow or a friend.

19.4. But if I know the good judgment of that most excellent woman, she won't let you drown in a useless grief and will tell her own story to you as a model to follow. I was a witness to it, too. She had lost her husband right in the middle of a sea voyage; she loved him very much and had married while she was still very young. She took on the burden of the loss, her grief, and her fear at the same time, and brought his body away from the shipwreck after she survived the storm! **19.5.** Isn't it true that the exemplary deeds of many women lie in obscurity? If she happened to have lived in the straightforward olden days, when it was obligatory to admire virtue, can you imagine how much competition among great poets there would have been to immortalize a wife who, without regard for her weakness or for the sea (that even the bravest men fear), put her own life in danger so her husband could be buried, and instead of worrying about her own funeral planned on his! The woman who gave her own life

---

38. Helvia's sister's name is not known.

in place of her husband is celebrated in the songs of all[39]—but it's a greater deed to ensure burial for a husband at the risk of your life. A love that acquires less with equal danger is greater. **19.6.** After hearing this, no one will be surprised that during the sixteen years her husband was governor in Egypt[40] she was never seen in public, did not allow any native of Egypt into her house, asked nothing of her husband, and made sure nothing could be asked of her. As a result, the province—known for being indiscreet and clever at insulting governors, in which even those who avoid blame don't avoid bad reputations—admired her as if she was their one and only model of propriety. And this is very difficult in a place where people like dangerously clever jokes and every kind of free (and loose) speech. Even today Egypt still prays, but never expects, to see another woman like her. It would truly have been something if the province had approved of her after sixteen years—it's much more so that it took no notice of her. **19.7.** I'm not bringing these things up to praise her—running through them so lightly cheats her—but so you understand that she has a real nobility of spirit. Ambition, greed, all the good and destructive things that come with power, none of them conquered her. The fear of death did not terrify her as she watched the ship go down after it was damaged. And she—hanging on to her husband's dead body—didn't try to figure out how she could survive instead of how she could get him out of there. It is appropriate for you to show an equal measure of virtue and recover from your grief. Make sure that no one can think you are ashamed of being my mother.

20.1. But since it's inevitable that you're not keeping a close watch over any of your children at the moment and that, although you've done all you can, your thoughts turn to me sometimes (it's not that you love them less, but that it's natural to put your hand more frequently on the place that hurts), here's how you should imagine I am: as happy and as positive as in the best of times. And these *are* the best of times, since my spirit, free of obligations, has time for its own work, sometimes even to play with less serious pursuits or, rising up eager for the truth, to understand its own nature and the nature of

---

39. That is, Alcestis, who agreed to die in place of her husband Admetus, but was brought back from death by Heracles.

40. A very prestigious post, only held by individuals the emperor trusted deeply because Egypt was key for grain supply to Rome and of strategic importance.

the universe. **20.2.** My spirit looks for answers first in the earth and
how it is arranged, then in the state of the sea that surrounds and its
tides. Then it looks at the frightful space that lies between the earth
and heaven, a volatile area with thunder, lightning, high winds, and
all kinds of precipitation. And then, after crossing through the lower
regions, it bursts through to the highest point and takes pleasure in the
most spectacular beauty of the gods: it becomes aware of its immortality and travels into what was and what will be forever.

Select Biographical Information
for Key Individuals

Marcus Antonius   Best known in English literature as Marc Antony. Born in 83 BCE, Antonius fully supported and benefited from Julius Caesar during his military and political ascendancy. He emerged from the turmoil after Caesar's assassination as one of the *triumvirate* (with Octavian and Marcus Aemilius Lepidus) charged with avenging Caesar and restoring the Republic. Antonius was given charge of the East and soon formed an alliance and relationship with Cleopatra, both of which caused significant disruptions to his relationships with Octavian (because he was married to Octavian's sister Octavia). These problems compounded the already fragile political situation and led to the failure of the *triumvirate* in 33 BCE and the beginning of civil war. Marcus Antonius died in 30 BCE after Octavian's forces defeated him at Actium in 31 BCE.

Lucius Junius Brutus   Brutus was widely cited as the person who precipitated the formation of the Republic by killing the last of the kings of Rome, Tarquinius Superbus. His kinswoman Lucretia was raped by Tarquinius' son, and subsequently killed herself; Brutus claimed vengeance, but there is little doubt that his motivations for deposing the kingship were as much political as personal. Portrayed as a hero of liberty and honor, Brutus became an example of dedication to liberty for the Stoics of the first century CE, so much so that the name Brutus by itself evoked the ideals of the Republic. Brutus was, along with Lucretia's husband Lucius Tarquinius Collatinus, the first consul of the Republic.

Marcus Junius Brutus   Born in 85 BCE, Brutus is best known as one of the chief conspirators who planned and carried out the assassination of Julius Caesar in 44 BCE. He was captured and killed in 42 BCE after he lost the Battle of Philippi to Octavian.

Marcus Porcius Cato   For Seneca, Cato embodies Stoic discipline, study, and virtue, and often even exemplifies the Stoic wise man. A principal player in the tumultuous mid-first century BCE, Cato the Younger (who had a famous great-grandfather with the same name) became legendary by Seneca's time for his steadfastness in the face of political and moral corruption and his conservative, vocal opposition to the reforms of Julius Caesar. Following Pompey and the senatorial faction to Greece, Cato continued to oppose Caesar even after Caesar's victories at Pharsalus in 48 BCE and Thapsus in

46 BCE. Finally fleeing to Africa, Cato attempted suicide in 46 BCE, falling on his sword rather than submitting to Caesar's power. His sword taken from him, he tore the life from his body with his bare hands. The figure of a heroic Cato became popular in literature almost immediately after his death, and under the empire he symbolized resistance to the emperor's rule.

CHRYSIPPUS   See Introduction, "Seneca and Stoicism."

Marcus Tullius CICERO   Cicero was a principal actor in the tumultuous first century BCE. Coming to Rome from a family not previously involved in politics, Cicero worked hard to build and maintain alliances. Instrumental in suppressing the rebellion in 63 BCE known as the Catilinarian Conspiracy while consul, he later encountered serious political retribution, suffering exile from 58 to 57 BCE. On his return, he became embroiled in the shifting politics of the 50s BCE and, unable to chart an effective middle course, finally withdrew to his estate. Although he supported Octavian in his rise to power, he was executed in 43 BCE during the proscriptions that accompanied the *triumvirate* among Octavian, Marcus Antonius, and Marcus Aemilius Lepidus. Cicero had angered Marcus Antonius with a series of damaging speeches and letters.

CLEANTHES   *See* Introduction, "Seneca and Stoicism."

Marcus Licinius CRASSUS   Reputedly the richest man in Roman history, and certainly believed in antiquity to be so, Marcus Licinius Crassus became one of the more important figures of the middle years of the first century BCE. A strong financial supporter of Caesar, Crassus entered into a power-sharing agreement with Pompey and Caesar in 59 BCE that preserved a fragile peace between these two rivals. Later, as a consequence of that agreement and perhaps in order to win military glory, Crassus campaigned in Parthia in 53 BCE, where he was killed (and his legions utterly destroyed).

Manius CURIUS DENTATUS   Curius Dentatus was an important figure of the beginning of the third century BCE, the victorious general of the Samnite War, who held the consulship three times. He used personal funds to finance the building of an aqueduct for Rome and was known for being incorruptible and untouched by wealth.

DEMETRIUS (the Cynic)   A Cynic philosopher from Corinth who lived in Rome during the first century CE and was a close friend of Seneca.

EPICURUS   See Introduction, "Epicureanism."

GRACCHI   Tiberius Gracchus (ca. 168–133 BCE) and then Gaius Gracchus (ca. 159–121 BCE), almost a decade after his brother's assassination, proposed and enacted a series of legislation aimed at social, economic, and judicial reforms, especially land reform. Gaius too was murdered. The period of the Gracchi brothers is generally considered a turning point in Roman Republican politics, leading to the extensive and bitter conflicts of the first century BCE.

Gaius GRACCHUS   See *Gracchi*.

Tiberius GRACCHUS   See *Gracchi*.

OCTAVIAN   After the Senate officially recognized him in 27 BCE, Octavian was officially named "Augustus" (originally an honorific title).

Gnaeus POMPEIUS Magnus   Pompey the Great was a figure of immense significance in the last stage of the Republic. He rose to power in the early part of the first century BCE through his military accomplishments rather than family connections, and always struggled within the relatively closed political culture of Rome. He allied himself with Julius Caesar through marriage. Along with Marcus Licinius Crassus, he brokered a political partnership with Caesar in 59 BCE. After his influence declined, he was returned to prominence by the senatorial elite to answer the threat of Julius Caesar. Pompey became the champion of this faction, but was eventually defeated by Caesar's troops in Pharsalus in 48 BCE. After this defeat, Pompey's sons Sextus and Gnaeus raised an army in Spain, but were defeated by Caesar in 45 BCE, soon after which Gnaeus was executed. Octavian executed Sextus a decade later.

Marcus Atilius REGULUS   Consul in 267 BCE and 256 BCE, Regulus was for the Roman Stoics one of the most famous role models of perseverance and principled action. After the Carthaginians captured him in 255 BCE and sent back to Rome to arrange for a prisoner exchange, he returned voluntarily to Carthage to face execution to honor the oath he made to his captors. According to some sources, on his return to Carthage—in addition to other tortures—his eyelids were cut off, and he died from sleep deprivation.

Publius RUTILIUS Rufus   Consul in 105 BCE, and charged and convicted falsely for extortion in 92 BCE.

Lucius SEJANUS   Sejanus was a low-ranking equestrian soldier who rose to great power and influence under the reign of Tiberius (14–37 CE). As Tiberius withdrew from public life in stages, Sejanus, in his capacity as prefect of the Praetorian Guard, consolidated power in his absence. (The Praetorians were the emperor's honor guard, and the only troop force permitted inside Rome's boundaries at that time.) Sejanus' plans became known to the emperor who quickly ordered his execution. Seneca may have had close ties to Sejanus and his circle during the reign of Tiberius.

Lucius SULLA Felix   Lucius Cornelius Sulla (138–78 BCE) began his career under Gaius Marius in the African campaigns of the Numidian and

Jugurthine wars. After rising in power to compete with Marius and marching on Rome with his armies twice to secure concessions and power from the Senate, Sulla was made dictator. Author of a number of important pieces of legislation and constitutional reforms during this time, Sulla also instituted the notorious proscriptions, as a result of which many Romans were executed summarily and their property confiscated. Relinquishing power in 79 BCE, Sulla died in 78 BCE.

Publius Vatinius   A partisan supporter of Julius Caesar during his years in Gaul, Vatinius was chiefly of service while he was tribune of the plebs in 59 BCE when he supported Caesar's ambitions for a five-year extension of rule over the province of Gaul. Rising to the *praetorship* in 55 BCE and the consulship after Caesar's victory at Pharsalus, Vatinius was eventually rejected by his own troops in Macedonia in 44 BCE and surrendered himself to Marcus Junius Brutus.

Zeno   See Introduction, "Seneca and Stoicism."

GLOSSARY OF LATIN WORDS
USED MORE THAN ONCE

agnomen See *nomen*.

atrium The *atrium* was the formal entrance hall of a Roman house. It was an open space, both upward (with roofs shaped to catch rain and direct it inward to a pool called the *impluvium*) and outward to the street. The *atrium* usually housed the *imagines* of the family and was the initial approach for all who encountered the family for political, business, or personal reasons. The *salutatio* took place in the *atrium*.

cliens Although this term describes any free person who is under the protection of a social superior (usually in exchange for economic or political support), *cliens* most often designates a freedman (ex-slave) who by law owed the same obligations to his former master. The status and relationships of clientage, on both ends, were hereditary.

cognomen See *nomen*.

consul The highest elected position under the Roman constitution, the two consuls for each year held authority over civic and especially military matters. Their grant of *imperium* was considered superior to that of other magistrates.

curia (1) The Senate house at Rome; (2) the formal division of citizens into voting groups that constituted the Roman Assembly (*comitium*).

fasces The symbols of *imperium*, an ax (for execution) and rods (for beatings), the *fasces* were carried before magistrates with *imperium* by *lictors* as a visible symbol of their authority to rule on law and to exact punishment. The number of rods differed for magistrates with different degrees of *imperium*.

imago (pl. *imagines*) The image, often in wax, of an ancestor who had achieved senatorial rank. The *imagines* were mounted in the *atrium* of a household and worn by actors during elaborate funeral processions.

imperium The supreme authority to impose law, exact punishment, and command troops, *imperium* was granted to elected and appointed magistrates by the Senate, in degrees according to rank and for specific spheres of authority or command (called *provinciae*). *Consuls, praetors,* and *dictators* and their surrogates could hold *imperium*. This word was also the Roman term for the extent of Roman control and influence, the Roman Empire.

213

maiestas   Technically a criminal charge for damage to the dignity and power of the Roman people, the word came to describe the legal mechanism adapted to prosecute those who threatened the emperor, and then those responsible for libel or slander of the emperor and his family.

nomen   Roman citizens generally had two or three names. The *praenomen* was the personal name, and there were very few to choose from (e.g., Gaius, Marcus, Lucius, etc.). The *nomen* is the gentilic (clan) name and almost always ended in –ius (e.g., Julius, Flavius, Claudius, etc.). The *cognomen* (or known-by name) can indicate the branch of the family, or be another given name, or be a nickname like Celer (swift) or Felix (lucky), or the town or tribal name of a provincial citizen. The *cognomen* was often reserved for members of the nobility in the Republican period, and sometimes reflected some important event, characteristic, or military achievement. In some cases, *cognomina* could be passed down through families. Adoption or the granting of freedom added additional names, based on the name of the adopting male. Girls were generally given their father's *nomen*, feminized, and rarely a *cognomen* or a nickname. Apparently some girls were simply numbered: Prima, Secunda, Tertia, etc. Women did not change their names when they married.

nomenclator   A slave specifically chosen and trained for the ability to remember names and relationships.

pontifex   One of a small group of priests who had extensive influence on many matters of state religion and of family (e.g., inheritance, marriage, etc.). The position of head *pontifex* (the *pontifex maximus*) was held by the emperor, following the tradition of Augustus.

praefectus   (*vigilum, annonae*) Any appointed administrative or leadership role in a variety of military and civil contexts. During the empire, some praefectures became important steps of a career progression for those of equestrian rank. As such, they were positions of significant power and authority.

praenomen   See *nomen*.

praetor   An elected position with *imperium* that had authority especially over legal matters. Individuals with *praetorian imperium* could also lead troops in battle.

primipilaris   The chief or senior centurion of a legion. For lower classes, this was an important position to hold to gain access to senior administrative and military positions. It came with an automatic grant of equestrian rank.

princeps   (pl. *principes*) During the empire *princeps*, following the tradition of Augustus, was an unofficial title of the emperor; literally means "chief man in the state."

proconsul   An individual granted consular *imperium*, usually for a specific period of time and purpose.

rostrum   (pl. *rostra*) A speaker's platform, especially the one at Rome, decorated with the prows of defeated ships.

sacer   Literally means subject to capital punishment or sacrifice to a god. Any object or person deemed *sacer* therefore belonged to a god. The Valerio–Horatian Legislation of 450 BCE restored the sacrosanctity of the *tribunes of the plebs* and anyone harming these individuals would become *sacer* to Juppiter (and thus subject to capital punishment) because they had violated a sacrosanct official (Cato was tribune in 59 BCE when the event recounted in *De Constantia* 1.3 took place).

salutatio   A greeting, especially the dawn greeting given to an important man by his clients (see *cliens*) and dependent friends.

tribune of the plebs   An early addition to the Roman political system (the traditional date is 494 BCE), the *tribunus plebis* acted originally on behalf of the largely politically disenfranchised lower classes (the *plebs*). As well as being able to pass universally binding legislation through the *plebeian* assemblies with *plebiscites*, a *tribune* possessed the ability to veto (literally meaning "I prohibit") the act of any magistrate, sometimes by physically interposing his body. Tribunes were sacrosanct (see *sacer*). The ten annual tribunes at the end of the Republic played pivotal roles in the upheaval that led to the *principate*, and Augustus was careful to maintain supreme *tribunician* power as the basis for his authority as emperor.

triumviri   Any board of three men elected or formed by legislation for a specific purpose on behalf of the Roman state. In Seneca's writings this usually refers to the *triumvirate* of Octavian, Marcus Antonius, and Marcus Aemilius Lepidus, formed by law after the assassination of Caesar in 43 BCE to avenge his death and restore order to the Republic.

Index of Historical Persons

Abbreviations

Prov.	*On Providence*
Const.	*On the Resolute Nature of the Wise Man*
Marc.	*Consolation to Marcia*
Vit.	*On the Happy Life*
Ot.	*On Retirement*
Tranq.	*On the Serenity of the Spirit*
Brev.	*On the Shortness of Life*
Poly.	*Consolation to Polybius*
Helv.	*Consolation to Helvia*